The SPY CATCHER TRIAL

THE SCANDAL BEHIND THE #1 BEST SELLER

MALCOLM TURNBULL

Salem House Publishers
Topsfield, Massachusetts

First published in the United States
by Salem House Publishers, 1989
462 Boston Street
Topsfield, MA 01983

Printed in the United States

Library of Congress Cataloging-in-Publication Data

Turnbull, Malcolm, 1954–
    The spycatcher trial / by Malcolm Turnbull.
      p.   cm.
    Includes index.
    ISBN 0–88162–422–5 : $18.95
    1. Great Britain—Trials, litigation, etc. 2. Wright, Peter,
    1916– —Trials, litigation, etc. 3. Heinemann (Firm)—Trials,
    litigation, etc. 4. Freedom of the press—Australia. 5. Book
    industries and trade—Law and legislation—Australia. 6. Wright,
    Peter, 1916– Spycatcher. 7. Intelligence service—Great Britain.
    I. Title.
    LAW <TRIALS A&E Spycatcher 1989>
    345.41′0231—dc19
    [344.105231]   88–37126
                                               CIP

DEDICATION

For my wife and (learned) friend,
Lucinda Hughes Turnbull

ACKNOWLEDGEMENTS

THIS BOOK CHRONICLES THE greatest adventure of my life. L'Affaire Spycatcher raised a great many serious issues about official secrets, the rule of law and democracy generally. But it was also an enormous lark and I enjoyed every minute of it. I hope this book conveys how much fun we had.

I am very grateful to everyone who made the case possible and in particular to Peter Wright and Margaret Thatcher without whose not dissimilar determination a thoroughly unmeritorious piece of litigation would never have seen the light of day.

This is my first book and it would not have been finished without a lot of encouragement from many friends. Especially my mother Carol Lansbury. The book benefitted from being read in draft form by Kerry Schott, Neville Wran QC, Paul Greengrass, David Hooper, Antony Larkins QC, Sandy Grant and my skillful editors both at Salem House and at Heinemann in Australia.

I am particularly indebted to the many tactful editing suggestions from Antony Larkins, although not, I fear, as grateful as those referred to in the passages he persuaded me to remove.

In this as in all things my greatest debt is to Lucy.

THE SPYCATCHER TRIAL
DRAMATIS PERSONAE AND GLOSSARY

Aitken, Jonathan   born 1942, journalist and Conservative MP. He tried to persuade the British Government not to press on with the *Spycatcher* litigation and correctly predicted the result would be disastrous for Britain.

Alexander, Robert   born 1936, barrister and leading counsel for the British Government in their (unsuccessful) efforts in the United Kingdom to stop *Spycatcher*. Now Lord Alexander.

Allason, Rupert   born 1951, author and Conservative MP. Author of many works on intelligence based on highly confidential sources with MI5 and MI6. His book *A Matter of Trust: MI5 1945–72* was of utmost importance in the *Spycatcher* trial.

Armstrong, Sir Robert   born 1927, civil servant, Secretary of the Cabinet and Head of the Civil Service 1981–87 and as such the Prime Minister's principal adviser on intelligence matters. British Government's principal witness in the *Spycatcher* trial. Extremely close to Prime Minister Thatcher and often described as the most powerful man in Britain. Retired in 1987 and created Lord Armstrong.

Bailey, Sir John	born 1928, lawyer and civil servant. Treasury Solicitor (the British Government's senior non-political legal officer) from 1973 to date. Responsible for much of the legal strategy employed by the British Government in the *Spycatcher* trial.
GCHQ	Government Communications Headquarters, Britain's secret organization for eavesdropping on international telecommunications. Works closely with the National Security Agency in the United States.
Grant, Sandy	born 1954, managing director of Heinemann Publishers Australia, the publishers of *Spycatcher* in Australia. He provided all-important moral and financial support for the defense of Peter Wright.
Greengrass, Paul	born 1956, journalist and television director. He was the "ghostwriter" of *Spycatcher* itself, and was responsible for much of the research used by the defense in the *Spycatcher* trial.
Havers, Sir Michael	born 1923, barrister and Conservative MP, British Attorney-General 1979–87, created Lord Chancellor 1987, now Lord Havers.
Hawke, Robert J.L.	born 1929, Rhodes Scholar, trade union secretary and politician. Labor Prime Minister of Australia from 1983 to date. He decided Australia should give token support to Britain in the *Spycatcher* trial.
High Court of Australia	Australia's ultimate court of appeal, equivalent of the United States Supreme Court.
Hooper, David	born 1948, English solicitor and Old Etonian who provided considerable as-

sistance to the defense team in the *Spycatcher* trial.

Hughes, Tom born 1923, barrister and member of the Australian House of Representatives 1963–72, Attorney General of Australia 1968–70, since then Australia's leading advocate. Father of Lucy Turnbull. He represented Wright at one of the preliminary High Court appeal hearings in Australia.

Kinnock, Neil born 1942, university tutor and Labor member of the House of Commons. Leader of the Opposition in the House of Commons 1981 to date.

Kirby, Justice Michael born 1939, barrister, President of the New South Wales Court of Appeal 1948 to date. He sat on the first appeal from Justice Powell's decision.

Mason, Sir Anthony born 1925, barrister, Solicitor-General of the Commonwealth of Australia 1966–69, judge of the New South Wales Court of Appeal 1969–1972, judge of the High Court of Australia 1972 to date. Chief Justice of the Commonwealth of Australia 1987 to date. He presided over the second, and final, appeal from the decision of Justice Powell.

McHugh, Justice Michael born 1935, barrister, Judge of the New South Wales Court of Appeal 1984–1988. He sat on the first appeal from Justice Powell's decision. He has recently been appointed to the High Court of Australia.

MI5 Unofficial name for the British Security Service which is the intelligence service responsible for counter-espionage and counter-terrorist work within Britain. Responsible to the Home Office.

MI6	Unofficial name for the British Secret Intelligence Service which is responsible for gathering intelligence outside Britain. Its existence has never been officially admitted by the British Government. Responsible to the Foreign Office.
Perman, Brian	Managing director of William Heinemann Limited in the United Kingdom, the parent company of the Australian publisher of *Spycatcher*.
Pincher, Chapman	born 1914, veteran journalist specializing in intelligence matters, close links to MI5 and MI6, author of numerous books including *Their Trade is Treachery* which he wrote with assistance from Peter Wright.
Powell, Justice Philip	born 1930, barrister, appointed judge of the Supreme Court of New South Wales in 1977. He presided over the *Spycatcher* trial.
Robertson, Geoffrey	born 1944, barrister and author. An old friend of Malcolm and Lucy Turnbull, he had provided some advice to Heinemann in England about *Spycatcher* and later directed them to Malcolm Turnbull.
Rothschild, Lord Victor	born 1910, served in military intelligence and has advised both MI5 and MI6. Member of Europe's greatest banking family, intimate adviser of British Prime Ministers of both political persuasions, was responsible for introducing Peter Wright to Chapman Pincher prior to Wright providing information to Pincher for *Their Trade is Treachery*. Also made the financial arrangements for Wright to be covertly paid his share of the royalties of *Their Trade is Treachery*.
Schaap, William	born 1943, New York lawyer specializing in military and intelligence matters. He

gave expert evidence for Wright at the *Spycatcher* trial about CIA policies on intelligence memoirs.

Simos, Theo   born 1934, barrister and leading counsel for the British Government in the *Spycatcher* trial and later Australian appeals.

Street, Sir Laurence   born 1926, barrister, appointed judge of the Supreme Court of New South Wales in 1965, Chief Justice of New South Wales from 1974–1988. A third generation Chief Justice he presided over the first appeal from the decision of Justice Powell.

Thatcher, Margaret   born 1925, barrister and Conservative MP. Prime Minister of Great Britain from 1979 to date. Her personal determination to suppress *Spycatcher* was the driving force behind the *Spycatcher* litigation.

Turnbull, Lucy   born 1958, lawyer and assistant defense counsel in the *Spycatcher* trial.

Turnbull, Malcolm   born 1954, lawyer and defense counsel for Peter Wright in the *Spycatcher* trial.

Whitlam, Gough   born 1916, barrister and member of the Australian House of Representatives from 1952–1978. Prime Minister of Australia from 1972–1975. He gave evidence in support of Peter Wright at the *Spycatcher* Trial.

Wright, Peter   born 1916, MI5 officer and counter-espionage specialist. Author of *Spycatcher*.

CHAPTER 1

JANUARY IN SYDNEY WAS hot and sticky. The courts
were shut, the streets were empty, the phone was silent.
No self-respecting lawyer was in his office unless he was
particularly poor or unusually optimistic. The rest of my
learned friends were at the beach, or if they were particularly prosperous, skiing in Europe. However, my partner Bruce McWilliam and I had established a new legal
practice. We had officially opened for business on January
1, 1986. And more in hope than expectation, we stood
ready for action.

We were not starting a new practice without clients.
For the last three years we had looked after Australian
media magnate Kerry Packer's legal problems, as his in-
house lawyers. After three years of that I decided we
should branch out and take on some more clients. Packer
offered no objection and so "Turnbull McWilliam, Attorneys and Solicitors" was born. One of our first well-
wishers was an old friend, Geoffrey Robertson. He is
widely known in Australia as the host of a television panel
show called "Hypothetical." In England he practices at
the Bar.

After the usual pleasantries, Geoffrey got down to the
purpose of his phone call. "I act for William Heinemann
Limited, the book publishers, in London. Their Australian

subsidiary is endeavoring to publish a book written by a former MI5 officer, Peter Wright. Someone at Heinemann in London was fool enough to leak this to a gossip columnist at the *Observer*. The Government read about it, commenced proceedings and have obtained an interlocutory injunction[1] from the Supreme Court of New South Wales barring publication."

This was the first I had heard of Peter Wright. His court skirmish with the British Government had received practically no publicity. Robertson explained that he thought Wright had a good case, but that a long line of Australian lawyers had advised them they had no chance of winning at all. "Two Queens Counsel, and three junior barristers have all said it was a dead loser. Their London solicitor, David Hooper, is here in Sydney trying to sort it out. Could you have a talk to him?"

"How committed are Heinemann to fighting this case?" I asked him. "Not much," he replied. "I think Hooper is the only person on our side, apart from myself, who wants to press on." It sounded like an interesting case. "Tell Hooper to call me, I will be happy to meet him."

I was then thirty-one years of age and had been practicing law in Sydney for five years. I had been educated at Sydney Grammar School and then read Arts and Law at the University of Sydney, graduating BA, LLB in 1977. During my time at University I worked as a journalist, first as a freelance writer for a leftish weekly called *Nation Review*. In 1976 I wangled a seat for myself in the New South Wales parliamentary press gallery and began covering that political bear pit for *Nation Review*, for Radio 2SM, owned by the Catholic archdiocese of Sydney, and for Television Channel 9, owned by Kerry Packer. I was serving, simultaneously, Marx, God and Mammon.

My time as a political reporter coincided with my second last year at law school and I engaged my friend, John

---

1. A temporary stay.

O'Sullivan, to take lecture notes for me. He took a carbon copy of all of the lectures and I paid him $30 a week plus the cost of carbon paper and extra writing paper. I met Packer in 1976 when I was supplementing my journalistic income by writing copy for advertisements for Doyle Dane Bernbach, then run by a friend of Packer's, John Singleton. Two years before Packer had inherited a vast magazine, newspaper and television empire from his legendary father Sir Frank Packer.[2] In 1977 Packer offered me a full-time position on the *Bulletin*, his weekly national news magazine.

I wrote about politics and law for the most part and started a rather irreverent column about legal matters which regularly enraged the more conservative members of the legal profession. I remember the then Chief Justice, Sir Harry Gibbs, chiding me for referring to judges in the column by their surname alone. He felt it was contempt of court to refer to a judge other than as "Mr. Justice Bloggs." I felt if surnames were good enough for prime ministers and presidents, they were certainly good enough for judges.

At the end of 1977, when I finished my law degree, I was awarded a Rhodes Scholarship. The publicity attached to this award came to Kerry Packer's attention and he appointed me an assistant to his astute deputy chairman and finance director, Harry Chester. For the eight months until I left for Oxford I worked closely with Packer and Chester and came to know both very well.

Packer is an unconventional managing director and threw me in at the deep end. In a very short time, I found myself negotiating a takeover with the Trade Prac-

2. The Packers are an Australian media dynasty whose rivals are the Murdoch and Fairfax families. While Murdoch and Fairfax dominate the newspaper scene, Packer's television network is overwhelmingly pre-eminent and many astute observers regard him as the best television operator in the world.

tices Commission and then the establishment of an Australian edition of *Playboy* with Christie Hefner in Chicago. Packer seemed happy with my efforts and we stayed in close touch during my two years at Oxford.

I arrived at Oxford in September 1978. I had spent about four weeks getting there, including a raft trip down the Colorado River with my father. I lived at Brasenose College in a room so damp I suspected frogs were breeding under the wallpaper. Still by Oxford College standards, it was quite luxurious. During my time there I freelanced for a number of publications in Australia and America. I also obtained a position on the *Sunday Times.* My time there coincided almost exactly with the period the newspaper's publication was suspended, in 1978 to 1979.

A long history of industrial disruption led to management giving all the workers a choice of signing a new industrial agreement or being stood down. The printers refused to sign and were duly laid off. The journalists did sign and management felt duty-bound to keep them all on the payroll despite the fact that no newspaper was being published.

I had met the editor, Harold Evans, some years before during a Cambridge Union debate. He was impressed with my speech and offered me a job on the spot. We stayed in touch and when I got to England he asked me to work for the *Sunday Times.* I accepted his offer together with his assurance that "We'll be back on the streets in a couple of weeks." His optimism continued unabated for ten months and as a consequence instead of having ten holiday months the journalists would spring into action every two weeks or so, write enough copy to fill a paper and then realize that a reopening was still some time off.

By the middle of 1979 the situation was becoming very unsatisfactory. My tutors at Brasenose had noticed my lengthy absences in London and threatened to send me down unless I concentrated on my studies. On the other hand I was hardly making a name for myself in Fleet Street, working for a paper that didn't exist. So with considerable regret I left the *Sunday Times,* about six weeks before it came back. I returned to Oxford and from then until June 1980 became a model student, working long hours in the Bodleian Law Library.

I married Lucy Hughes in March 1980. Lucy and I had been courting, as it used to be termed, for about two years, although she was still living in Sydney studying law at Sydney University. During my first year in England, Lucy came over to England during each of her vacations and we corresponded almost daily. Her last visit was in November 1979. I realized I could not bear to see her return to Australia again. So she stayed and we were married four months later. We lived first in a flat in North Oxford and then in a tiny cottage covered with roses, at Cumnor.

Lucy is the eldest child of the Honorable Thomas Eyre Forrest Hughes, QC. A distinguished Queen's Counsel, he had been Attorney-General of the Commonwealth from 1968 to 1970 during the short-lived Gorton Government. He left politics in 1972 and quickly became recognized as the leader of the Bar in Australia, a position he maintains today. The Hughes family were all Roman Catholics although both Tom and Lucy were somewhat lapsed by 1979. My own religious background was almost nonexistent although I had been baptized in the Presbyterian Church, my forebears having built the first nonconformist church in Australia, at Ebenezer, in 1809.

We decided we would be married in the Cumnor church and approached the vicar, Neil Durand. The vicar remonstrated with us, pointing out that Lucy as a Catholic and I as a Presbyterian were not part of his flock. "Your petty sectarian approach is unconstitutional, Vicar," I responded. "The Church of England is the religion of the state. You are a servant of the Crown, not materially different from an ambassador or an admiral. It is your constitutional duty to prevent fornication in your parish and marrying us is a good start." The vicar was rather more scholarly than he let on and slyly observed that he wasn't entirely in agreement with me on his constitutional position, but nonetheless felt persistence should be rewarded. "After all, if the Church of England can include bishops who doubt the divinity of Christ, it should be broad enough to take in you two."

So we were married in the Cumnor Church. Geoffrey Robertson stood in for Lucy's father and the small wedding party adjourned for lunch to "The Bear and Ragged Staff." It has been a good match. Lucy combines the best qualities of her father and her more artistic mother. While being intellectually first class (she topped her final year at law school) she has an artistic and gentle spirit. In the eleven years I have known her I doubt I have seen her depressed on more than three or four occasions. My best friends would concede I am a little more volatile in temperament.

We returned to Australia in September 1980, and encouraged by Lucy's father I was admitted to the Bar of the State of New South Wales. The legal profession in New South Wales is modelled upon that of England and thus there is a strict division between barristers and solicitors. You practice as either one or the other. For the most part the system works as it does in England, with barristers concentrating on court work and solicitors on legal work that does not involve appearing in court as an advocate. Unlike England, however, solicitors do have the right to appear as advocates in the courts, although when they do exercise that right they appear unrobed. But by and large, solicitors do not appear as advocates, particularly in the superior courts. The reasons for this are somewhat contentious, but there is no doubt that some judges and almost all barristers manifest considerable hostility to solicitor advocates. The Bar guards its turf with great jealousy; when suggestions were made to fuse the solicitors' and barristers' branches of the profession into one, the barristers reacted with almost hysterical opposition.

The conservatism of the barristers and judges is most obvious when it comes to their court dress. A barrister not only wears a wig, but a wing collar and bands (like a clergyman), a special black jacket and a long black gown. The judge's attire is even more elaborate. Senior barristers who are given the honorary title of "Queens Counsel" wear silk gowns and more elaborate jackets. This anachronistic attire often looks quite becoming in the ancient halls of justice in London but is very out of place in the modern court rooms of Australia and quite uncomfortable in the heat of an Australian summer.

The two major political parties in Australia are a mildly conservative Liberal Party and the mildly socialist Labor Party. Although originally modelled on English political parties their ideological differences are now so slight that they are closer to the Republicans and Democrats than their English counterparts. I had renewed my membership of the Liberal Party upon returning to Sydney and in March 1981 I contested the Liberal Party's pre-selection for the very safe seat of Wentworth. I came second in a field of twenty, beaten by only four votes. Had I won the preselection ballot, I would have certainly been elected as a member of the House of Representatives. I remained involved in the Liberal Party for a few more years, contesting preselection for a State parliamentary seat two years later.

With these fine conservative political antecedents I was rather puzzled when some British Tories later sought to represent me as a dangerous left-winger. However the political scene in England and Australia is now so different that "conservative" or "left" labels are not readily transferable; they mean different things in Australia and England. Overall I had a great deal of sympathy for Mrs. Thatcher's Government. I do not believe in socialism and applaud her privatization of state-owned industries, but unlike Mrs. Thatcher I do not believe that freedom should only reign in the economic sector. Freedom of competition is important, but no more important than freedom of speech or freedom of information.

My practice at the Bar prospered. My notoriety as a journalist, my connections with Packer and my father-in-law all helped my progress. On November 10, 1982 Packer asked me if I would be interested in returning to work for him as an in-house lawyer. He nominated a very substantial salary and I said that I would think about it. Before I had much time to consider the offer, my father was killed in a light airplane accident. I was particularly close to him and was shattered by his death. For a while, I lost the will to work at the killing pace of a barrister. Moreover I had inherited a number of interests in hotels, together with a grazing property where he lived. All that would require time. I told Packer I would accept the offer on the basis that we would both reconsider the situation after twelve months.

At that time my intention was to return to the Bar after what I hoped would be a sedate year in the corporate world. I would have time to tidy up my father's affairs. I would spend more time with Lucy and our new baby, Alexander, born in August 1982. So I rented my chambers for one year and joined Kerry Packer's company, Consolidated Press Holdings Limited. Packer's legal affairs had for many years been conducted by Australia's largest firm of solicitors, Allen, Allen and Hemsley. They in turn invariably retained senior Queens Counsel, especially my father-in-law, to represent Consolidated Press in any litigation. Allens expected that I would be like my predecessor as in-house lawyer and funnel business to them. Instead I started to do all of the work myself. I hired Bruce McWilliam from Allens and within twelve months we were handling all of the legal work of the Packer empire. We quickly demonstrated that you don't need large law firms and expensive barristers to provide good legal service.

I still planned to return to the Bar, but my plans were thwarted when Packer came under the attention of a Royal Commissioner, Frank Costigan, who had been originally appointed to investigate the affairs of a rather sordid trade union, the Federated Ship Painters and Dockers. Costigan construed his terms of reference to include an inquiry into criminal conduct in general and in what was one of the blackest episodes in Australian legal history he targeted Packer, first for tax evasion and then, most improbably, for drug trafficking and murder. The Costigan Royal Commission was described by me as practicing "a new McCarthyism" and it is difficult to find a satisfactory parallel other than the McCarthy witch hunts. However where McCarthy hunted communists, Costigan was hunting the rich and powerful and many were happy to see the plutocrats humbled. Costigan denied Packer any opportunity to answer the charges against him. The allegations against Packer appeared likely to destroy him, his family and his company, and in the circumstances I could not leave him. It took three and a half years before all of Costigan's allegations were disproved and Packer received a public apology from the Federal Government.

The Costigan affair kept me at Consolidated Press, but it also taught me a lot about law and propaganda. Allegations about Packer were systematically leaked from within the Royal Commission to the press. It heard evidence against Packer in secret hearings at which Packer could not be represented. Tackling Costigan by conventional means was futile and I persuaded Packer to counterattack with a violent public attack on Costigan. We launched our campaign with an 8000-word press release written by me which was printed in full on the front page of every newspaper in Australia, none of them owned by Packer. I followed that up with press and television appearances whipping up opposition to Costigan's Star

Chamber tactics. I realized that propaganda was not enough, however, and when a fresh inquest was opened into the death of a man Costigan said had been murdered by Packer, I appeared for Packer. The Coote Inquest proved not only that this allegation was false but also that Costigan's inquiry had been conducted with breathtaking incompetence. We fought fire with fire and won.

My efforts on Packer's behalf certainly made me notorious. I became very unpopular with my former colleagues at the Bar who resented my use of the media to defend a client. So I became a solicitor. The rules regulating solicitors' practice were much more liberal than those regulating barristers. I had no dislike for the Bar, but I knew that the sort of work I was doing could not be done by a barrister. Barristers were prevented by their professional "ethics" from talking to the press. Barristers only acted on the instructions of solicitors. So a client could not call a barrister direct, he had to hire a solicitor first and then a barrister. These sorts of restrictive work practices were regularly decried in blue collar industries, but the lawyers had managed to retain them. I wanted to practice in the way American attorneys do and deal directly with the clients and act as the advocate. I was doing this for Packer, but I also wanted to establish a reputation as a good lawyer, not simply as Kerry Packer's lawyer. So we set up Turnbull McWilliam with a view to attracting other clients and broadening both our client base and our expertise.

The news from Geoff Robertson in early January 1986 seemed almost too good to be true. For reasons of discretion, Robertson was not prepared to go into much detail on the phone. The full story up to then was only revealed when David Hooper called on me the following day. Hooper was an improbable scourge of the British establishment. Educated at Eton and Balliol, he was the third son of a distinguished ambassador, Sir Robin Hooper. He was a partner in a London firm, Biddle & Co., and had published a very witty and well-written book about famous libel cases. Of course I didn't know any of this when Hooper arrived in my office, although by the time he had opened his mouth I could have guessed most of it. He was red in the face and sweating profusely. His tall and lean form was clad in what appeared to be his tropical rig: baggy white pants, an open-necked striped shirt, and a large straw hat. He had been, he said, at the cricket. Hooper speaks with a languid upper-class accent, affects an occasional stutter and generally gives the impression of being much calmer than he is. On this occasion however he was obviously very downcast.

The book had been a great secret, he said, until someone leaked to the *Observer*. News that Wright was planning to publish his memoirs was published in a diary item in the *Observer* on March 31, 1985. The British Government engaged Stephen Jaques Stone James as their solicitors in Sydney and fired off letters to Wright and Heinemann on August 20, 1985. The managing director of Heinemann Australia was Nicholas Hudson. He sought the advice of Tony Smith, a senior partner of Gillotts, a large firm of solicitors in Melbourne. He gave a noncommittal reply to the letters from Stephen Jaques and on September 10, 1985 the British obtained injunctions against Wright and Heinemann in the Supreme Court of New South Wales.

"Somehow or other, the case became a complete shambles. Gillotts advised that Wright needed to be separately represented, so another Melbourne law firm, Corrs Pavey, were brought in as his solicitors. Each firm of solicitors briefed senior and junior counsel and since Gillotts did not have a Sydney office, Gillotts retained a Sydney firm of solicitors, Ebsworths, to act for them in New South Wales. They all advised us the case was hopeless: a less than one percent chance of success, they told us, and would cost many hundreds of thousands of dollars to fight."

I knew most of the Sydney Bar very well. I interrupted Hooper. "Who were these pessimistic barristers?"

When Hooper mentioned their names, I was very taken aback. All of them were very distinguished and successful lawyers, and one was widely regarded as the foremost equity lawyer in Australia. Whether the advice was correct or not, it had certainly come from impeccable sources.

"Anyway," Hooper continued, "by the end of October we had been advised to give an undertaking not to publish the book until a full trial of the matter. We had twenty-four lawyers involved on our side; our costs were already well over $200,000. We had been advised we had no chance of success and naturally enough the clients wanted to chuck it."

"What about a second opinion?"

"Geoff sent us off to one of his more radical friends at the Bar. He also says we can't win. He says that there is no Australian public interest in the book being published and thinks we should get the case transferred to England. We told him we had absolutely no chance of winning in England, and his only reply was that we had even less chance of winning here. The Treasury Solicitor has offered to settle the case if we agree to permanent injunctions. He has graciously offered not to make us pay his costs. Heinemann are pretty well minded to do it."

"What about Wright?" I asked.

"Well, I have just been down to Tasmania to see him. He's about all that's keeping the case alive, apart from me. Wright says if Heinemann pull out he will fight on himself, although I can't see how he can. He's broke, you know."

So the legal team for the defense were unanimous that the case was hopeless. They correctly saw that an important part of the defense was the argument that much of the material in Wright's book *Spycatcher* had already been published and was therefore no longer confidential. However the lawyers apparently believed that in order to mount this defense it was necessary for all of them to read every known spy book and indeed some of the lawyers actually started on this task.

By the end of 1985 the picture was as bleak as it could be. A huge team of lawyers had achieved absolutely nothing except convey the gloomiest possible advice to their clients and run up $200,000 in costs. The lack of progress by this legal army was astonishing. No written advices or memoranda were prepared on any of the legal issues in the case. No draft affidavits for Wright were prepared nor was a proof of evidence. Heinemann were profoundly depressed, and Hooper's visit was to see how the case could be given a decent burial. Fighting it was out of everyone's mind, except Hooper and Wright himself.

I told Hooper it seemed that I was the lawyer of last resort. He agreed. "You see, I know these fellows are very bright and so on, but I don't think they're right and neither does Robertson. It's just that we can't get anyone to agree with us."

"I agree with you. We have to give the Government a copy of the book and force them to specify the passages they say are objectionable."

"I rather think they'll object to the lot."

"If they do, we have to fight for the lot, but on the other hand if we can get them down to particulars we may be able to negotiate a few cuts and at least still get a book out of it. Do you want me to act for you?"

"I can't retain you now. The clients are still very depressed about it all. Will you write me an advice and give me a firm and *very* low quote to do the case? I may be able to persuade them to fight on if they are satisfied it won't cost them much."

The proceedings had actually been brought by the British Attorney-General. Indeed the case's official title was "Her Majesty's Attorney-General in and for the United Kingdom v. Heinemann Publishers Australia Pty Limited and Peter Maurice Wright." The British Attorney-General was Sir Michael Havers. Generally regarded as somewhat more liberal and easy-going than his Prime Minister, Havers filled a curious political role. While he was a member of the Government and often had to effect government policy, in much of his legal work he had to act in accordance with his own independent judgment, while in other areas he was simply the Government's (very distinguished no doubt) lawyer and paid mouthpiece. His independent role was particularly so in criminal matters where he had the ultimate responsibility, free of any political influence, of deciding who should be prosecuted or not. In civil matters he sometimes acted independently, and at other times on instructions from the Government. At the trial the question of the Attorney's independence in the *Spycatcher* case would become a key issue.

Hooper gave me copies of two affidavits (sworn statements) which had already been sworn by Sir Robert Armstrong and used in the proceedings so far as the evidence for the interlocutory orders. I knew nothing of Sir Robert Armstrong when I first read the affidavits; as I read them it became apparent that he knew nothing about Wright's book. This was not unexpected, as at this state the Government had not seen the manuscript. In the affidavits, he said he was the Cabinet Secretary and the Prime Minister's principal advisor on intelligence matters. He described how Wright had served in MI5 from 1955 until 1976 in extremely senior positions, becoming aware of much sensitive information. Armstrong had not seen the manuscript of the book, and his affidavits were a chronicle of the kind of damage a book by a former intelligence officer may cause. He said that Wright had signed a Declaration in 1955 stating he was aware of the provisions of the Official Secrets Act. Section 2 of that Act prohibits any person from revealing any "official" information. I knew that this Act had been the subject of some considerable controversy in England, particularly since "official information" apparently included any governmental information whatsoever. Moreover an English civil servant could not defend himself against prosecution by arguing that his disclosure of official information was in the public interest. The Official Secrets Act imposes a total obligation of secrecy on all government employees no matter how junior and no matter how trivial the information. It was this total and undiscriminating obligation of silence that Armstrong was seeking to have enforced against Wright in Australia.

The English Official Secrets Act did not, however, apply to Australia, and so Armstrong argued in his affidavits that this total obligation of silence was part of an implied contract which Wright had with his former employers and which an Australian court would enforce. He went on to argue that if Wright were to reveal any information he learned while in MI5 this would damage the reputation of MI5 with other friendly intelligence agencies, add to the knowledge of hostile intelligence agencies and generally set a bad example to other officers both serving and retired.

I had more than a little sympathy for Armstrong's argument. After all, one could hardly run an intelligence service if its former officers could willy-nilly publish books about their activities. On the other hand it is perfectly obvious that there was a lot of information about the intelligence services which was already well known. Moreover, some information would become out of date and quite innocuous if published. In short all Armstrong proved in his affidavit was the obvious: a former MI5 officer *could* publish a book the contents of which *might* damage security. He did not address the particular question of whether Wright's proposed book *actually* did have such damaging contents.

I wrote to Hooper on January 16, 1986 and advised him that in my view there were at least three strong defenses: first, the book disclosed evidence of criminal activities by MI5 and in my view an Australian court could not suppress the publication of evidence of such criminality; second, if MI5 was penetrated by the Russians in the way Wright said it was, what possible harm could be caused by the publication of the book? third, a great deal of the information in the book had already been published. It could not be considered confidential and worthy of protection.

We would argue that once an intelligence secret ceased to be a secret, it was in the public domain and anyone, including former intelligence officers, could write about it. The philosophy behind our case had been stated by Justice Sir Anthony Mason of the Australian High Court [Australia's ultimate court of appeal, equivalent to the United States Supreme Court] in a case called *Commonwealth v. Fairfax.* That case in 1981 involved an attempt by the Australian Government to stop the publication of certain Foreign Office documents and cables. Sir Anthony Mason had refused an injunction to the Government, saying that governments could only restrain the publication of confidential information if they could establish that the information was still secret, and most important, that its publication would cause real detriment, not just embarrassment and public debate and controversy. A number of academic writers had criticized this decision saying that it made the task of governments seeking to suppress leaks of information far too difficult. Since that decision, however, Justice Mason had become Chief Justice of the High Court. I had little doubt that the principles in *Commonwealth v. Fairfax* would never be overturned, at least while Sir Anthony was Chief Justice.

I concluded my advice by optimistically opining that the British Government would settle the case before a final hearing. "I would be very surprised if the British Government would want Mr. Armstrong [sic] to be cross-examined about the British Security Service in public in Sydney." In short my view was that we would have about three months of tough interlocutory skirmishing and then when the British realized they would have to face a public trial, they would sit around the table and agree on a deal, probably involving the censoring of nominated passages in the book.

I could not have been more mistaken in assessing the British Government's attitude. We all underestimated their determination. The following week I met Paul Hamlyn, the chairman of Octopus Books, which had recently swallowed up Heinemann. Hamlyn is a shy and enigmatic man. He is a German Jew who at seven years of age emigrated, with his family, from Germany to England in 1933. His pediatrician father established a practice in fashionable St. Johns Wood. Paul Hamlyn had made millions out of book publishing. In his rise to the top he had made a great many friends on the left of politics, including the Australian Prime Minister, Robert Hawke. Hamlyn therefore stood somewhat apart from the English establishment. He was a plutocrat/socialist. He knew that a previous potential publisher of Wright's memoirs, Hamish Hamilton, had been frightened off by MI5, and he was not disposed to being pushed around by MI5, Mrs. Thatcher or anyone else for that matter. On the other hand Hamlyn is not the stuff martyrs are made of. He had no wish to throw good money after bad and he obviously had grave doubts whether I was the right man for the job. I concluded the meeting with Hamlyn none the wiser about him.

By February 5, Heinemann had made up their mind. I was officially retained. We immediately struck a snag. Heinemann were opposed to my running the public domain defense. First, they had been advised previously that it would be ruinously expensive to prove that this page in *Spycatcher* had been published here and that page there; second, as publishers they did not particularly like an argument which could be summarized as saying: let the book be published because it's old hat anyway. Hooper and I managed to persuade them to let me run the case as I saw fit.

The British Government had filed Armstrong's two affidavits in late 1985. Heinemann and Wright had given undertakings to the court not to publish any material learned by Wright in the course of his work with MI5 until the case had been finally dealt with at a full trial. Moreover the defense had failed to file any affidavits in answer to those of Armstrong. On February 10, I first appeared for Heinemann and Wright and asked the court to extend the time for the defense to file some evidence. At the brief hearing, before a junior judicial officer revelling in the quaintly medieval title of "Master," the solicitor for the British Government, Richard Feetham, a partner of Stephen Jaques Stone James, asked the court to order Heinemann and Wright to file evidence as to why they wished to retain me as their solicitor. Master Greenwood was puzzled by this and Feetham explained that the Government was concerned that my close connections with the press might result in some confidential material leaking out. I observed that his own firm acted for the John Fairfax newspaper group which included a weekly journal that specialized in intelligence exposés. Master Greenwood wearily observed that litigants could retain whichever solicitor they pleased and it was none of Feetham's business who acted for Wright. He gave us another month to submit an affidavit.

It was about this stage that I became aware of Paul Greengrass. Paul was a producer employed by Granada Television and had, together with John Ware, produced the 1984 World in Action program "The Spy Who Never Was" which featured a lengthy interview with Peter Wright in which he stated he was "99 percent certain" that Sir Roger Hollis, Director-General of MI5 from 1956 to 1965, had been a Soviet spy. During the preparation of the Granada program Wright had discussed his "dossier" on Soviet penetration of British intelligence and with some reluctance Greengrass had been persuaded to help Wright turn his rather heavy material into a readable and hence saleable book.

Greengrass' identity as the "ghostwriter" was a great secret at the time. He feared that if his role became public he might be prosecuted under the Official Secrets Act since he still lived in the United Kingdom and under Section 2 of that Act it was an offense to receive "official" information, which Greengrass certainly had done. Our efforts to conceal his identity only extended to not making any _public_ admissions of his role since both Hooper and I accepted that our telephones and faxes would be intercepted by the British and that it was possible our offices would be bugged also. Certainly Hooper's would have been since he lived in England. I had my doubts whether ASIO, Australia's equivalent to MI5, would be willing to bug an Australian lawyer's office at Britain's behest. But we had to assume it would be done.

Greengrass was also an unlikely enemy of the British Establishment. While he lacked Hooper's wealthy background and elitist education, he was politically conservative, had a sneaking respect for Mrs. Thatcher and had a number of very good friends in the CIA, who regarded him as sound. He did however look like a Trotskyite bombthrower. His straight black hair came well below his collar and he wore an evil looking moustache. He generally had a day's growth and looked rakishly villainous. Greengrass' greatest dislike was for those whom he regarded as upper-class twits, and on occasions he gave me the distinct impression he put Hooper in that class (which was unfair). Greengrass was a mine of information about intelligence matters. He had read every book published in English about spies and many works published in French also. It was pointless my trying to cross-reference _Spycatcher_ with previously published works and so we asked Greengrass to do this job. He took some persuading. He had written the case off as a legal cock-up and told me so, repeatedly. Over a few telephone conversations I gradually won his confidence and he set to work. It was a huge task and proved to be of critical importance.

At the publishing end, Heinemann had sacked Nick Hudson as managing director of their Australian subsidiary, the first defendant in the case, and replaced him with "Sandy" Grant. Alexander Beresford Grant is an Australian who had joined Heinemann from the United Kingdom. At the outset he had little input to the case, the decisions were being made in London by Brian Perman, the managing director, and Nicholas Thompson, the chairman of William Heinemann Limited. Grant is a very calm person and stands, therefore, in complete contrast to Brian Perman whom we christened Panicking Perman for his late-night telephone calls agonizing over the political risks of the case. While they would not now admit to it, I have little doubt that at this stage Heinemann thought that my ferocious conduct of the case for a few months would persuade the British Government to come to the negotiating table. Nobody had any idea the British Government would fight the case all the way. It just didn't seem important enough. It occasionally got a couple of paragraphs in the *Observer,* but really only because of journalist David Leigh's interest in intelligence stories. There is no doubt that had the book been published in early 1986 it would have sold only about 50,000 copies worldwide.

Since intelligence agencies do not like admitting to their bugging activities we knew that it was most unlikely that they would be prepared to use telephone taps as evidence to prosecute Greengrass. It also provided us with splendid opportunities for misinformation. Hooper and I had numerous conversations about lines of cross-examination for Armstrong which were entirely fictitious.

"Is that you Hoops?"

"Absolutely, I have just come back from seeing Boris. He can't get us any pictures, or any clear ones."

"How clear are they?"

"Well, I don't think you can be sure it is Armstrong. Boris says it's Armstrong. Apart from the old Etonian tie on the door, there's nothing to indicate it's Armstrong."

"Can you see the mole?"

"No, can't pick that up. I'm just not sure it's Sir Bob. Even though Boris is financing the case I don't really trust Russians."

"Spending the bloody roubles is hard. How much vodka can a man drink . . ." and so on. The quality of these conversations was not high and generally demonstrated a lamentably ribald lack of respect for our opponents, because with an eleven-hour time difference between Sydney and London, they generally occurred late either in my night or Hooper's night, and not infrequently after one of us had returned from a very good dinner.

Hooper became quite enthused by the possibilities for misinformation and sent me numerous fax messages describing the news he was receiving on a regular basis "from my old chum at MI5." This "old chum" was particularly scathing, according to Hooper, about the forensic talents of the Treasury Solicitor and his Australian lawyers. We rather enjoyed the prospect of our opponents reading the intercepted messages and wondering whether, just possibly, we might not have been pulling their leg.

CHAPTER 2

———————

WHILE GREENGRASS BEGAN TO tackle the particulars of public domain and painstakingly note where the contents of *Spycatcher* had been previously published, I arranged to visit Wright. I flew from Sydney to Hobart on Monday, February 24, 1986. I took my portable computer and printer so that I could prepare his affidavit, print it and have him sign it all on the spot.

Wright had given me his address: Duloe Arabians, Slab Road, Cygnet. As I drove down through the Tasmanian forests to the picturesque old timber port, I recalled the brutal history of Tasmania which belied the chocolate box scenery. When the British settled Australia as a dumping ground for convicts, they chose Tasmania as the home for the worst prisoners and Van Dieman's Land, as it was then known, became a byword for cruelty and despair. In one of the least known and most efficient exercises in genocide the British annihilated the entire aboriginal population in the early nineteenth century. Since those bloody beginnings Tasmania has become a quiet, largely rural, backwater of Australia and at Cygnet, in the south of the island, Peter Wright had chosen to live almost as far away from England as he could without travelling to Antarctica. I asked for directions, and while I negotiated the narrow lane up to Peter's farm, I had visions of an unpretentious horse stud farm, but instead was confronted with a vision of rural poverty rarely seen in Australia. "Duloe Arabians" was about thirty acres in size. The fences were falling down. The horses seemed well fed, but none were broken in. The whole place was in disrepair, and the house was a two-room hovel which compared unfavorably with some swagmen's shacks I had seen in the bush.

The Wrights were obviously stoney-broke. What little money Wright had when he left England in 1976 had been spent on his horse stud business. The bottom had fallen out of the market for Arab horses and his pension was barely enough to feed his horses, let alone himself and his wife Lois. Wright's frailty was obvious. He could not walk more than a few yards without pausing for breath and all of the physical work around the farm was done by his wife Lois whose robust good health made even worse the pale, almost cadaverous, appearance of her husband.

Wright may have looked like death warmed up, but he certainly talked like someone with plenty of life in him. He began with a bitter complaint about the publishers and the lawyers. His complaints were not entirely unreasonable. I persuaded him that I was cut from different cloth. Although he was frail, the years of sickness and frustration had not dimmed Wright's brilliance. He could not concentrate for long periods, but there were still flashes of genius. I felt that Peter would have been a frightening man to work with, so sharp was his intellect.

By this stage I had read the draft manuscript, and I asked Wright whether he felt there were any secrets in the book.

"Not if I can help it. The only material which has not been published before is some of the stuff about my methods of detecting illegal radio transmitters and receivers. This technology, which I developed in the late fifties and early sixties all depended on certain characteristics of valve radios which became completely obsolete with transistorized circuits."

"Would any hostile intelligence service find your book useful?"

"Oh, I'm sure there are a few of my Russian counterparts, now in retirement, who would have a good laugh about it. But their current technical people would be about as interested as an armored corps officer is in Roman chariot design."

At this stage the British Government had not been given a copy of the manuscript, as I had proposed to hand it over together with Wright's affidavit. I was very struck by the datedness of the material in the book. I asked Wright whether he thought the British feared he might reveal other information, not in his manuscript.

"They might. I spent a lot of time in Northern Ireland, you know. But I won't reveal anything about that. Malcolm, it would be easy for me to make this book very sensational indeed. But that's not my point, you see, I really only want to make a case about Soviet penetration."

"Your book goes a lot further than that Peter. It reads like a memoir."

"Oh yes, well Greengrass said my dossier was too heavy-going and so he persuaded me to put in all this personal stuff, conversations, atmosphere, to make it interesting. Paul said if no one reads it it won't do any good and of course he's quite right. You see when I started writing all this stuff I wanted to give my dossier to Thatcher. But she wouldn't read it. She would just hand it back to MI5. So the only alternative is publishing."

I had not read Wright's dossier and suggested that I might take half an hour to do so. I had to agree with Greengrass. When Wright left MI5 in 1976 he was a bitter man. On a personal level he was bitter that his pension was as low as it was. When he joined MI5 on September 1, 1955 he had been employed as a scientific officer with the Admiralty for nearly fifteen years. Because of MI5's peculiar status Wright had to leave his Civil Service job, join a private employer and then join MI5. There was a no-poaching agreement between MI5 and the Civil Service and this shuffle apparently served to honor it, at least superficially. His pension with MI5 was entirely discretionary but he was told that he would be given credit for his years of service with the Admiralty. As it happened he was not. Accordingly when he retired in 1976 after 36 years of highly sensitive work he retired on a pension of a few hundred pounds a month.

But a far more important source of bitterness lay in the failure to identify with certainty the Russian mole that Wright and others believed had gnawed away at the very soul of MI5 throughout the fifties and sixties. The generation who ran MI5 and its sister organization, MI6,[1] during the fifties and sixties was a deeply disappointed one. The British secret services had performed with great courage and cunning in the Second World War. They had succeeded in cracking the German secret military codes, they had parachuted agents into occupied Europe to stir up resistance against the Germans. While it was ultimately the massive resources of the United States which won the military war, the British felt they had won the secret war. But before the garlands of victory had even started to lose their lustre, Guy Burgess and Donald McLean defected to Moscow in May 1951. Kim Philby was accused of treachery and, quite mistakenly, cleared. It was clear to everyone, and in particular the Americans, that the generation which had been educated in the England of the thirties had been extensively penetrated by the Soviet intelligence services. Whatever damage was done by these long term Soviet moles was as nothing compared to the destruction of trust which followed the

---

1. MI6, or the Secret Intelligence Service, is the British intelligence organization which conducts espionage activities outside Britain. MI5's activities are limited to within Britain.

paranoia and suspicion created by their suspected presence.

Men like Wright began to see Soviet interference with every MI5 operation which failed. When in 1963 Sir Antony Blunt confessed to having been a Russian spy the mole hunts began in greater earnest than ever. The story of those mole-hunts is the story of Wright's own book, but suffice it to say that when he left MI5 in 1976 he was convinced that Sir Roger Hollis, Director-General of MI5 from 1956 to 1965, had been a Russian agent. Wright believed that the British establishment had joined ranks to protect Hollis both before and after his death. He was not alone; James Jesus Angleton, counter-espionage head of the CIA, shared his views as did many others. The suspicions destroyed the essential trust and collegiality required in any secret service as intelligence officers spent more time investigating their colleagues than the Russians.

Wright had insufficient means to live in England and so retired to Cygnet in Southern Tasmania. He had a daughter living there and he could acquire land cheaply, at least by English standards. He started to breed Arab horses and spent most of his savings on purchasing a few good sires to start his breeding program. Horse-breeding is generally an expensive hobby for the very rich and it is certainly not recommended as a retirement calling for impoverished ex-spies. But more than the financial pressure, Wright found the isolation of Southern Tasmania very troubling indeed.

He had been privy to some of the weightiest secrets of the free world, he had spied on presidents and prime ministers, he was at the very center of the fight against the Soviets, the IRA and any other enemies of Britain. Suddenly he left all that behind to live in a remote part of Australia's smallest, sleepiest state. His old friends and colleagues were all at the other end of the world and would never call in for Sunday lunch and an update on office gossip. A powerful intellect which had grappled with the wilderness of mirrors now had nothing more to contemplate than the relative mundanity of horse-breeding. With no new challenges to divert it, Wright's brain returned to the problems of the past.

From his exile in Cygnet he dreamed of finding the answer to the riddles, of finding the additional evidence which would expose his enemies and prove him right. He began working on a detailed memorandum on Soviet penetration of British intelligence. This document, which Wright described as his "dossier" went through many versions and one version of it formed the basis of Chapman Pincher's *Their Trade is Treachery* which in 1981 had revealed, for the first time, that Sir Roger Hollis had been investigated as a possible Russian spy. The version of the dossier which I read was the one Wright had tried to get to Thatcher in 1984 following the television interview on the British "World in Action" program. It was dense with detail, dates, code names and close analysis. It was a professional intelligence officer's report. *Spycatcher,* on the other hand, while containing the same message, was couched in the language of popular literature.

Chapman Pincher was a legendary political journalist. He was born in 1916, in British India, and was thus older than Wright, but in considerably better health. Pincher is a staunch conservative and has acquired the manners and bearing of an English country gentleman, illustrating his own recent book about the *Spycatcher* affair with a portrait of himself shouldering a fishing rod. He made his reputation as a journalist with successive "scoops" often about intelligence matters. Pincher's close connections with the conservative military and defense establishment were legendary and in his 1978 book *Inside Story* he had boasted of his "unofficial" work as an agent for MI5.

I read the dossier and returned to talk to Wright. I was puzzled by his involvement with *Their Trade is Treachery*. There appeared very little in *Spycatcher* which was not in either *Their Trade is Treachery* or the second Pincher book on Hollis, *Too Secret Too Long*. Hooper had told me that Wright had been a source of Pincher and had hinted darkly that Wright had received some money from Pincher. (Later I was to learn that this amount was thirty thousand pounds.) It was an unattractive combination. The British could argue that we should not be able to rely on a public domain defense if the previous publications had been caused by Wright himself, acting in breach of confidence.

"Peter, they are going to say that you acted wrongfully in providing information to Pincher for *Their Trade is Treachery*."

"No, they won't. If I breached the Official Secrets Act, then so did Pincher. It's illegal to receive official secrets, you know."

"Well do they know that you gave the information to Pincher?"

"Of course."

"Well, why haven't they come after Pincher, or even you before?"

When I asked this Wright became deliberately vague. "Do you need to know about this now, for this affidavit?"

I confessed I did not. "Very well," said Wright, "We shall discuss that when we need to, later. There is someone else involved whom I don't want to hurt."

I was puzzled by Wright's answer but realized that I was acting for a man who had spent his whole life practicing the arts of deception. "Peter, if you can't answer a question honestly I would rather you told me so. I can't accept half-truths or lies from you. I have to know the truth or know I cannot know anything. Do you understand?"

"I promise to tell you the truth, Malcolm, when I can. But I may never be able to tell you the truth about some things."

"Such as?"

"My work in Northern Ireland, for example. Satellite surveillance. A lot of things. This is a safe book compared to what I could write."

I was puzzled by Wright's motives. It has often been suggested by his critics that his only motive in writing *Spycatcher* was money. There is no doubt that he was short of money and desperately wanted to make some before he died. Wright feared he had very little time left and was anxious to provide for his wife, Lois. On the other hand he knew that *Spycatcher* was all old material. At this time we had not the faintest expectation of a massive trial coupled with a political brawl. Everyone's expectations for the book were fairly modest. If Wright were lucky he might get $100,000 out of it. Had Wright really wanted to write a bestseller, he could have revealed more current secrets. He chose not to do so.

The most intriguing part of *Spycatcher* was Wright's claim that in 1974 up to thirty officers of MI5 planned to destabilize the Labor Government of Harold Wilson. Wright and some of his colleagues suspected Harold Wilson, Prime Minister of Great Britain, as being a Russian spy. So they started to gather material about his Soviet connections with a view to leaking them to the press and forcing his resignation. This allegation was not new, Wilson himself had suspected that the intelligence services were planning to overthrow his Government, but Wright was the first participant to admit to being involved. The Wilson plot, as it became known, was potentially very helpful for me. No court could suppress evidence that the intelligence services were plotting to overthrow an elected Government, or in other words doing precisely what they were supposed to be preventing.

Yet the Wilson plot was only mentioned in passing in Wright's book. When I tried to discuss it with Wright he became frustratingly vague and ambiguous. I sensed then that there was a lot more to the Wilson plot, and to Wright's role in it, than he had related in *Spycatcher.*

"I don't want to discuss it with you, Malcolm. Greengrass has insisted this go in the book, I would rather leave it out. There are people who could be hurt by any more detail. Look, this book is about Russian spies, it isn't about MI5 plotting against the Government . . . even if it was run by a crook like Wilson."

"Well, what do you want to prove in this book?"

"I want to prove that Hollis was a spy; if I can do that I will be happy."

There was more to his motivation, however, than a desire to expose Hollis. An important factor in Wright's thinking was to create a public debate about intelligence in general and Soviet penetration in particular. He wanted people to sit up and take his arguments seriously. Vanity was important also. Wright was frustrated by having led a life of so much achievement and receiving no thanks or public recognition for it. A life of total secrecy can seem very exciting at the time, but in the autumn of a man's life he becomes bitter at the anonymity, particularly when he contrasts his position with others who are laden with honors as they publish their own flattering memoirs.

I asked Wright how he felt about Armstrong's claim of total silence. "You're out of it now, Peter, but if you were still in MI5 how would you feel about an old fellow like you writing his memoirs about the good old days?"

Wright became particularly didactic. "Now look Malcolm, I know more about vetting books than anyone. It is absolute rubbish to say that whatever I write about MI5 will be damaging. We used to leak stuff into the newspapers and into books all the time. It depends on what I say. My book is all old hat in operational terms. It uses history to show how the Russians worked, and how they are almost certainly working today. The Americans let people like me publish their memoirs; you just have to show them to the office first and they cut out what they think is still sensitive. Armstrong doesn't know what he's talking about. It's not hard working through a book and deciding what is damaging and what isn't. I vetted Kim Philby's book *My Silent War* for MI5 when we got an advance copy from the printers."

Chapman Pincher published *Their Trade is Treachery* in March 1981 and set off a big debate about the extent of Soviet penetration in MI5. However, Pincher's book was quickly defused when Mrs. Thatcher told the House of Commons a few days later that in fact Hollis had been cleared by an independent inquiry conducted by Lord Trend, and that the evidence against Hollis all related to events during the Second World War which could equally be attributed to Kim Philby or Anthony Blunt.

Wright told me Mrs. Thatcher had misled the House of Commons. "The evidence against Hollis was all post-war. It couldn't have been laid at the door of Philby or Blunt. The Prime Minister was given a misleading brief by MI5." Pincher was not able to debate with the Prime Minister in the way that Wright (probably mistakenly) thought he was. Wright's faith in Pincher and Thatcher was shaken to the core. The last real chance for his dossier, his obsession perhaps, had been dismissed without any worthwhile debate. The Hollis skeleton was out of the closet . . . but to what purpose?

"All that's happened is that the Hollis thing has been exposed. Bloody Pincher actually said that there was no present problem of penetration of the intelligence services."

"You don't agree with that?"

"Of course not, that's the whole point. Hollis is dead now, but what about the people he appointed and groomed to succeed him? The system is no better now than it was then. It needs reform root and branch. You can't just say that the Hollis thing was an aberration. It's only a symptom of a serious disease.''

To prepare Wright's affidavit, I set up my computer and printer on the floor of his shack and started to take down his words. We went through the main points in Armstrong's affidavits, briefly, and then we went back over the words improving the grammar and syntax.

First Wright denied that his relationship with the British Government, as an officer of MI5, was contractual. This point was important. The Government argued that Wright had been employed under a contract, like a normal employee in civilian life. They argued that there was an implied term in this contract of service which prevented Wright from ever publishing anything about his work as an MI5 officer regardless of whether that information was already well known, regardless of whether it was out of date and regardless of whether it contained evidence of crimes or treachery.

We had to argue that Wright was not employed on a contract at all. We said that whatever obligations he owed to the British Government were no more than the normal obligations imposed on any recipient of confidential material. A person who receives a confidence from another cannot be stopped from publishing the information unless it is still confidential and its publication would cause some real detriment. At the heart of our defense was going to be a contention that everything in *Spycatcher* had already been published and therefore was no longer confidential. The horse had bolted. We were going to argue that, since most of this material was at least twenty if not thirty years out of date, there could be no damage done to the Government by that information being published.

Contracts normally involve both parties having obligations to the other. But servants of the Crown traditionally were owed no obligations by the Crown. Their relationship with the Crown arose out of the Royal Prerogative, a murky doctrine with its roots deep in the

Middle Ages. Murky or not, it was an important legal issue in the case. Wright explained in his affidavit how he had been obliged to leave the Civil Service to join MI5 and how he had been advised that he could be sacked at a moment's notice without reason, that he was not entitled to any pension. In short, the employees of MI5 had no rights at all. This pointed to a non-contractual relationship. Ultimately, however, the crucial fact on this issue was that MI5 was regarded as part of the defense forces of the United Kingdom. Therefore, we argued, its relationship with its officers was the same, in legal terms, as that between the Crown and servicemen. There was no doubt, as a matter of law, that servicemen did not have contractual relations with the Crown.

As we learned later, the contract argument was particularly important for the Government because they needed to find some basis for establishing that Wright owed an obligation to the Crown which was wider than the legal obligation of confidence. At this stage, however, I genuinely believed that once the Government saw the manuscript, realized it was full of old, well-known tales of battles long ago, they would negotiate an end to the litigation. But their purpose was more ambitious than that.

The Government wanted to establish that Wright had an obligation not to publish anything about his life in MI5 regardless of whether the information was common knowledge, out of date, trivial, revealed treason or whatever. In short, a total obligation of silence regardless of what the former officer wished to publish. One of the Government's main objectives in the case was to deter any other officers, present or former, from writing their memoirs. The case was to be a show trial, although at the time they had no idea that it was the Government's conduct which was to be on trial, not Wright's. The absolute doctrine of silence had some amusing aspects: as the Government's counsel later told the court in Syd-

ney, even the MI5 canteen menu could not be revealed.
The Government's attitude was rather like that of the
prohibitionists of alcohol. Because some people used alcohol to excess they justified banning it for everyone.
Similarly the Government wanted to ban all intelligence
memoirs simply because it was possible that they could
contain damaging material. This "principle" of confidentiality was, as we were to argue at the trial, no principle
at all. A better way of balancing the need for security
and the public interest in information about intelligence
was to allow memoirs so long as they were vetted first.

After two days in Tasmania I returned to Sydney and
filed Wright's affidavit, together with the manuscript of
the book. I asked the solicitors for the Government to
tell us which passages of the book they considered to
contain confidential information and offered to negotiate
cuts of any material which was objectionable. In the light
of all that followed my optimism about an early settlement
was quite remarkable. On March 17, 1986 I wrote to
the managing director of Heinemann Publishers Australia
and advised him:

> Generally the case seems to be progressing fairly well.
> The British Government's lawyers have most of the
> manuscript now and I have the matter listed on the
> 24th of March to seek an order obliging them to
> provide us with full particulars of all the passages which
> they claim to be confidential and why. Once we get
> those particulars the case will become manageable and
> it may even be that once they realize how much of
> the book has already been put in the public domain
> by other authors, they will back off.

On March 24 we came before Mr. Justice Phillip Powell.
He was the judge on duty in the Equity Division of the
Supreme Court and was handling as a matter of routine

all interlocutory matters of this kind on that day. He
ordered the Government to file a Statement of Claim.
This meant that the Government would spell out its case,
we would then spell out ours in a Defense and they would
then file a Reply. Once these documents, called pleadings,
were all filed we should have a clear idea of what the
issues were going to be.

I had argued only one case in front of Phillip Powell,
and I had never met him socially. He was fifty-five years
of age and had been a judge for nine years. Powell was
a child of the Great Depression, born in 1930. His father
was a piano-tuner, as had been his grandfather before
him. Phillip Powell was educated at state schools, matri-
culating from Sydney Boys High School to the University
of Sydney where he graduated with a BA and an LLB.
Sickness prevented him achieving outstanding honors in
his Arts degree, but he won first-class honors in Law and
graduated with the prize in Equity. He practiced as a
solicitor for a few years before being admitted to the Bar
of New South Wales in 1954.

He practiced almost entirely in the field of commercial
and equity law and acquired a reputation as both a first-
class lawyer and a good facts man, by which his fellows
meant that he was both sound in academic terms and a
practical advocate to boot. As he progressed at the Bar
his practice expanded to include cases involving trade
union disputes and industrial accidents. He took silk in
1970 and was elevated to the Bench in 1977. Phillip
Powell is a workaholic, even by the fanatical standards
of the legal profession. One of the more senior judges,
becoming exasperated with Powell's high standards, complained: "Powell, if you had your way no one could be
admitted to the Bar unless he had a first-class honors
degree, had been an articled clerk and had practiced for
three years as a fully certified solicitor." "Quite right,"
said Powell, unrepentant. For this reason he has a terrifying reputation among the younger and less experi-

enced members of the profession who find his readiness
to make good the deficiencies in their education rather
intimidating. On the other hand one of his jobs is to look
after the court's Protective Division which deals with
exnuptial custody cases, suits between de facto spouses,
and applications under the Mental Health Act. His common sense and compassion for these unhappy people have
become a byword.

Powell was a member of the Citizens Military Forces
(equivalent of the National Guard) and was commissioned
a captain in an infantry regiment. He served for a time
in infantry intelligence, but was never at any time an
intelligence officer, and certainly was not connected with
counter-espionage. I was a little apprehensive about him
trying the case. Cases like this which sought injunctions
were invariably heard before a judge alone and so Powell's
personality was going to be much more important than
it would be in a jury case. While he is almost completely
apolitical in a party political sense, I had heard he was
a fairly conservative man, and with his army background
likely to be sympathetic to the claims of government in
a case of this kind. However on the 24th Powell was very
businesslike. He said the case had dragged on too long
and that it was high time to get "the matter into the
marketplace." He rejected the Government's pleas for
more time and gave them until April 16 to file a statement
of claim, with us having a further week to file a defense.
He relisted the matter for April 28th. I wrote to Heinemann about this and concluded, "I think they may try
to settle before the 28th."

The Government's statement of claim arrived on April
16. It claimed that Wright owed two distinct sorts of
obligation. The first was a contractual obligation not to
communicate to any person other than a person to whom
he was authorized to communicate it, any information
which had obtained owing to his position as an officer of
MI5. The second obligation was outlined in this way:

Further or in the alternative, during the period of the
second Defendants service, the second defendant obtained information and information was imparted to
him in confidence, so as to import a duty on his part
to the Crown to keep such information confidential.

I wrote to the British Government's solicitors on April
29 and asked them for particulars of this statement of
claim, in particular of their claim that the book contained
confidential information. They replied by saying that *every
line of the book,* with the exception of those chapters which
referred to Wright's pre-MI5 days, was confidential.

Our defense was filed on April 24. In answer to the
claim that Wright owed a contractual duty never to write
about his work in MI5, we said there had been no
contract. We said that the Government's case was an
attempt to enforce in Australia the Official Secrets Act,
by indirect means. It has long been a principle of international law that the courts of one country will not enforce
the penal or public laws of another. Thus an English
criminal law cannot be enforced in Australia, nor can an
English taxation statute be enforced here. The reason
for this unenforceability is that those obligations which
are in fact manifestations of the sovereign power of one
country cannot be enforced in another without diminishing that other nation's own sovereignty. We argued that
the whole relationship between Wright and the British
Government was such a manifestation of sovereign power
and therefore no incident of that relationship could be
enforced in Australia.

My wife, Lucy, was charged particularly with research-
ing and framing this aspect of our argument. If we were
right, then the whole British case was misconceived, regardless of the contents of the book. But it was a difficult
and technical area of the law, and different people could
quite easily take totally different views. We had to concentrate on winning the case on its merits, and that meant

the merits of the book. So we argued that the contents of the book were either:

(a)   in the public domain and no longer confidential;
(b)   already known to the security services of the Soviet Union;
(c)   so out of date its publication would not even if it were still confidential and not known to the Soviet Union, damage the interests and activities of the Plaintiff;
(d)   evidence of treason by members of the British Security Service and therefore should in the public interest be published; and/or;
(e)   evidence of crimes and other unlawful acts committed by the British Security Service and therefore publication should not be suppressed.

We provided the Government with extensive particulars of these defenses. As for the defense that the book contained evidence of crimes and treason, we provided a long list of crimes disclosed in the book, ranging from conspiring to murder to burgling diplomatic premises to switching number plates in breach of the English Motor Traffic Act. Most important perhaps was the allegation that up to thirty officers of MI5 had been involved in a plot to destabilize the government of Harold Wilson whom they apparently suspected of being a Russian spy. This was treason of the worst kind. The agency chartered to defend the realm was trying to undermine it. In chronicling these particulars I was particularly indebted to a young English barrister called Abigail Lochtenberg who helped me with the case for a few months before moving on to more lucrative activities in the heady world of bull market company flotations.

So far as the particulars of prior publication were concerned, I am afraid I persecuted Greengrass until he produced a line by line annotation of the book which

disclosed that there was practically nothing in the book
which had not been published before. The irony of this
was not lost on those with a sense of humor. The publishers at Heinemann became rather downcast as their
lawyer prepared to argue there was nothing new in their
book!

In late April I travelled to England on some business
for another client and took the opportunity to visit the
Treasury Solicitor, Mr. John Bailey, at his office in Queen
Annes Chambers, near Victoria Station. The Treasury
Solicitor is the principal legal officer of the British Government other than the Attorney-General and the Solicitor-General. I called on him with David Hooper who
was looking forward, he told me, to my having a dust-
up with Bailey. I gathered Hooper and Bailey were not
fond of each other.

Hooper in fact was bubbling with anticipation. "Do
you think you might swear at him, a little. You know
what I mean, the way you swear at me all the time?"

"Fuck off, Hooper," I replied, much to his satisfaction.

Bailey's building was subject to extensive security precautions at the time owing to a Libyan bomb scare, and
after five minutes of checking bags and coats we were
admitted to the presence.

Bailey is a short, perfectly formed man, with jet black
hair swept back over his forehead. He is a neat little
fellow, entirely without humor, at least on that occasion.
His companion taking notes was the assistant Treasury
Solicitor, David Hogg.

Bailey began by expressing surprise that we were still
pressing on with the case. "Mr. Hooper, I thought we
had almost reached agreement that your clients would
agree to permanent injunctions if each party paid its own
costs."

Hooper smiled, too smugly, I thought. "I rather think
the emphasis should be on almost."

"I see, so you are pressing on."

"Absolutely."

I then started to explain to Bailey the object of our mission.

"Mr. Bailey, whatever you may think of him, in our view Wright is a genuinely patriotic man. He sincerely believes his book can do no harm to the Security Service."

"No doubt, but now that I have read it, I believe it to be much worse than I had originally expected. Much worse."

I was stunned by this. Had the man read the same book?

"Wright believes that there is nothing in the book which is not either well known or so out of date as to be innocuous. Now, if there are some nuggets of confidential information there which we have missed, will you spell them out so we can consider deleting them?"

"We can't do that, Mr. Turnbull, our objection is to the book as a whole. Each passage is as bad as any other."

"Look, I know that is your official position, but the book is twenty years out of date. There's nothing new in it. This case is going to develop into an embarrassing political row, about nothing. It is simply not worth the effort. Why can't we negotiate? You did so with Nigel West."

I was referring there to the case of Rupert Allason, a Tory MP who writes about intelligence matters under the pseudonym "Nigel West." His book *A Matter of Trust: MI5 1945–72* was published in 1982 and was regarded by many as the reply of the pro-Hollis faction to *Their Trade is Treachery* since it argued that Hollis had not been a spy. West had received extensive assistance and some confidential MI5 documents from one of Wright's former colleagues, Arthur Martin. When Martin realized that West proposed to actually quote extracts from the documents, thereby pointing unequivocally at him as a source, he panicked and told MI5 about the project. The Gov-

ernment had obtained an interlocutory injunction against
it and then negotiated a few deletions from the book,
finally agreeing on a manuscript which could be published.
This blue-pencilling approach was all we asked them to
undertake.

Bailey was quite obdurate. He proceeded to lecture
me, quoting cases to me as though he were an irritated
university tutor and I a particularly dense undergraduate.
I said: "If I can't persuade you, can you please take
instructions from your clients. I really believe you are
overlooking the political implications of this case and you
should discuss this very carefully with your political mas-
ters. They, after all, will carry the can if the case goes
wrong."

Bailey was obviously offended by my suggestion that
he was answerable to the elected representatives of the
people and replied testily: "I don't need to get instructions
from anyone."

I, too, became annoyed. "Well, who do you think you
are? You are a lawyer with a client. Your duty is to seek
instructions from the client, isn't that right?"

Bailey rather pompously replied: "I am in a special
position."

Bailey's smugness made me furious: "You'll be in a
rather special position after everyone has blamed you for
this disaster. I'd get to work covering my own position
if I were you, Mr. Bailey. You'll wish you'd never heard
of Peter Wright by the time the case is over. Don't you
understand? The case is bad news for the Government,
even if you win it. You must clearly explain to the
Government and the responsible ministers the very serious
political risks of pursuing this case."

Bailey changed color a little and said that of course
these decisions were not his to take. Discussions would
continue. The conversation drifted into small talk until
it was time to leave. As I put on my raincoat, Bailey said:

"Your client Mr. Wright, he's a very sick man, isn't he?"
I replied that he was, though mentally he remained sharp.

Bailey took me by the arm, gripping it hard for emphasis, and said: "Well you tell him from me that he'd better seek some medical advice before he comes to court. He'll get no quarter in the witness box on account of his ill health."

I was shocked. Either Bailey was trying to scare Wright, or he had a very black sense of humor. "You tell Armstrong from me, Mr. Bailey, that whatever happens to Wright, he will be politically ruined by this case."

Bailey was delighted that he had got under my skin. As we left his office he patted me on the back. "Well, well, young man, we'll see what you're like on your feet, won't we?" If he had not been so short, I am sure he would have patted me on the head.

Bailey had made it abundantly plain that settlement was out of the question, but naively I still imagined we would be able to settle the case. I felt that if only we could bring it to the attention of one of the responsible politicians, we would be able to talk sense. I could not believe that someone as experienced and realistic as Margaret Thatcher would want to embark on such a fruitless exercise. Wright after all was one of her admirers. He held extreme right-wing views, suspected the Labor Party was riddled with Communists, shared her dogmatic determination, and in intelligence matters his only complaint against Mrs. Thatcher was that she was insufficiently alert to the perils of international communism.

Back in Sydney we worked to provide full particulars of the defense. Abigail Lochtenberg and my wife Lucy catalogued all the crimes, large and small, that could be found in the book. We turned Greengrass' annotations into legalese and in due course presented the British with reams of particulars. These demonstrated that practically every piece of information in *Spycatcher* had been previously published. Only one name was mentioned of a serving officer, and he was about to retire anyway. All of the MI5 premises had been previously identified. No defectors or informants were named who had not been previously identified elsewhere. As we ploughed through all the detail, Lucy turned to me and said: "You know if this was published as a book review of *Spycatcher* it would be remaindered the following day."

"I know, if the British are really smart, they will let us prove there is nothing new in the book and then drop the case completely."

It wasn't until June 24 that we were back before Justice Powell. I asked His Honor to set an early hearing date. My opponents objected to this, complaining that we had not provided sufficient particulars of the public domain defense. Their attitude was deliberately obstructive and time-wasting. For instance Wright's book referred often to Sir Dick Goldsmith White, a former head of both MI6 and MI5. We stated that his identity had been disclosed before in, say, Nigel West's book *A Matter of Trust*. Although there was an index to that book, the Government's lawyers wanted us to spell out every passage where his name was mentioned. I ended up photocopying the index and sending it to them with a rude note.

The mention on June 24 was significant for another reason. Bill Caldwell, the barrister then representing the Government, arrived in court a little late waving facsimiles of the *Observer* and *Guardian* for June 22 and 23 respectively. The two articles detailed some of the more interesting allegations Wright had made in his book about MI5 misconduct. They repeated Wright's allegation that there had been a plot to overthrow Harold Wilson as Prime Minister by certain disaffected MI5 officers, that MI6 had plotted to assassinate Colonel Nasser, that there had been extensive burglaries and buggings of various diplomatic premises in London and so on. It was the first I had heard of this leak and I was as puzzled by it as I think the judge was. Caldwell however went on to suggest, none too obliquely, that the leak had come from my office. I exploded. I demanded to know whether he had instructions for such an allegation and when it was apparent he did not, I characterized his recklessness as "consistent with the lowest traditions of the Bar." Justice Powell, as always, quickly poured oil on the troubled waters, Caldwell conceded he may have been a little rash, the allegation was withdrawn and all, I thought, was well.

In England, however, the consequences of the leak were disastrous. The Government took action there against the two newspapers and in a series of cases that finally found their way to the House of Lords,[2] the newspapers were injuncted, pending a trial of the matter which was heard before Justice Scott in London in December 1987.

The leak gave the Government the opportunity to get the English courts to express their views on the matter and I knew that the English judges would be much more likely to go along with the philosophy of Sir Robert Armstrong than would their Australian colleagues. I was very concerned that the English hearings would result in nasty precedents which might influence the Australian proceedings. I was right. Sir John Donaldson, Master of the Rolls,[3] wrote a leading judgment in the Court of Appeal in which he succinctly expressed the Government's philosophy on this matter:

The background to these proceedings is well known. Mr. Wright was for many years a member of, and

---

2. The House of Lords is the upper house of the British Parliament, similar to the US Senate, except that most of its members are hereditary peers and the balance have been appointed for life. Its "judicial committee" consisting of the most senior British judges is also the ultimate British court of appeal, similar to the US Supreme Court or the High Court of Australia.
3. The Master of the Rolls is the President of the Court of Appeal, the intermediate appellate court of Britain. Sir John's predecessor was the great reformer, Lord Denning.

held senior posts in the British Security Service. The Security Services of this and other countries are popularly referred to as "Secret Services" and indeed until fairly recently there was no official admission that the British Service existed. I mention this matter because it illustrates the unique character of the obligation of confidentiality which is implicit in the acceptance of appointment in the Security Service. Thus, it is a lifelong obligation, wholly unaffected by retirement. Naturally it extends to sensitive information or material, and on the evidence, Mr. Wright occupied positions in which, prior to his retirement in January 1976, he would have had access to information and material which to this day retains a very high degree of sensitivity. However the obligation also extends to mundane matters which in any other context would have no confidentiality. Thus it is the obligation of officers of the Service to keep confidential the .very fact that they are so employed, where they are employed and every aspect of their work. In a word, in so far as it lies in their power, their duty of confidentiality extends to making and keeping it "the Service that never was.

Sir John's philosophy underlined the peculiar hypocrisy of the Government's position, which is best summed up by the phrase "official secrets." Organizations like MI5 and MI6 may be officially secret in that their officers are not permitted to speak publicly under their own names. But unofficially they are far from secret as the dozens of books about their activities have shown. This philosophy concentrates on form rather than substance. It is bad form for intelligence officers to be seen speaking to the public, but if they provide extensive material to a journalist who does not quote them as his source, that is acceptable. Either way the information is in the public domain. Either way intelligence officers have talked. As a matter of substance, there is no difference.

On July 2 we received a Notice to Answer Interrogatories addressed to both Wright and Heinemann. Interrogatories are questions relevant to the disputed factual issues raised in the proceedings, which one side in litigation serves on the other. The answers have to be sworn as true. Interrogatories are designed as pre-trial procedure to obtain admissions from your opponents and thereby sharpen the issues for the hearing. They are particularly important when your opponent is a corporation or, as in this case, a government. I was concerned that a number of matters I wanted to get answers on would not be matters Armstrong had particular knowledge of. I feared he might simply say "I don't know" quite honestly. The interrogatories would oblige the Government to make inquiries and find the answers from their files, retired officers and so on.

The Government's interrogatories were largely directed to formal matters of evidence, but there was a sinister aspect. They sought to know the names and addresses of each person who had participated or contributed to the composition of the manuscript. They wanted to know the names of his agents and the names of any other persons to whom it had been disclosed. We objected to answering these questions on the grounds that they were irrelevant and designed solely to find some more victims for the Government's prosecutors. Our real concern was Greengrass. He lived in the UK and was very much within the grasp of the Director of Public Prosecutions.

Our interrogatories were to cause much more grief. Part of our defense was that the book contained evidence of serious crimes and improprieties on the part of MI5. So we itemized the most important of these allegations and in our interrogatories asked the Government whether they were true. For example, Interrogatory No. 27:

27. Did officers of the British Secret Intelligence Service, otherwise known as MI6, or any other officers

or employees of the British Crown, develop any plan
or operation which had as its goal the assassination of
Colonel Nasser, then head of the State of Egypt?

Other interrogatories from our side included questions
about the Government's prior knowledge of the publication of Chapman Pincher's *Their Trade is Treachery* and
Too Secret Too Long and also Nigel West's *A Matter of
Trust.* The Government refused to answer any of these
questions on the grounds that they were irrelevant. If we
were able to persuade Justice Powell that the prior publications were relevant to the case, then the trial could
be turned on its head. Instead of being a case about why
Wright should be allowed to publish *Spycatcher*, it would
become a case about why the Government allowed Chapman Pincher and Nigel West to publish their books. I
was already deeply suspicious about the circumstances in
which both these books were published.

Changing the focus of the case from Wright's conduct,
to the conduct of the Government in allowing Pincher
and West to publish their books, was the most important
strategic objective we had. While I was fond of Wright
and admired his sincerity, I had to accept that to many
people he would be seen as a man who had knowingly
set out to breach the obligations imposed on him by the
Official Secrets Act. Judges are conservative people. Being
part of the machinery of government, they have developed a deep respect for authority and order. Wright was
unlikely to find many admirers among them, and if the
litigation went right through the Australian court system,
in due course eleven judges would consider his case: one
trial judge, three judges on the New South Wales Court
of Appeal, and up to seven judges on the High Court
of Australia.

On the other hand if we could demonstrate that the
Government's policy on official secrets was a hypocritical
one and that safely conservative writers like Pincher and

West could publish without restraint, the judges would be outraged. While they respect authority more than most, they also expect Governments to act consistently and honestly. If the Government's conduct started to look unattractive, then Wright's might appear more appealing.

By August things were changing at the Government's camp. Theo Simos QC became involved in the case. Simos, then fifty-two, is a distinguished lawyer with considerable expertise in equity and constitutional law. He quickly recognized that the Government's statement of claim needed amending and so on August 11 they amended it to frame their claim against Wright in absolute terms which reflected the views of Sir John Donaldson.

With the Government objecting to answer almost all of the interrogatories we had served upon it, and Heinemann and Wright objecting to answer some of theirs the case came before Justice Powell on August 12, both sides moving for orders that the other answer the interrogatories objected to.

It was at this stage that the Government took a significant, perhaps fatal, decision. The Government's case was that Wright owed an absolute duty of silence. It didn't matter whether he wanted to publish material which was out of date, common knowledge, evidence of crimes. He had to stay mum, no matter what. Our interrogatories of course were largely aimed at making out our defenses that the book contained evidence of crimes and that in any event its contents had been previously published by other authors, in circumstances where the Government could have stopped those other authors but had failed to do so.

Theo Simos was faced with a dire choice. If Wright's absolute duty of silence was correctly stated, then all of these defenses were irrelevant and no answer to the statement of claim. Therefore the interrogatories were irrelevant. In order to persuade the judge that his clients did not need to answer them he would have to limit his case to this argument and win or lose upon it. My instructions were to keep the case as short and economical as possible, and I invited Theo to ask the judge to limit the case to this one proposition. That would involve a short legal argument the result of which would determine the case.

With the benefit of hindsight, I do not doubt the Government wished that they had taken this route. They would have almost certainly lost, but at least they would have been seen to make an effort and they could then put down their defeat to legal technicalities easily remedied by legislation and special contracts for intelligence officers. They always claimed they were fighting for a principle of total silence which transcended normal obligations of confidentiality. They should have limited their arguments to that principle, and if the principle was wrong, accepted defeat with grace.

Had they done this, they would never have become involved in the merits of Peter Wright's particular book. Armstrong would never have been cross-examined on the Government's dealings with Chapman Pincher, there would have been no political fallout and *Spycatcher*, when it was published, would have only sold a few thousand copies.

The Government of course wanted to have two bites at the cherry. If they couldn't succeed on their claim that no book of this kind should ever be published, they then wanted a fall-back position by which they could argue that Wright's book *in particular* was dangerous. As long as they wanted to argue this second alternative position, the interrogatories would then become relevant and necessary to show whether or not Wright's book was indeed really dangerous.

After two days of argument the Government realized they were caught. Either they limited their case to the absolutist argument of total silence, or they answered the interrogatories. The implications of this were terrifying.

The Government would have to answer on oath whether or not MI5 had been systematically breaking the law by bugging embassies, burgling consulates and generally doing the sort of thing law enforcement agencies are meant to stop.

Urgent talks occurred between London and Sydney overnight. A solution was found. The next morning Theo rang me and asked me what our attitude would be if the Government admitted that everything in Wright's book was true. This admission would be made "for the purposes of the proceedings" only. The case would therefore proceed on the basis that MI5 had burgled embassies, plotted to assassinate Nasser and so on. This admission had another advantage. It prevented me from cross-examining Armstrong about the truth of Wright's allegations. I was not particularly concerned about that since it was obvious that almost all of Wright's allegations were well before Armstrong's time and he would be able, quite honestly, to say he did not know anything about them.

I extracted another admission from the Government. In 1985 Cathy Massiter, a former MI5 officer, who had resigned only months before, made a number of grave allegations about MI5's bugging of civil libertarians, left-wing politicians and trade unionists. I had told the judge that I proposed to rely on these allegations to assist my making out a case that MI5 was a criminal organization which should be given no assistance by the courts. The Government also admitted that everything in Massiter's allegations was true.

Lucy and I now became confident that we had a good chance of winning. We should now be able to turn the tables and fulfil the threat I had made to Bailey: the Government's practice on official secrets was to be on trial, not Peter Wright's book.

CHAPTER 3

THE INTERLOCUTORY VICTORY OVER the interrogatories had also established a very important principle.
The previous publications of Pincher and West were
relevant matters for the trial. I started to plan a long
cross-examination of Sir Robert Armstrong which would
seek explanations for the rather inconsistent treatment
of Pincher, West and others on the one hand and Wright
on the other.

While I was beginning to relish the prospects of the
trial, I still wanted to settle the case. Even though I was
confident of success, I realized that all litigation is risky
and that at best we had a 60 percent chance of victory.
So I telephoned an old friend, Jonathan Aitken.

Aitken is the Conservative MP for Thanet East. He is
a cousin of the great Lord Beaverbrook and at forty-six
is still regarded as a bright young man. Jonathan's career
spans journalism, finance and politics. I had come to know
him through my father-in-law while I was at Oxford.
Later we worked together after Kerry Packer's acquisition
of 23 percent of TV-am Ltd, of which Jonathan was
chairman. He is a liberal Conservative and steadfastly
opposed to the Official Secrets Act. He has a special
interest in official secrets, however, having been unsuccessfully prosecuted for breach of the Official Secrets Act

after he published some leaked information about British involvement in the Biafran War.

Jonathan knows everyone in London. He lives in a fine house in Lord North Street, formerly occupied by Brendon Bracken, and I knew that if anyone could get the ear of the Prime Minister he could. I explained to Jonathan that neither I, Wright nor Heinemann had any desire to proceed with a bitter fight against Sir Robert, Mrs. Thatcher or the British Government.

"I have a great admiration for Thatcher, Jonathan, as you well know. But she must be told that the case is now on a collision course. The Government must be getting misguided legal advice."

"Why are you so sure you will win?" Jonathan asked.

"Well, we are now going into the trial on the basis that everything in the book is true, we have already established that there is practically nothing new in the book, and unless the trial judge proposes to ignore what the High Court said in *Commonwealth v. Fairfax,* I think we have to win."

"I understand the Government are very confident that the judge will find Wright has a contract which overcomes the Australian law."

"Believe me, the contract argument is hopeless. What I think has happened is that John Bailey, the Treasury Solicitor, is like most lawyers with a disaster on his hands, he does not want to admit it to his clients. Thatcher and Armstrong have obviously got much more important things on their plate than this little brouhaha and as a result they simply don't realize how grim their prospects are."

"Have you tried to talk to Bailey?" Jonathan inquired.

"Of course. He's a smarmy patronizing tall poppy. He told me to tell Wright to get medical advice before he gets in the witness box because he'll get no quarter from the Government when he's cross-examined. I have offered him a solution which you should pass on to the Government. Get them to send a top security officer out to

Sydney for a without prejudice meeting. He must tell us what's in the book which is really sensitive. As long as he is being sensible we'll cut that material out. Then the case will be settled and honor will be satisfied, we can agree on a joint statement so that no one on our side crows about winning and the whole thing will be forgotten in ten days."

"But I gather they see this as a means of stopping other would-be Peter Wrights from doing the same thing," Jonathan protested.

"No doubt, but that's how misguided they are. If Wright lived in America there would not even be a case. The First Amendment would not allow Britain to ban this book in the United States and so any other would-be author simply has to move there rather than Sydney. The answer to the general problem is to implement proper written contracts with intelligence officers which provide for the same sort of official vetting of manuscripts that the Americans have."

Jonathan made notes of the telephone conversation and passed them on to Sir Michael Havers. At first Havers seemed interested, but finally he wrote a stiff note rejecting any such offer of a deal. Subsequently I learned from one of Thatcher's aides that the Prime Minister herself had ruled out any compromise. I had obviously been far too harsh on Bailey. He had explained the risks to his client, but she was not prepared to take them.

Many observers of the *Spycatcher* litigation have regarded the Government as making a huge tactical error in admitting that the allegations in *Spycatcher* were true. Certainly the admissions caused a real political embarrassment for the Government in London. Here was a book filled with allegations Mrs. Thatcher had denied in the Commons, being branded as "true" for the purposes of a court case in Sydney.

Fleet Street was predictably unimpressed with this legal maneuver. Try as they might the British Government could not convince that the admission was merely "technical." The *Evening Standard* summed up the mood when it described the admissions as "MI5 Charade." The editorial writers were not slow to observe, in scathing terms, that the very allegations of criminal conduct which the Government had persuaded Sir John Donaldson to suppress in London were now officially "true" in New South Wales.

But what else could they have done? The only realistic choice was to limit their case to the absolute doctrine of confidence, and if that was found to be wrong in law, give up gracefully. From my point of view, I was in two minds about agreeing to the proposed admissions. My strategy at that time was based on a firm belief that the case would settle. I did not believe for one moment that the Government would be mad enough to allow such a relatively trivial matter to develop into a full-scale political drama.

So I was trying very hard to find a way out for the British Government, a face-saving solution that would allow it to drop the case with honor. At the time I felt that had I insisted on answers to the interrogatories, Justice Powell would have ordered them answered. I also felt we would have been successful in the Court of Appeal. The risk we ran by insisting on the answers was that the Government would enlist the support of the Australian Government (as they were later to do) in a claim that the national security of Australia precluded answers being given. Such a claim would have been spurious and in the long run doomed to founder, but by the time it had been argued up to the Australian High Court the trial would have been delayed for at least a year. On the other hand had we fought that battle and won, the British might have chucked the whole case in. Rightly or wrongly, I decided to accept the admissions and press on for a trial as soon as possible. I felt that they would be most likely to settle when Sir Robert realized he had to actually get on the plane to come to Sydney to give evidence. I completely underestimated their steely, albeit misguided, determination.

The political embarrassment caused by the admissions in Sydney and the proceedings against the *Guardian* and *Observer* in London meant that for the first time the case became really newsworthy. I had received remarkably few calls from journalists before the hearing about the interrogatories, and now they became frequent. Since my dealings with the press have been the subject of some criticism it is worth describing my approach.

From the outset I knew that the *Spycatcher* case had the potential to become a big political story. But I genuinely believed it would be settled long before a hearing. I was not relishing the notoriety the case would bring if it did get to a trial. But it was an important part of my strategy for effecting a settlement that the case receive a lot of publicity. Naively I imagined that the case was being pushed by MI5 and some rather unworldly lawyers, like John Bailey. At that time I felt that once Mrs. Thatcher cottoned on to the risks inherent in the litigation, she would order that a settlement be negotiated. Of course as history proved, the opposite was the case.

I had in the past defended clients in the press and on television. When I used television and radio to defend Kerry Packer from the attacks of the Costigan Royal Commission, I received a great deal of praise and criticism, the latter mainly from lawyers who felt that such public appearances were unseemly.

I did not agree with their criticism then, and the intervening years have not caused me to change my mind. While I think lawyers have their main function in the courts, if their client's cause requires media appearances they should not shrink from it. Packer's position was such that unless the damage to his reputation was repaired quickly, he could have been forced out of business. Traditional legal methods were just too slow, especially since

Costigan had denied Packer the normal procedures of natural justice. For him, there was no alternative.

But *Spycatcher* was different. Winning the support of the media was not really material to winning the trial. The newspapers would always be sympathetic to anyone who took on the Government, in any case. It was very important, however, that we ensure the media understood the basis on which we were defending the case. In particular I had to counter the very misleading line that Wright wanted to obtain "a charter for leaks." Moreover, I knew that Powell would be very unhappy if he felt the real battle was going on outside his courtroom.

Lawyers in Australia (and the United Kingdom) are rather hypocritical about their relations with the press. The "ethical" prohibitions against giving interviews to the media have largely evaporated so far as solicitors are concerned, but they still apply to barristers. Their purpose is to stop "advertising" or "touting" for business. They are part of the whole structure of restraint of trade that most professions have erected about their members.

That is why barristers are permitted to speak to the media about their cases so long as they do so "off the record" and are not quoted. This is precisely the sort of hypocritical practice I was to criticize the Government for. It involves the exercise of influence without taking responsibility. I was already reading articles quoting "Governmental legal sources" giving various views about the litigation and I knew that this came from someone in the Government's legal team, probably in London.

So I resolved that I would not make any contentious statements to the press other than on a fully attributed and hence quoted basis. On occasions when I did provide background information to the press and make "hard" information available to them, such as copies of submissions handed up in court and general descriptions of the issues, I would not agree to be quoted by any journalists. But I resolved that where I decided to say something which was subjective, or calculated to help Wright's case, I would do so on the record. This did not stop some journalists attributing all manner of extravagant remarks to me about the case. I began to prefer the electronic media which at least had to put up with what I said; even though they could edit me, they weren't able to put words in my mouth.

As the case progressed and public attacks were made on Wright and his advisors, largely from sources "close to the Government," I had to become much more openly outspoken. If the Government wanted to have a public slanging match, I was more than happy to oblige at my end.

The admissions saved the Government from answering the questions about all the allegations of illegality in Wright's book, but the judge still ordered them to answer the questions which were directed to the Government's prior knowledge of Nigel West's book *A Matter of Trust* in 1982. *A Matter of Trust* is a history of MI5 from 1945 to 1972 and contains an incredible amount of detail. It is perfectly obvious that most of it must have come from sources inside MI5.

On September 16, 1982 Sir Robert answered two questions I had posed for him about *Matter of Trust*. The first answer simply confirmed that the book had been published after the Government had obtained an interim injunction to restrain publication. There were negotiations and the book was published as a result. In answer to the question "Were the said proceedings settled on the basis that the book could be published?" Sir Robert answered: "The proceedings were stayed by consent following discussions between the parties to the proceedings the Plaintiff being satisfied that those matters contained in the manuscript which the Plaintiff believed had been obtained by the Defendant in breach of a duty of confidentiality owed to the Crown would be removed." This answer was later proved to be false, but even then I felt it must be wrong. The answer suggests that the Government had everything removed from the book which the Government believed West had obtained from an MI5 or ex-MI5 source. It was well known that his source was Arthur Martin, one of Wright's colleagues in the mole-hunts. One had only to read the book to recognize that there was still a huge amount of previously unpublished material.

However an even more important piece of evidence came to light in August. In the judgment of Sir John Donaldson in the English Court of Appeal the previous month, he had addressed the contention, made by counsel for the newspapers, that much of the contents of *Spycatcher* had been previously published by Chapman Pincher in *Their Trade is Treachery* and *Too Secret Too Long*. Sir John observed: "In the case of Mr. Chapman Pincher's published works, no-one with authority to authorize publication may have known of what was intended before it was done." Pincher wrote to the *The Times* on August 21 and observed in part as follows:

While my publishers and I took extreme precautions to prevent the security authorities from seeing the script of the first relevant book, *Their Trade is Treachery*, in advance of its publication in March, 1981, we failed. Unknown to us, photocopies of the book were being circulated in MI5, MI6, the Cabinet Office and the Prime Ministers Office several weeks in advance of publication. So the Crown had ample time to obtain injunctions. Instead after meetings of which I have been given details by some of those present, it was decided to do nothing because it was agreed that, in the event of litigation, the Crown would have to make too many damaging admissions. Two days before publication the publishers received a letter from Sir Robert Armstrong assuring them that there was no intention of interfering with publication of the book in any way.

The additional interrogatories served as a result of this letter to *The Times*, together with Sir Robert Armstrong's sworn answers are set out below:

148.Q.   Were photocopies of the manuscript of the book "Their Trade is Treachery" in the possession of any, and if so, which, officers or departments of the British Crown prior to the publication of the said book in March, 1981?

148.A.   Photocopies of the manuscript were in the possession of officers of the Crown prior to publication of the said book in March, 1981.

149.Q.   If the answer to the foregoing interrogatory is yes, when did photocopies of the said manuscript first come into the possession of any servants or agents of the British Crown?

149.A.   In or about February, 1981.

150.Q.   Was consideration given by the Plaintiff or any other servants or agents of the British Crown to restraining the publication of the said book prior to its publication?

150.A.   The Plaintiff was advised that it had no basis to restrain the publication of the said book.

The last answer was staggering. I knew immediately that there was a large whale in the bay. What lawyer would give such ridiculous advice? Here was a book filled with information obviously received from either serving or retired MI5 officers. Pincher said as much in the foreword. The information is about as damaging as could possibly be imagined: for the first time it was revealed that Sir Roger Hollis, head of MI5 from 1956 to 1965, had been investigated on suspicion of having spied for the Russians. In these circumstances the Government obtains a copy of the manuscript of the book weeks before publication. It could have obtained an injunction on the basis that the information in the book was avowedly obtained in breach of the Official Secrets Act in five minutes flat, and I knew that any lawyer who advised the contrary was a knave, because, frankly, there is no lawyer alive who could be so great a fool.

The interrogatories were just one aspect of pre-trial procedures. On July 10 I had served on the Government's solicitors a Notice for discovery of documents. The Discovery procedure obliged them to produce for our inspection all documents in their possession, custody or control which were relevant to any fact in issue between the parties. The Government's lawyers obfuscated and no discovery was made until, despairing of resolving the matter informally, I went back to Justice Powell and obtained an order for discovery from him. Powell was suitably unimpressed by the Government's failure to comply with the rules of court and in his final judgment records the following:

> Although I had earlier been assured by counsel for the British Government that no formal Order for Discovery by the British Government was necessary as Discovery would, if requested by the Defendants' solicitor, be given, Discovery, although requested by the Defendants' solicitor had not been given by October 3, 1986, on which day the proceedings were, at the request of the Defendants' solicitor relisted before me.

The Government filed a list of documents on October 28, 1986, not one of which related to anything other than Wright's conditions of employment. In particular none related to the Pincher or West books. We went back to court and on November 5, after two days' ar-

gument, Justice Powell ordered, for the second time, that
the Government provide discovery of documents relevant
to the issues raised in the defense, which included the
previous publications by Pincher, West and others. The
Government filed another list of documents on November
12, 1986 which was no more enlightening than the previous one and so I took them back to Justice Powell who
on November 14 ordered for the third time that they
provide discovery of documents relevant to the previous
publications and some other issues. Then, the Friday
before the trial was due to begin, Theo Simos QC announced that the Government wanted the trial date va-
cated, or postponed indefinitely, so that the British Government could appeal his ruling on discovery to the Court
of Appeal.

I thought Justice Powell was going to explode. His
normally placid countenance became thunderous and he
complained bitterly about the British Government's failure to comply with the Rules of Court. He refused to
vacate the trial date.

In retrospect the Government's conduct was quite disgraceful. It was perfectly obvious back in August that the
issues of prior publications were relevant. They had been
pleaded in our defense and the Government had not
bothered to move to strike them out. Had they felt
aggrieved by this they could have gone to the Court of
Appeal then, but rather than doing so they left their
application to the Court of Appeal until the last possible
moment.

CHAPTER 4

Two weeks before the trial was due to begin, on November 17, Peter and Lois Wright came up to Sydney from Tasmania. Lucy and I collected them at the airport and took them to the Cranbrook Private Hotel, a small hotel located a kilometre from our house in Rose Bay, a harborside suburb about five kilometres from the city.

I had spent very little time with Wright before the trial and had looked forward to spending the two weeks going over his evidence with him. But the battle over discovery completely thwarted my preparation plans. Instead of preparing for the trial we were fighting interlocutory skirmishes about the documents we had requested from the British Government. It was very frustrating.

We parked Peter in a spare office at Turnbull McWilliam and he and Lois worked away compiling notes about previous publications. Peter also started to draft a monumental list of people he suspected of having been Russian spies. As it got longer and longer I wondered whether the KGB had more representatives in England than in Russia. He was a charming if demanding guest in the office. He kept the secretaries busy providing him with whiskies and sandwiches.

Peter is quite bald and in November the sun is blazing hot in Sydney. He had brought a floppy sun hat with him, but left it in a taxi. He asked me where he could buy a replacement and I directed him to R. M. Williams, the Bushman's Outfitters in Castlereagh Street. He returned with the large bush hat which became his trademark. It caused so much attention that even Sir Robert Armstrong was moved to ask Peter at court where he could buy one for himself!

Two others arrived to complete the team. David Hooper arrived a few days before the trial began. He had prepared some large folders of material concerning previous publications on intelligence matters and was an expert on the tortuous twists and turns of British policy on official secrets. Hooper was flown out at Heinemann's expense.

The Old Etonian Hooper was part of the establishment, and to some extent lacked the objectivity of an outsider. This paradox amused me, since much of the British Government's case was based on the premise that Wright, as an insider, had some special perspective on intelligence life. Yet my own experience had convinced me that insiders generally lost sight of the wood for the trees.

The key to Hooper of course was that he was really two people. On the one hand he was Eton and Christchurch and very respectable, and that side of his character admired, if not adored, Armstrong who had reached a pinnacle of Establishment ambition. But lurking in the background was another, much more radical, Hooper persona which despised the establishment and delighted in tweeking its nose.

Hooper's nascent radicalism did not extend so far as to make fun at his old school. One evening later in the case when we relaxed with a few bottles of wine, the conversation became a little disrespectful of Armstrong's (and Hooper's) old school, Eton. Hooper lost his good humor. "I say, you can keep school right out of this." And so as not to offend him, we did.

The second, and in many ways the most important member of the defense team was Paul Greengrass. For reasons I never fully understood, Heinemann in London treated him like a leper. Despite the fact that he had ghost-written the book and had compiled a monumental amount of information about prior publications, Heinemann refused to pay his airfare to Sydney. Fortunately the resourceful Greengrass was able to persuade the *Observer* to pay the airfare to Sydney in return for an exclusive pre-trial picture of Wright and his advisors. I have little doubt that if he had not been able to get to Sydney, we would not have won the case at all.

As soon as Paul arrived we started to expand our particulars of public domain which demonstrated that there were no "revelations" in *Spycatcher*. His memory was almost photographic and as we went through *Spycatcher* line by line he would say "Right, stop there, there is a reference to that in a French book about the intelligence services . . ." and then he would find the page reference and we would note it down. Greengrass, having no money at the time, stayed at our house for the five weeks he was in Sydney. He is a father of two small children, and so had little difficulty getting on with our rowdy offspring Alexander, then four and Daisy, then two.

Greengrass was a natural lawyer, in the sense that all he lacked to be a great advocate was a law degree. I have never met a non-lawyer who better understood the nature of litigation and tactics of cross-examination. He also understood the way the British establishment thinks.

He was very anxious the day he arrived, and later in the day suggested that he and I might have a quiet drink "not in the office." He insisted it be somewhere that I normally didn't patronize. Since I rarely drink in bars, or hotels, it wasn't hard to find such a place and we repaired to a wine bar at Kings Cross. We found a table down the back, and Greengrass began to talk.

"You know how Peter provided the information to Pincher for *Their Trade is Treachery?*"

"A little," I replied. "Peter seems very sensitive about it. I know he received some money from Pincher. It's not going to look good in court."

"Has he told you about Victor?" Greengrass was referring to Wright's great mentor, Lord Victor Rothschild, of the great banking family, a confidant of Prime Ministers, spymasters and financiers. Also a great scientist. Rothschild was almost the personification of brilliance, wealth and power.

"Victor Rothschild? Well, there's masses about him in the book of course, but Peter hasn't said much about him at all. I am a little worried about this, of course. We are trying to present Peter as an idealist, and his receiving £30,000 from Pincher for giving him the information about Hollis does make him look rather greedy, if not grubby."

Greengrass took a deep breath and began. "Okay, here we go. One of the things you've got to understand about Peter is that he is incredibly socially insecure. He never felt completely welcome with the establishment people at MI5. They always let him know he was a bit on the outside. Now, Victor Rothschild was different. He was very kind to Peter, introduced him to people, made a fuss of him. In return Peter kept Victor posted about what was going on at MI5."

"Was he allowed to do this?" I asked.

"Peter says that Furnival Jones authorized him to talk to Rothschild.[1] Victor was always part of that intelligence world, but a little outside it. He seems to have been close to everyone, but no one. Do you know what I mean?"

"Not really," I said. "But how does Rothschild fit into the Pincher business?"

"Right, now when Blunt was exposed in 1979 everyone started looking about for the next mole. Rothschild thought he might be accused. He writes to Peter and

---

1. Sir Martin Furnival Jones, head of MI5 from 1963–1972.

invites him over to England. Peter says he wants to get his dossier about Hollis and the Russians to Thatcher. This is late 1980 now; Thatcher's only been in power for eighteen months. Rothschild tells him the best way to go is to write a book, he introduces him to Pincher, Pincher comes out to Tasmania, sees Peter and gets the information about Hollis, then he comes home and writes *Their Trade is Treachery*. Meanwhile Rothschild funnels half the royalties to Peter via his own Swiss bank account."

"Good God, Paul. Rothschild was responsible for *Their Trade is Treachery?* He could go to jail for that."

"Let me finish. I have made sure my friend in the CIA knows about this. I told them all about it a few months ago."

"What did he say?" I asked.

"He laughed."

"I think it's a conspiracy, I think the Government wanted *Their Trade is Treachery* published. I think Rothschild was given the job of organizing it."

Greengrass smiled. "You're as paranoid as Peter. I think this intelligence stuff has got to you."

The news about Rothschild was startling. If Greengrass was telling the truth then Rothschild had conspired with Pincher to pay Wright for revealing Government secrets. Not only had Rothschild, Pincher and Wright breached the Official Secrets Act, but Rothschild had clearly arranged for Wright to be paid money so that he would break the law.

Journalists regularly breach the Official Secrets Act by receiving Government information and prosecutions are rare, no doubt because Governments do not want to unnecessarily alienate the press. But Rothschild was in a different category. He was a war hero who had defused bombs during the blitz on London. He was a great scientist and part of the world's wealthiest and most powerful financial family. He had worked for MI5 and MI6, particularly in the Middle East, he had been a close advisor of successive British Prime Ministers. He was Establishment with a capital "E." I simply could not believe that Rothschild would lend himself to such a criminal enterprise without getting at least *covert* authorization first.

One of Rothschild's former colleagues at No. 10 Downing Street was the British Government's principal witness Sir Robert Armstrong. Robert Temple Armstrong was born in 1927. His father was Sir Thomas Armstrong, head of the Royal Academy of Music. Sir Robert was educated at Eton and Oxford and joined the Treasury in 1950 when he was twenty-three. He is a first-class musician and apparently considered a career in music before he finally opted for a bureaucrat's life.

His rise through the Civil Service was also a series of connections with powerful mentors. He was successively private secretary to Roy Jenkins, as Chancellor of the Exchequer, Ted Heath, as Prime Minister,[2] and Harold Wilson as Prime Minister. Before that he had been Secretary to Lord Radcliffe's committee of inquiry into the monetary system. After spending a year with Wilson in 1975 he was moved to the Home Office where he ran the police department, and in 1977 became Under-Secretary. Two years later he succeeded Sir John Hunt as Secretary of the Cabinet and head of the Civil Service.

At the time of his appointment most of the profiles were highly flattering. Indeed they ought to have been. His whole career up to that time had been faultlessly executed. However Laurence Marks, writing in the *Observer* on July 15, 1979, sounded a note of caution:

> Those who don't like him complain that he is a manipulator obsessed with bureaucratic equilibrium, a what-e'er-is-best-administered-is best sort of man, uncomfortable with those who take a stand on principle.

2. It was during Heath's prime ministership in 1970–74 that Armstrong worked closely with Rothschild who was the Prime Minister's principal policy adviser and head of the "think tank."

On the other hand Armstrong is plainly a sensitive and artistic man. He writes beautiful prose. His panegyric for his friend Anthony Rawlinson who died climbing in the Alps is as elegant a farewell as any friend could ask for. He is also a precise man, a master of detail. One observer wrote in 1986: "Armstrong has the qualities to have been professional head of the civil service at any time since 1870."

Nonetheless his discharge of his office differed markedly from that of his predecessors. He became a public figure in the way civil servants rarely do. He acquired a reputation as the Prime Minister's fix-it man. The four episodes which marked his reign at No. 10 prior to the *Spycatcher* trial were the banning of trade unions at Government Communications Headquarters at Cheltenham, the substantial increase in salary scales for senior civil servants, known as the "top people's pay" affair, the Anglo-Irish agreement and Westland. In February 1986 the *Spectator* had this to say about the Cabinet Secretary:

> The view is taken that whatever his technical competence, he has absolutely no feel for politics; so the greater his sway, the greater his scope for getting the Government into trouble.
>
> There is little doubt that this is precisely what happened, both over the decision to ban trades unions from GCHQ and over top people's pay. Both of these were classic Armstrong operations. They were conducted in great secrecy: only a specially selected group of ministers was fed a carefully limited amount of briefing; no contradictory views, information or political advice were allowed to surface until the decision was irrevocably taken—and then into a political crisis.

His rather fumbling political hand was particularly apparent during "the Westland affair." That episode involved a dispute between the Prime Minister and the

Minister for Defense, Mr. Michael Heseltine, concerning a foundering British owned helicopter company called Westland. Heseltine was supporting a European consortium in its efforts to acquire the company, whereas it was believed the Prime Minister would prefer an American company to acquire it.

The Solicitor-General had written a letter of advice to the Minister for Trade and Industry, Leon Brittan, which was critical of certain remarks made by Heseltine. This letter was leaked to the press by the press secretary at Trade and Industry. The leaking was approved by certain officials at No. 10 Downing Street. Needless to say this leak caused a great scandal, and it was Armstrong who appeared before a parliamentary committee to give his own version of the events. Instead of the various press secretaries involved giving their own evidence, Armstrong privately interviewed them and then gave his own summary of what had occurred. Armstrong's version of events was that there had been a "misunderstanding" between officials at Trade and Industry and others at No. 10. In particular his version exonerated the Prime Minister or her press secretary, Mr. Bernard Ingham, from any complicity in the leak which had gravely damaged Mr. Heseltine.

The accuracy of Armstrong's assessment could not be tested because the Government refused to allow any of those people actually involved to give evidence. His handling of the rather mild cross-examination by the committee was widely praised. However Labor MPs called for his resignation and accused him of having been the agent of a cover-up. The committee report was mildly critical of Sir Robert.

This affair and a number of other less significant events gave Armstrong a reputation for being very much Thatcher's man. He had become, in many eyes at least, a hired gun prepared to do almost anything in the service of his boss.

When I read Armstrong's evidence before the Westland Committee, I was not particularly impressed by either his answers or the questions from the committee. Significantly Armstrong had only spent a day before the committee, but a really effective cross-examination may often take many days. A man like Armstrong had to be worn down, humiliated a little. He had to have his own verbal dexterity and cleverness flung back in his face. Armstrong plainly revelled in his own cleverness, in his ability to write with a sufficient degree of ambiguity to allow a number of interpretations. That was not the sort of cleverness which helps a man in the witness box.

But whatever Armstrong's enthusiasm for litigation may have been during the Westland inquiry, it appeared to have been diminished somewhat when he set off for Australia to give evidence in November. Annoyed by some press photographers at the airport, he lashed out at one with his big red official briefcase and smashed his camera. Having done this he retreated into a lounge for a few moments and then, having composed himself, returned to apologize and ask if "we could do that again." He had great faith in human nature if he expected the cameramen to agree to let him stage a more sedate entry!

It came as no surprise, therefore, when I heard that the British High Commission in Canberra had requested that Sir Robert be allowed to enter and leave the court by the more discreet judges' entrance. This item found its way into the press. Its publication had the desired effect of ensuring that Sir Robert came in the front door with the rest of us.

It was during this pre-trial period that I received disturbing news from an unusual source. It appears that Attorney-General Sir Michael Havers was fond of sharing the heavy burdens of his great office with certain companions at the Garrick Club in London. One of his companions regularly related Sir Michael's remarks to a friend who passed them on to me. The Garrick source proved to be invariably accurate, and as the case progressed and the pressure on Sir Michael increased, the more he confided to his fellow members at the Garrick.

The first piece of intelligence from this source was that Sir Michael had been overheard in the Garrick *pissoir* exulting in his own cleverness. He had, he said, persuaded Bob Hawke, the Australian Prime Minister, that the Australian Government should give evidence in support of Britain. He added that Australia might even intervene in the proceedings and effectively take over the running from Britain.

This was bad news indeed. One of my best arguments was that there was no evidence to suggest that publication of the book would be against Australia's public interest. I was determined to keep the case limited to a straightforward battle between the British Government and us Australians, into which latter team I included Wright, who after all had taken out Australian citizenship. Support from the Australian Government could muddy the waters.

I immediately arranged for a friend to speak to Hawke. It turned out my information was correct. Thatcher had apparently rung Hawke, and without knowing too much about it the Australian had agreed to lend a hand. That was all he knew, he said, the Australian Attorney-General, Lionel Bowen, was handling the details. I knew Bowen distantly but not well enough to contact him directly. He was sixty-four and a conservative member of the right-wing faction in the Labor Party. This meant in practical terms that any arguments about free speech, civil liberties, dangers of unchecked spy services and so on would fall on deaf ears. On the other hand if I could persuade him that helping Thatcher would start a real brawl in the Caucus,[3] that might appeal to him.

3. The Caucus consists of all of the Labor Party members of Parliament which meets separately to determine policy on legislation, elect cabinet ministers and so forth. There is an uneasy balance

I spoke to Bowen's private secretary, Brian Burdekin. He confirmed that they were planning to help, but had not decided how much. He told me that Bowen did not wish to discuss the matter with me personally and had suggested I discuss the matter with the Solicitor-General, Dr. Gavan Griffith. Before doing that I wrote a strongly worded letter to Bowen with copies to the Prime Minister and the Foreign Minister, Bill Hayden.

In my letter to Bowen I stressed the motives of the British:

> In our view the British Government's only motive for seeking to suppress the book is that information in the book is evidence that the Prime Minister of the United Kingdom, Mrs. Margaret Thatcher, made a false statement to the House of Commons in March, 1981 concerning the investigations into Sir Roger Hollis. In other words the efforts to suppress this book are essentially political efforts by the Government of the day of the United Kingdom to prevent political embarrassment for that Government and its advisers.
>
> Your Government has built upon the achievements of the Whitlam Government in showing the world that Australia is a truly independent nation. Australia should not run to Mrs. Thatcher's whistle. It should not protect Britain from the consequences of its past crimes. It should not condone the breaching of international conventions to which it is a party.

I phoned Hayden and explained my position at more length. The Prime Minister and the Defense Minister, Kim Beazley, were the most supportive of the move to help Britain. They had been pushed very hard by ASIO

---

between the factions and any Labor Prime Minister spends much of his time ensuring that the dissension in the Caucus room stays there and does not emerge into the public eye giving the impression of party disunity.

and ASIS[4] who saw this as a chance to prove their loyalty to the British. Hayden was very skeptical about the intelligence community and delighted in relating how he had been obliged to ban ASIS from training with any "sharp objects or guns" after a training exercise in a Melbourne hotel (designed to simulate the rescue of a hostage) had resulted in half a dozen officers being arrested by the local police after the manager objected to the secret servicemen demolishing a hotel room door with a sledge hammer.[5]

The following day a very disturbed Hayden telephoned me. He said that he was very concerned about my telephone line. "I can't go into detail, but yesterday I was asked by another senior minister if I had spoken to you. I demurred somewhat, and he then went on to tell me almost word for word everything which had been said." The inference was obvious.

I discussed the matter with Dr. Griffith on a number of occasions. Gavan Griffith is a Melbourne barrister with liberal leanings. I was unable to persuade him that Australia was best out of the case. He told me the decision had been made, and there was nothing he could do about it. Nonetheless it was still very important to me to be sure that the nature of Australia's intervention was as innocuous as possible.

Griffith told me that an affidavit would be filed in similar terms to Armstrong's affidavits. I ascertained from

---

4. ASIO, the Australian Security Intelligence Organization, was founded in 1949 and its objectives and structure are very similar to MI5. ASIS, the Australian Secret Intelligence Service, was established in 1952 and is also based on its English counterpart, MI6.

5. This extraordinary exercise produced some entertaining litigation as the Victorian Police sought to prosecute the secret servicemen, who in turn claimed their identities should be protected. When it reached the High Court of Australia, Chief Justice Mason wryly observed that the case had all the hallmarks of "a law school moot [exercise] based on the adventures of Maxwell Smart."

other sources that a number of senior Australian civil servants, including the head of Foreign Affairs, had refused to sign it. Finally on November 14 as we trudged back from court after yet another interlocutory fight about discovery we received an affidavit by Michael Henry Codd, the Australian Cabinet Secretary. As I read it I was truly relieved. It was about as innocuous a document as decency would allow. Australia was going to lend some support to the British, but no more than absolutely necessary.

Over the weekend before the trial began, the English press began to arrive. It was an impressive rollcall. The *Guardian* sent Richard Norton-Taylor, the *Observer* David Leigh, the *Times* was represented by Stephen Taylor, the *Financial Times* by Chris Sherwell, the *Independent* by Robert Milliken, the *Express* by Ross Benson. The BBC sent its Hong Kong correspondent Brian Barron and Channel 4 had David Walter and Trish Lawton. Channel 4 was also represented by a team preparing a television re-enactment of the trial, which was eventually broadcast in England the day after the trial concluded. Dennis Wolfe and Claudia Milne were the two producers and they engaged a young barrister, Heather Rogers, as their legal expert. (Heather later went on to appear as junior counsel for the *Guardian* in the English *Spycatcher* case.)

Greengrass knew most of the English journalists well and Lucy and I quickly established a good rapport with them. In particular we saw a lot of Norton-Taylor, Leigh, Trish Lawton, Claudia Milne and Heather Rogers. Claudia and Heather were particularly neurotic when they arrived. All the interlocutory maneuverings had the potential to delay the trial until the following year or even worse of resulting in an early settlement! That would play havoc with their program plans. I sometimes felt as if they regarded all the participants in the trial in Sydney as scriptwriters for their re-enactment. Norton-Taylor and Leigh were particularly helpful. They had an excellent insight into Armstrong's character, having observed him closely for some time, although it is safe to assume they were not admirers of his mandarin style.

This collection of hard-drinking journalists added a rather carnival air to the proceedings. When we arranged the *Observer's* exclusive photograph of Wright surrounded by his advisers we even had a few folders on the desk with Armstrong's name spelled out in the Cyrillic alphabet. "What's that" the photographer asked. "Oh, that's just Sir Bob's KGB file. Boris dropped it in this afternoon."

David Leigh had an unbecoming experience on the Saturday night before the trial. I was in my office working during the afternoon. Lucy was somewhere else in the office, as were Hooper and Greengrass. The telephone rang and the editor of the *Sunday Times* asked for my comments about a story he proposed to run the next day. It was a scoop of some sort, revealing some of the details of Nigel West's dealings with MI5. Just as I was explaining all this to Greengrass, David Leigh walked in. He had heard most of the story before I noticed him. Greengrass turned on him. "Leigh, you must undertake not to call the *Observer* and tell them about the story." David Leigh rubbed his hands in mock sincerity. "Oh, gentlemen, I am an honest journalist. I would never take advantage of a confidence overheard in an office." He then started to move towards the elevator. Greengrass grabbed him and despite his protests that not a word of this would be shared with his editor, we kept him under surveillance in my office for an hour or so. The deadline ticked away; within a few hours it would be too late for Leigh to call the *Observer* and get them to run a story spoiling the *Sunday Times'* scoop. So we decided we would all go out to dinner. Leigh sat in the middle of the backseat with Greengrass on one side, and Hooper on the other. Lucy sat in the front and I drove. Leigh complained: "The only thing that is missing is a gun at my head. You bloody kidnappers." His captivity was short-lived. By the time his dinner was over, it was, in our opinion, too late for him to call his own paper, and so we released him from custody. "It's too bloody late now, you bunch of fascists, I've been better treated in Nicaragua."

From the week before the trial until it ended, I was rarely at home. I worked in the office seven days a week and most nights until 11:00 p.m. I was well behind in my preparation. Instead of preparing to cross-examine Armstrong I was wasting my time on all the interlocutory arguments about discovery. I was being "papered" by the British. They knew that our resources were very limited and set out to distract me from the task at hand. I like to think they underestimated my capacity for living without sleep.

CHAPTER 5

THE TRIAL WAS DUE to begin on Monday, November 17. If the Government's tactics were designed to distract me from the real issues of the case, then they had certainly succeeded.

On Monday morning we were all in the Court of Appeal as Theo Simos sought special leave to appeal from Justice Powell's ruling on discovery of documents. The bench was composed of the Chief Justice, Sir Laurence Street, the president of the Court of Appeal, Michael Kirby and a third judge, Michael McHugh. They indicated they would hear the application on Wednesday, and so the trial proper began at 2:00 p.m. on Monday, with the discovery question hanging unresolved.

The British Government were represented by Theo Simos QC, Bill Caldwell QC and Bill Gummow QC with Richard Feetham of Stephen Jaques Stone James instructing them. In attendance was a supporting team from Mallesons plus the Treasury Solicitor, John Bailey, his assistant, David Hogg, and another lawyer from London called Susan Marsh whom we suspected of working in the MI5 legal department. Messrs. Simos, Caldwell and Gummow were wigged and gowned and sat at the Bar table on the left-hand side. Another important member of the British team was Ivor Roberts, a Foreign Office relations man who was brought out to make sure the British press got "the line" right. He spent most of the time assuring the English hacks that Sir Robert was doing frightfully well, all this accompanied by lashings of free champagne at the Wentworth Hotel. On the right sat myself, dressed in a business suit. Assisting me were my wife Lucy Hughes, David Hooper and Paul Greengrass. These three sat at a small table behind me. Since Lucy was not admitted to practice at that stage, she was not permitted to sit at the bar table. My mother, Coral Lansbury, soon joined the defense team, although in a supporting capacity only. She is a successful novelist and academic who lives in Philadelphia. She was not out in Australia especially for the spy case, but being a keen amateur student of courtroom tactics, was more than fascinated. Sitting beside her was the distinctive figure of the Honorable Antony Larkins QC, Lucy's godfather and a retired judge of the Supreme Court. He had an unnerving effect on everyone in the court since he invariably went to sleep and snored when the evidence or argument became a little dull. The first sign was when his monocle fell out of his eye, and if one was alert this could be a hint to get the case moving on a little.

The Australian Government was also represented by no less a personage than the Solicitor-General of the Commonwealth, Dr. Gavan Griffith QC. His junior was Alan Robertson. Dr. Griffith told the court that he expected to remain silent for most of the proceedings and would only intervene if questions of public interest immunity, otherwise known as crown privilege, arose.

The case began with Bill Gummow reading out Armstrong's four affidavits which had been filed in the proceedings. The affidavits were all on the same theme; each one was longer than the last and each said much the same thing. Armstrong's evidence was more by way of argument than evidence. It did not deal with any specific passages in the book and was a long list of the sort of damage a book written by someone like Wright could possibly cause.

Gummow has a flat, tedious voice. A confirmed bachelor with few interests outside the law, Gummow was regarded as a first-class academic lawyer rather than an advocate. As the junior of he three QCs it was his task to read the affidavits. The tortured Whitehall prose intoned in Gummow's featureless drone made it a very dull opening, for a gallery crammed with the international media.

Armstrong's affidavits explained that the practice and policy of the British Government had always been to reveal as little as possible about the work of the intelligence services. But he added, in a sentence that was to dog him later:

> It is not the policy of the British government that no information about the work of the Security Services should ever be released. The practice and policy is that, when in the view of the government information may be disclosed without risk of damage to national security, it should be done by way of official publication, based on official records with a view to giving a comprehensive and accurate account . . .

As examples of such "comprehensive and accurate" official accounts Armstrong referred to Mrs. Thatcher's statement to the House of Commons in 1979 about Blunt and in March 1981 responding to Chapman Pincher's *Their Trade is Treachery* and it's allegation that Sir Roger Hollis had been a Russian agent.

He then went on to list examples of the sort of damage a book like Wright's could do. These included the following types of information it could reveal:

(a) Information about the methods of working, the sources of intelligence and the structure of the Security Service.

(b) Information about the nature and extent of liaison between the UK Security Service and the security services of other countries.

(c) The knowledge that the Security Service has of the activities of hostile intelligence services.

(d) Information about people who have assisted the Security Service in its work.

(e) Identification of members of the Service and premises used by the Service.

This summary does less than justice to the lengthy affidavits sworn by Sir Robert. But they served to develop two themes. The first was that a person in Wright's position could reveal information which might damage the Service. This theme was never really pursued by the Government because they refused to take issue with our contention that while Wright *could* write a damaging book, *Spycatcher* was in fact quite innocuous. The second theme was that if Wright were allowed to publish, this fact alone of unauthorized publication would make other intelligence services and those who provide information to MI5 less likely to trust MI5. In short, to paraphrase Sir John Donaldson, MI5 must be seen to be leakproof.

After Armstrong's affidavits Gummow read the affidavit of Michael Henry Codd. Codd's affidavit had only been filed the previous Friday. He was (and still is) the Secretary of the Australian Prime Minister's Department and Secretary to the Cabinet. He was therefore Sir Robert's Australian counterpart. He had held that position since February 11, 1986 and in that capacity was chairman of the Secretaries Committee on Intelligence and Security which was the senior bureaucratic body in the Australian intelligence hierarchy. He observed that Australia's intelligence agencies liaised with those of other friendly countries, including Britain. His main objection however was that if Wright were allowed to publish, other intelligence agencies may think that sensitive material provided

to Australian intelligence agencies was not properly safe-
guarded under Australian law. Furthermore he added,
somewhat more tortuously, that if Wright were allowed
to publish, Australian agencies would lose faith in MI5,
and other agencies who provided information to Australian agencies and who knew Australian agencies provided
information to MI5 would be less likely to provide information to the Australian agencies in case it was provided to MI5.

Finally an affidavit was read from an anonymous de-
ponent who claimed to have been an officer of MI5 when
Wright joined and claimed to have indoctrinated Wright
into the obligations of secrecy required of MI5 officers.

The court adjourned for the day, and we returned to
my office to prepare for the first day of cross-examining
Sir Robert. My routine on that day, as on all the others,
was to work on at the office until 9:00 or 10:00 p.m.,
then I would have dinner with Lucy, Greengrass, Hooper
and a few of the journalists, and then return to the office
at about 6:00 a.m. the following morning. The following
day, November 18, was hot. Peter and Lois stayed in the
office. Just before Lucy, Greengrass, Hooper and I set
off for court a number of large cardboard boxes arrived
from Wright's former solicitors, Corrs Pavey Whiting and
Byrne. One of them contained a whole file of correspondence between Chapman Pincher and Peter Wright.
Greengrass recognized it and said he had read it back in
1984. Peter thought it had all been lost. I did not have
time to do more than glance at it, and we hurried out
across Hyde Park to the Supreme Court. Each of us was
carrying at least two large bags full of books and folders
and the walk through Hyde Park was hot and sticky. By
the time we got to the courthouse we were red-faced and
steaming. It must have looked odd as we ran the gauntlet
of the international news camera crews who haunted the
courts.

The Supreme Court of New South Wales consists of forty judges and is the highest judicial body in the State of New South Wales. It occupies the bottom half of a huge, office tower with the Federal Courts occupying the top half. Banks of elevators hurry litigants and their lawyers up and down and the daily jostle of wigged barristers, nervous witnesses and frantic solicitors gives the very modern building a thoroughly Hogarthian atmosphere. The courts building is at one end of a large square dominated by an old statue of Queen Victoria. As we crossed that square each morning a team of television crews competed for the best pictures, occasionally tripping each other up in their enthusiasm.

The British Government no doubt took some comfort in the thoroughly British appearance of the court proceedings, which included barristers and judges wigged and gowned, a royal coat of arms on the wall behind the judge and English law reports piled high on the bar table. But they failed to perceive that while Australia appeared to be very British, the reality of Australian life, including its legal system, had moved on.

Only a few years before it was still possible to appeal from the Supreme Court of New South Wales to the Privy Council, a court made up of English judges whose principal function had been to hear appeals from the colonies.[1] Australia, like Canada, has the Queen of England as its Head of State. The lawyers are particularly Anglophile. Until recent years Australian courts almost automatically applied English precedents, partly because of the possibility of final appeal to the Privy Council.

So it was no surprise that Sir Robert beamed with the confidence of a man among friends as he sat in the body of the court clutching his large red despatch box. In the flesh he looked fit and robust, but his face lacked the

---

1. A number of British Commonwealth countries still retain appeals to the Privy Council including New Zealand.

fine features one normally associates with a well-bred Englishman. He could have easily passed for an Australian. He had none of the mannered effeminacy that is so common with Englishmen of his background. He looked and talked like a tough and practical man of the world. Next to him sat John Bailey the Treasury Solicitor. As the case wore on and the lamentable state of the Government's preparation became more and more apparent one would have expected Bailey to look a little perturbed, but he seemed to have a constant smirk on his well-scrubbed face.

The witness box where Sir Robert was to spend the next two weeks was located on the left hand side of the courtroom in front of, and a little beyond, the bar table. Theo Simos and his two juniors sat in the middle of the bar table; the Australian Solicitor-General sat on the extreme left hand side near the witness box. As counsel for the defendants I sat alone on the extreme right hand side. On the right hand side of the court, facing the witness box, is a jury box into which had crammed most of the foreign press. I moved my lectern to the far right-hand corner of the bar table so that I looked straight across the courtroom at Armstrong. He on the other hand looked at me, with the press gallery over my shoulder. I knew he would find the view of the press gallery very disturbing. He could not escape it, without appearing to avoid eye contact with me.

Sir Robert was sworn in and I began to cross-examine. I had no idea of where to start. I had let it be known in the press that Armstrong would be cross-examined for days, and we certainly had plenty of material, but I was very worried that he might adopt a low-key and unresponsive approach. I needed to get him talking and debating with me. How to begin?

I decided to feel him out, so I started with something which I knew was peripheral. I drew his attention to the 1985 television interview by Catherine Massiter, a former

MI5 officer who alleged that MI5 had been systematically bugging the phones and houses of left-wing trade unionists, members of anti-war groups and civil libertarians. Armstrong responded by saying that Lord Bridge had investigated allegations of illegal phone-tapping and had found there had been no breaches of the law. Lord Bridge had published none of the evidence which he considered in his inquiry, a four-day inquiry which allegedly considered over 6000 taps! The report was nothing more than a conclusion.

He explained that in matters of national security it was inappropriate for the reasons behind the conclusion to be published. In Armstrong's world the public (which included anyone not in the Whitehall establishment) had no business knowing about the intelligence agencies notwithstanding that their taxes pay for them and their liberties are being regularly infringed by them.

Tuesday November 18, 1986

Q. It would not be very satisfactory if, for instance, his Honor could simply say *"I find for the defendant,"* and keep the reason secret?

A. We are dealing with rather different matters here.

Q. You would agree that that would be unsatisfactory in the administration of justice?

A. I am not an expert in the administration of justice, but I'm sure you're right.

Q. What is there in the Massiter Case that compels you to contend that it is satisfactory for Lord Bridge to simply publish his conclusion and none of the facts upon which it was based?

A.   Because it may not be possible to publish, to make public all the evidence on which the conclusions are based. And that being so, the purpose of having somebody of the independence and stature of Lord Bridge of Harwich is to assure the public that where it is not possible for reasons of national security to give reasons, somebody of that stature and independence has satisfied himself that this is right.

Q.   So the public have to put their faith in Lord Bridge in his four-day investigation of the matter, being given all the evidence by the Security Service and the other relevant authorities and come to the right conclusion. It is a matter of trust, isn't it?

A.   It is a matter of trust, to coin a phrase.

So it was all a matter of trust. I recognized that this was the opening I needed. Sir Robert's whole philosophy involved the people trusting him, and it was blind trust he and his colleagues demanded. They would not deign to provide any information about their decisions. Their integrity was all the public needed to be satisfied of. Well, the time had come to show that that integrity was lacking.

Q.   Turning to a matter of trust, Sir Robert, may I give you a book? (Shown) This is a book called *A Matter of Trust: MI5 1945–1972* by Nigel West; is that right?

A.   Yes.

Nigel West's *A Matter of Trust* was a curious book. Packed with detail, it was a textbook compared to *Their Trade is Treachery* or indeed *Spycatcher*.

Q.   In interrogatory 31 you were asked
       whether proceedings were commenced in
       the United Kingdom by the plaintiff or
       otherwise for the Australian publication
       of the book that you have before you,
       and you answered: On October 13 the
       plaintiff commenced proceedings in the
       Queens Bench Division to restrain the
       publication of the manuscript on the
       ground that it contained the information
       obtained by him in breach of a duty of
       confidentiality owed by the Crown. The
       next question was: Were the said pro-
       ceedings settled on the basis that the book
       could be published? Your answer is: The
       proceedings were stayed by consent fol-
       lowing discussions between the parties to
       the proceedings, the plaintiff being sat-
       isfied that those matters contained in the
       manuscript which the plaintiff believed
       had been obtained by the defendant in
       breach of a duty of confidentiality owed
       to the Crown would be removed. Do you
       stand by that answer?

A.   I stand by that answer.

Q.   Before you swore these answers to the
       interrogatories you took care to ensure
       that your answers were in all relevant
       respects true and correct, did you not?

A.   To the best of my knowledge.

Q.   But you made inquiries to ensure that
       your answers would be correct, did you
       not?

A.   Yes.

Q.   Sir Robert, do I take it from your answer
       that you contend or you believe that there
       is nothing in the book before you which
       the author had obtained in breach of a
       duty of confidentiality owed to the Crown?

A.	I contended that when the Crown withdrew its injunction, it believed the matter to which it objected on the ground of duty of confidentiality would be removed.
Q.	Please answer the question. I will ask it again. Do you believe that there is nothing in the book before you which the author had obtained in breach of a duty of confidentiality owed to the Crown?
A.	I am afraid I couldn't answer that without reading the book again.
Q.	Is it not the fact that your answer states that at the time the book was allowed to be published by the consent order, the plaintiff, the Attorney-General of the United Kingdom, believed that all material West had obtained in breach of a duty of confidentiality had been removed? That is what the answer means, doesn't it?
A.	That is what the answer says.
Q.	Is that answer true?
A.	To the best of my knowledge, it is true as a description of what the Attorney-General believed at the time.

I knew these answers were incorrect. West's book had been barely affected by the agreed edits. My confidence here was not misplaced as we had got hold of a copy of the original manuscript of *A Matter of Trust* and when we compared it with the published version, the differences were minimal. Indeed the only excisions of any substance were the removal of some verbatim quotes from the Report into Soviet Penetration by Ronnie Symonds. The verbatim quotes would have made it far too obvious that West had received inside assistance.

It was important for us to establish that Armstrong's "absolute duty of confidence" was nonsense. In other words we wanted him to admit that not every publication of information about MI5 by former officers would cause damage to national security. This proposition may seem too obvious to worry about, but the Government's case always was that damage would be caused to national security just by Wright talking, even if the information in his book was on its face innocuous. We had tried very hard to persuade them to step down from this lofty plane of absolutism and to consider the contents of the book with a view to cutting out, or "blue-pencilling" the objectionable passages as they had done with West.

Tuesday November 18, 1986

Q. Do you say that those responsible believed that all of the material and information that Martin[2] gave to West was removed from the book before it was published?

A. I can say no more than that those responsible believed that previously unpublished information classified as secret and obtained in breach of a duty of confidentiality owed to the Crown would be removed.

Q. Of course, it is part of your case, is it not, that a former officer of MI5 was bound by his duty of confidentiality not to reveal information even if it is already in the public domain, even if it has already been published by other people?

A. Yes.

Q. Where do we draw the line there, Sir Robert? If a former member of MI5 is

2. A former officer of MI5 and MI6 who shared Wright's views about Hollis and who subsequently provided an enormous amount of inside material about the molehunts to Nigel West.

at a dinner party to whom all secrets are sacred, and someone says to him, "Was Anthony Blunt really a Russian spy?" and this fellow had been involved in the investigation of Blunt, do you say that is a breach then of a duty of confidentiality to say "Yes, he was?"

A. If this dinner party was taking place after the Prime Minister had made a statement [confirming Blunt's treachery] in 1979, I don't think that anyone would suppose that that was a serious breach of confidentiality.

Q. But it is a breach of confidentiality, you contend?

A. I don't think it can be, can it?

Q. It is your case, Sir Robert. You tell me. You tell me, is it or is it not?

A. This is now a matter which has been published with authority by the Crown.

Q. So if something has been published with authority then officers of the Service who learnt of that fact in their service and prior to the official publication are free to restate it; is that what you are saying?

A. They must be free. That is what the Prime Minister said.

Q. Are they allowed to say, are they allowed to confirm from their own knowledge that the Prime Minister's statement is correct?

A. I have never had to consider that matter. I don't know the answer, I am afraid.

Q. Can you give it some thought now and let us have an answer? This is central to the whole case—you would appreciate that, wouldn't you?

A.   I think that this duty of confidentiality is absolute, certainly. I am no lawyer but I would—on this specific case you mentioned—if somebody said they they didn't wish to contest the Prime Minister's announcement that Anthony Blunt had been a spy, I shouldn't think that was all that serious a breach of a duty of confidentiality. I suppose technically it is a breach.

Q.   What if a member of MI5 were to state at this dinner party, or even to a journalist for publication, that there was division of MI5 whose task it was to determine the Russian order of battle in London, would that be a serious breach of confidence.

A.   I should think that would be a breach of confidence.

Q.   Why then did the Security Commission say as much in the Bettaney Report?

A.   What did they say in the Bettaney Report?

Q.   In the Bettaney Report, with which you are quite familiar, the Security Commission states quite explicitly that Bettaney worked in a division of MI5 involved in ascertaining the Russian order of battle in London?

A.   That was a disclosure made with authority by the Security Commission, wasn't it?

Q.   The Security Commission would not have made that disclosure if it had thought that that disclosure would damage national security, would it?

A.   No doubt.

Q.   So therefore if an officer of MI5 said there is a division of MI5 which is involved in determining the Russian order of battle, he wouldn't be doing anything prejudicial to national security?

A. He could still be in breach of his duty of confidentiality to the Crown.

Q. But it would be a breach of confidentiality which would not damage national security?

A. It would depend on the information, wouldn't it?

Q. I put to you the information. We are talking about a division of MI5 that is involved in determining the Russian order of battle in London. You said it would be a breach of confidence. Do you say that it would be damaging to national security if he said that?

A. I think that everybody would assume that that was the case, but I think it is still a breach of his duty of confidentiality to say it.

Q. But it wouldn't damage national security, would it?

A. No.

Q. So you would concede, would you not, that there are breaches of this absolute duty of confidence which you contend for which, because of the content of the information, do not cause any detriment to the national security of Britain?

A. The information may not; the source from which it came might.

Q. You would agree with me that there is no absolute rule that simply because a former MI5 officer breaches what you contend is his absolute duty of confidence, there is no absolute rule that in breaching that duty he damages or causes detriment to national security?

A. No absolute rule.

Q. Now, Sir Robert, is it not the case that from the very time you and your colleagues were given Mr. Wright's manuscript, Mr. Wright has invited you or your government to tell him what passages in the book you contended were detrimental to national security?

A. I am only aware of one request or proposal to that effect.

Q. But it was made some time ago, was it not?

A. It was made some time ago.

Q. And you have declined to accede to that request, other than to state that Chapters 2, 3 and 4 are not complained of?

A. Correct.

Q. So there is an extensive amount of information in that book which has already been published, isn't there?

A. There is an extensive amount of informaiton as in those particulars which is in the public domain.

Q. Why is the publication of that material by Mr. Wright going to be detrimental to national security?

A. Our argument is that it is in breach of the duty of confidentiality.

Q. I know that is your argument and I can assure you I don't accept that. I do not want to canvass the law of confidence with you as you are not a lawyer. What I am asking is, accepting your contention that a real duty of confidence covers information which is already in the public domain, as you have described, why do you say that information which is in the public domain, if published by Wright, would cause detriment to national security?

A.   It may or may not be.

Q.   Sir Robert, with respect, how long has the government had the book?

A.   Since June, is it?

Q.   You had the whole book by June. June is five months. Are you able to give His Honor some considered view of those passages in the book which have already been published which you say will or won't damage national security?

Mr. Simos   I submit that this is all covered in Sir Robert's affidavit; it is all there.

Mr. Turnbull   I am testing propositions in the affidavit. With respect, I would be grateful if my friend would let me do it.

His Honor   I wonder, if one makes the question a little more precise, by suggesting that one cannot give chapter and verse—although Sir Robert may be able to—but give particular incidents which no doubt he would not wish to make public of particular items of information. I think that may be the problem.

Mr. Turnbull   If I approach it from another angle; Sir Robert, you would agree with me, wouldn't you, that not all of the information in the book, in the chapters of the book you have objected to, would, if published, cause detriment to the national security of the United Kingdom?

A.   I would argue that publication by Mr. Wright, even of some information which is already in the public domain in other ways, could cause detriment to the national security of the United Kingdom.

Q.   All of it?

A.   All of it could.

The cross-examination continued in this vein, punctuated by frequent objections from Theo Simos, who was acutely aware of the admission his witness was about to make.

Armstrong started to shift his ground, and suggest that the answer to the Interrogatory spoke of an expectation that confidential information in *A Matter of Trust* would be removed, leaving open the possibility that not all of it had been.

Q.	There was no "would," there was an agreed text. It was not "would be" removed.
A.	It is what the answer says: "It would be removed."
Q.	I am saying your answer is wrong.
A.	The proceedings were stayed by consent because the plaintiff was satisfied that those matters contained in the manuscript which the plaintiff believed had been obtained by the defendant in breach of a duty of confidence owed to the Crown would be removed. The answer is correct isn't it?
Q.	I do not wish to be offensive, Sir Robert, but it is almost weasel words . . .
Mr. Simos	I object. I do not know what "weasel words" means.
His Honor	That is because you do not have a dirty mind like me.
Mr. Turnbull	It has been judicially defined as meaning words which are devoid of content, just like an egg which has been sucked out by a weasel.

Finally Justice Powell intervened and asked the question one more time:

Q.   Sir Robert, are you able to answer the question which, as I recall it, was this. Do you agree that in Mr. West's book there is information which you would believe was obtained from former members of the Service in breach of their obligation of confidentiality to the Crown and the Service?

A.   Your Honor, I cannot say as a matter of fact whether the book contains such information but I believe it to be likely. I would further say that if it does contain such information, then that information was obtained in breach by those concerned of the duty of confidentiality which they owed to the Crown.

His Honor   Thank you. I am obliged to you.

Armstrong had now retreated considerably from the original answer to Interrogatory 33. It was not the case that "those matters obtained in breach of confidence" were removed from the text of *A Matter of Trust*, but rather only those matters which the Government and West's lawyers had agreed should be removed. I drove in hard on Armstrong insisting that his sworn answer to Interrogatory 33 had been designed to mislead:

Tuesday November 18, 1986

A.   I am sorry if I have misled His Honor and the court in this respect. But that was the intention of the interrogatory, it was that the answer should refer to those matters which had been the subject of negotiation and they were all matters which had been obtained by the defendant in breach of a duty of confidentiality.

Q.   You admit that answer was misleading, don't you?

A.   I say that it did not say "all."

Q.   It was misleading by omission, was it not?

A.   It was not intended to be so.

Q.   It was calculated to mislead.

A.   It was not calculated to mislead.

Q.   It was not intended by you to mislead, is that what you say?

A.   That is what I have just said. If it has misled, I regret that.

Q.   Sir Robert, your whole life has been involved in writing submissions, writing documents, writing memoranda, expressing yourself fully and clearly has it not?

A.   That is certainly part of my training and my duty.

Q.   And yet you are confronted with an answer which a court has ordered you to answer on oath and you answer it inadequately; why is that?

A.   I have not agreed that it was inadequate. I regret it very much if the answer is interpreted in that way.

Q.   It is not a matter of interpretation. How can it be a matter of interpretation? It is plain on its face. The answer states that the plaintiff believed that the matters in the book which were obtained in breach of confidence would be removed. It does not say "some of the matters"; it does not say "the matters we thought were too politically sensitive to let out of the bag." It says "the matters in the manuscript."

A.   It says "those matters contained in the manuscript which the plaintiff believed had been obtained by the defendant in breach of confidentiality owed to the

Crown." I cannot argue that that is an extensive covering of all the matters in the manuscript which were so obtained. I can only relate it to the matters which were removed as a result of agreement between the Crown and the publishers and the authors.

Q. Sir Robert, how high in your scale of values is telling the truth?

A. It reckons very high.

Q. Is it the highest?

A. There are a number of things which I would not wish to grade in order of priority.

Q. Would you tell an untruth to protect what you perceived as national security?

A. I would not wish to do so.

Q. You may not wish to do so. But can you tell us whether you would under no circumstances tell an untruth to protect national security as you saw it?

A. I do not think I can answer a question like that. I have not been faced with such a situation.

Q. You have never, happily, been put in a position where you had to tell an untruth to protect national security?

A. We can all imagine situations in which somebody might be put into that situation. For instance, the situation which you are put into if you are about to devalue your currency.

Q. Yes, I understand that.

A. And you may be forced, as indeed people have been forced, to say something which is untrue. I have fortunately not been put into such a situation.

Q.   A little while ago you said that you had
            not been. Now you are saying you cannot
            remember?

A.   I do not distinguish between those.

Armstrong's answer was unfortunate, because I followed it up by showing him a letter he had written to Mr. William Armstrong, the chairman of Sidgwick and Jackson, publishers of *Their Trade is Treachery*. He had written to his namesake on March 23, 1981 in these terms:

CONFIDENTIAL   March 23rd, 1981
    I have seen the extracts in the *Daily Mail* today from Mr. Chapman Pincher's forthcoming book *Their Trade is Treachery*. The Prime Minister is in my judgement likely to come under pressure to make some statement on the matters with which Mr. Pincher is dealing. I believe you will agree with me that, if she is to make a statement, it is in the public interest that she should be in a position to do so with the least possible delay. Clearly she cannot do so until she has seen, not just the extracts published in the *Daily Mail* but the book itself. I should like to be able to put her in a position where she could make a statement this Thursday [March 26th] if she should wish to do so.
    I should therefore be very grateful if you would be willing to make one or (preferably) two copies of the book available to me as soon as possible today or tomorrow.
    I can understand your need and wish to protect the confidentiality of the book until publication date, which is (I understand) March 26th. I can assure you that, if you are able to comply with my request, that confidentiality will be strictly observed, that the copies will not go outside this office and the Prime Minister's office, and that until the book has been published there will be no disclosure to the Press or the broad-

casting authorities of any part of the contents of the book.

I can also assure you that the only purpose of this request is to equip the Prime Minister to make a statement, if she should need or be minded to do so, with the least possible delay. The request is not made with a view to seeking to prevent or delay publication. And I can assure you that we shall not do so.

signed

Robert Armstrong.

Q.	That letter was calculated to mislead, was it not?
A.	It was calculated to ask for a copy of the book on which we could take direct action.
Q.	It was calculated to mislead Mr. Armstrong to believe that the Government did not have a copy of the book. Correct?
A.	It was calculated not to disclose to Mr. Armstrong that the Government had a copy of the book in order to protect the confidentiality of the source from which it came.
Q.	In fact a copy of the book had been stolen from the printers?
A.	No.
Q.	Where had it come from?
A.	I don't know where it had come from, but it had not been obtained by those means.
Q.	I am very assured by that, Sir Robert. Would you agree that Mr. William Armstrong on reading this letter would inescapably come to the conclusion that the Government did not have a copy of the book?

A.   Mr. William Armstrong had been taking strenuous steps to keep the book under very close cover and I was concerned to write a letter which did not disclose that we had a copy of the book.

Q.   You intended that letter to cause Mr. Armstrong—or is it Sir William Armstrong?

A.   Mr. Armstrong.

Q.   To cause Mr. Armstrong to continue in his belief that his security measures had been effective?

A.   To continue to his belief that the Government did not have a copy of the book.

Q.   And the Government did have a copy of the book?

A.   The Government did have a copy of the book.

Q.   It had the book at least for a month before the letter was written?

A.   I cannot answer for the exact period.

Q.   You said in answer to interrogatories that the Government obtained a copy of the book in or about February?

A.   That's right.

Q.   So it would be . . .

A.   . . . about a month.

Q.   You said to his Honor a little while ago that you could not remember an occasion when you had been placed in the unhappy circumstances of having to misrepresent the facts or to lie in order to protect the sources of MI5 or national security?

A.   I think I said that I had not been in a position where I had to tell an untruth. I think that was the nature of the question I answered.

Q. This letter is an untruth, is it not?

A. It is what I have said. It was designed to protect the confidentiality of the source and to avoid the disclosure that a copy of the book has been obtained.

Q. Sir Robert . . .

A. If that is misrepresenting, yes, it was.

Q. Do you understand the difference between a truth and an untruth?

A. I hope so.

Q. And a statement is true if it is an accurate representation of the facts, is it not?

A. I think that is certainly one definition of truth.

Q. And a statement is untrue if it misstates the facts, is it not?

A. If it misstates the facts. You say it misrepresents the facts.

Q. What is the distinction between misrepresenting and misstating the facts?

A. In this letter, as I have explained, it was designed, it was written so as not to disclose the fact that a copy of the book had been obtained.

Q. It misrepresented the facts?

A. If that was misrepresenting the facts, it was misrepresenting the facts.

Q. It did misrepresent the facts, did it not?

A. If it did so, if you say it did, if you say that is what this letter was doing, very well.

Q. Sir Robert, it is not what I say. I am asking you what you say. Do you admit that that letter misrepresented the facts as they were?

A.   It was designed, as I have said, not to disclose to Mr. Armstrong that a copy of the book had been obtained beforehand, and that was in order to protect the confidentiality of the source from which it had been obtained.

Q.   I will ask you the question again . . .

His Honor   Mr. Turnbull, I am not sure if we are making any progress. We may have fallen into an exercise in semantics. As I understand it, Sir Robert says, according to my note, that he would not wish to tell an untruth to protect the national security. He has never been put in a position in which he has been required to do so. However it is my impression—and I ask Sir Robert to assent or deny the accuracy of it—that he would not say that he would not be willing to mislead people if that were necessary in the national interest. Is that a correct assessment, Sir Robert?

A.   I would not wish to do so. But in this case, as I said, I said what I did say not so much to protect the national security as to protect the confidentiality of the source from which the book came.

His Honor   It certainly would be with the intention to mislead?

A.   Certainly with the intention that Mr. Armstrong should not be aware that the Government had already seen a copy of the book.

Mr. Turnbull   You said earlier that you had not been put in a position where you had to tell an untruth in order to protect national security or a source of the Security Services. I put it to you that in this letter you did just that?

A. I have already said that the letter was not written to protect national security but to protect the source, the confidentiality of the source from which the book was obtained.

Q. I put it to you that this letter contains an untruth. That is the question.

A. It does not say that we have already got a copy of the book, that is quite true.

Q. So it contains an untruth?

A. Well, it does not contain that truth.

Q. See, you could have written to Mr. Armstrong and said: Dear Mr. Armstrong, I read in the *Mail* that Pincher is publishing another one of his books, could you shoot me over an advance copy, and don't worry, we won't do anything to stop it. You could have done that, could you not?

A. Isn't that what the letter does?

Q. No. Please answer the question.

A. I thought that is what the letter did.

Q. No it does not. It does more than that. If you had written to the publisher and said: Dear Mr. Armstrong, I read in the *Daily Mail* that Pincher is writing a book. Don't worry, we are not going to do anything to stop it, can you shoot me over a couple of copies, I am sure that Mr. Armstrong would have been delighted, he could have taken his solicitors off standby and he probably would have brought the books around personally witha bunch of flowers.

A. He did not bring a bunch of flowers, but . . .

Q. Anyway, he was happy to bring the book around?

A.   The book came around. I don't know whether he brought it himself.

Q.   You went further than that. You went further than you needed to go to get a copy of the book. You conveyed to Armstrong, to William Armstrong, the clear impression that you did not already have a copy of the book, did you not?

A.   Yes, I did, because I was wishing to protect the confidentiality of the source from which we had obtained it.

Q.   And that impression was not a true impression, was it?

A.   Well, clearly we had a copy of the book.

Q.   So it contains a lie?

A.   It was a misleading impression. It does not contain a lie, I don't think.

Q.   What is the difference between a misleading impression and a lie?

A.   A lie is a straight untruth.

Q.   What is a misleading impression—a sort of bent untruth?

A.   As one person said, it is perhaps being economical with the truth.

Armstrong's answer, intended as a little joke, brought a gasp of disbelief from the courtroom. How could he be so candid about his own cynicism? It was as though he had summed up the whole Whitehall tradition. He was rattled now. The press gallery were laughing at him and some were sneering too. The confidence had gone and it was now a rather frightened Robert Armstrong who faced the cross-examiner. His minders, only ten feet away in the well of the court, could have been in Antarctica for all the help they could give him. He was all alone now, and he knew it. And as we went on, his answers became even more disturbing:

Tuesday November 18, 1986

Q.   So you regard it as worthy of the Cabinet Secretary of the United Kingdom to be economical with the truth for the purpose of conveying a misleading impression?

A.   In order to protect the confidentiality of the source on this occasion.

Q.   What assurance do we have from you that you are not doing this today in court?

A.   I am under oath in this court.

Q.   You do not convey misleading impressions under oath but you do when you are not under oath?

A.   I do not wish to do so at all under any circumstances. There are occasions when—as there was an occasion here— when it seemed necessary to do so. I regret that, but it seemed necessary.

Q.   Necessity is your guide, is it?

A.   It sometimes has to be.

Q.   Or to put it another way, expediency?

A.   I would say in this case, necessity.

Q.   Sir Robert, just so we understand the situation, when it is necessary you give misleading impressions when you are not under oath but you do not give them when you are under oath?

A.   I hope I have to give misleading impressions as little as possible.

Q.   We are talking about deliberate misleading impressions here. We often, all of us, give a misleading impression innocently.

Now, back to the question. When it is necessary you deliberately mislead as long as you are not under oath?

A.   I thought that on this occasion it was justifiable to write as I did in order to protect the confidentiality of the source from which the book was obtained.

This was extraordinary. I was offering him the chance to say, categorically, that he was not, under any circumstances, prepared to lie under oath. But he would not do so. Was this a case of Sir Robert absolving himself in advance, warning us, as it were, that his high office may require him to give deliberately misleading answers, even under oath?

Now, he no longer sat forward in the witness box, but leaned back as though trying to put as much distance between himself and the questioner. His integrity had been questioned and he was intelligent enough to know he had come out the worse. But now the questioning became in deadly earnest. The little matter of the Nigel West interrogatory could be explained away as a problem of semantics, the William Armstrong letter was perhaps only being economical with the truth. So I turned to what I would later contend was a deliberate lie.

We knew that the Government had received a copy of *Their Trade is Treachery* some weeks at least before it was published. Interrogatory 150 had asked Sir Robert the following question: *"Was consideration given by the Plaintiff or any other servants or agents of the Crown to restraining the publication of the said book prior to its publication?"* His sworn answer was *"The Plaintiff was advised it had no basis to restrain publication of the said book."*

I was certain this answer was false. I had no "inside" information on this score, as some journalists have suggested. But I simply could not accept that the Attorney-General could receive such patently mistaken advice as this. Pincher had made it perfectly clear in the foreword to *Their Trade is Treachery* that he had received secret information from former members of MI5 and Sir Robert conceded that this was obvious to the Government at the time it received the page proofs. The law on confidential information was very clear in such cases. Had the Government asked the courts for an interim injunction to stop the publication of *Their Trade is Treachery* they would have been successful, just as they had been in obtaining an interim injunction against Nigel West's *A Matter of Trust*. We had obtained a copy of an affidavit used by the Government in the Nigel West case. Sworn by one James Nursaw, it said no more than that the Government had reason to believe *A Matter of Trust* contained information obtained from a former officer of MI5. This short document produced a quick injunction. It was this action over West's book which gave the lie to their evidence about Pincher's. The case in respect of each book was, from a national security and legal viewpoint, identical. Yet in one legal action had been taken, and in the other it hadn't. Why?

Having laid the framework for our attack on this score I put the point plainly to Sir Robert just before the luncheon adjournment.

Tuesday November 18, 1986

Q.   So the view was taken that notwithstanding that the book contained information obtained in breach of confidence and notwithstanding that it had material publication of which could damage national security, you felt that any damage that would be caused could be fixed up by Mrs. Thatcher's statement in the Commons?

A.   The Attorney-General decided or was advised that he had no basis to restrain publication.

Q.   I am putting to you that the Attorney-General received no such advice at all.

A.   Why are you putting that to me?

Q.   Because if he received that advice he received it from somebody that should have not got through first year law.

A.   I cannot answer questions of law.

Q.   I imagine you cannot. But that is what I am putting to you. And I am putting it to you fairly now so that you know that that will be part of our case.

Sir Robert stuck to his guns after lunch and insisted that the whole decision was the Attorney-General's. Moreover he insisted that the decision was taken personally by Sir Michael Havers, and no one else. Sir Robert went further and insisted that this was not simply a decision of Havers, as proxy for the whole Government, but a personal one.

Q.   Sir Robert, you said before lunch that the decision to move to stop the publication of a book of the kind we are talking about today is one for the Attorney-General. Did you say that?

A.   Yes.

Q.   And his decision, or her decision of a woman, is final, that is to say once the Attorney has made up his mind no attempt to overrule that will be made by another minister?

A.   I said it was the Attorney-General's decision which did not engage the collective responsibility of the Government. It is not a Government decision, it is a decision of the Attorney-General as a law officer.

So we had an eminent lawyer, Sir Michael Havers, apparently agreeing with legal advice which would have disgraced an articled clerk. However, this curious tale became even harder to believe when Sir Robert stressed that the damage caused by *Their Trade is Treachery* was immense.

Tuesday November 18, 1986

Q. Did you advise the Attorney-General that you considered or did you or those with you in the Cabinet office, advise the Attorney-General that you considered this publication would cause damage?

A. I'm sure that the Attorney-General was advised that publication could cause damage, yes.

Q. By you or those in the Cabinet?

A. Not necessarily by me, possibly by the Security Service.

Q. So you would expect that advice would have been tendered by the Security Service to the Attorney-General about the possible damage?

A. Yes.

Q. Now Sir Robert Pincher's book *Their Trade is Treachery* revealed openly for the first time that there had been an extensive investigation into long-term Soviet penetration of MI5 and in particular into a former director-general of that service, didn't it?

A. Yes.

Q. The book was a bombshell, wasn't it, when it came out?

A. Yes.

Q.   Can you imagine anything more damag-
      ing to the credibility of the Security Ser-
      vice than the allegation that its director-
      general for nearly ten years had been a
      Russian agent?

A.   That is a very serious allegation.

Q.   Can you imagine anything more damag-
      ing to the Security Service than that al-
      legation?

A.   Few things, if any.

Q.   Did the Prime Minister express any views
      to the Attorney-General about publica-
      tion of this book?

A.   I think that she accepted the Attorney-
      General's decision.

I put forward an alternative explanation which met
with a predictable response.

Q.   Would you agree that Mr. Pincher is a
      journalist who is known for his conserv-
      ative views on political matters.

A.   With a small "c," yes.

Q.   Prior to April 1981 that there was already
      circulating in political and journalistic cir-
      cles rumours concerning the investiga-
      tions into Hollis?

A.   I believe there were.

Q.   It was around, yes. Now Sir Robert, you
      and the Prime Minister and the Security
      Service agreed to let Pincher write his
      book about Hollis so that this affair would
      come out in the open through the pen
      of a safely conservative writer rather than
      some ugly journalist on the left?

A.   It is a very ingenious conspiracy theory
      and it is quite untrue.

Q.   Totally untrue?

A. Totally untrue.

As I pressed him on the inconsistent treatment of Wright, Pincher, West and some others, Armstrong sought refuge behind the skirts of the Attorney-General. I returned to Arthur Martin who had admitted to providing information to Nigel West yet had not been prosecuted. Theo Simos, who no doubt recognized his witness was getting into deep waters, sought to protect him by objecting to the relevance of the questions. Simos complained that I was asking Armstrong about legal matters when Armstrong was not a lawyer.

Q. Sir Robert, when you became aware that Martin had admitted to having provided all this information to West, did you draw this fact to the attention of the law officers [i.e., the Attorney-General and Solicitor-General]?

A. I was not aware of that at that time but there were others who were quite clearly. It was drawn to the attention of the law officers for the purpose of the injunction against the West book, as you have seen from Mr. Nursaw's affidavit, therefore the Attorney-General would have been made aware of that matter.

Q. But the Attorney-General took no steps, as far as you are aware, to prosecute Mr. Martin?

A. I don't enter into the matter, as your Honor has said, I don't enter into matters of charges under the Official Secrets Act. That is for the Director of Public Prosecution and I think I am right in saying that any decision to prosecute had to be authorized by the Attorney-General in person.

Q.   But no such decision to prosecute was made.

A.   Clearly not.

Q.   Yet when Sarah Tisdall leaked to the press some documents concerning the Defence Minister's tactics in Parliament she was prosecuted under the Official Secrets Act wasn't she?

A.   Yes.

Q.   But surely the information Martin gave to West was more serious in terms of sensitivity than what Tisdall gave to the *Guardian?*

A.   The policy is consistent with practice. It does not have to be invariable in every case. In every case it is an exercise of discretion by the Attorney-General and I am afraid I can't tell you why the Attorney-General exercises discretion in one way in one case and another way in another.

Q.   Why has the Attorney-General, who is the plaintiff in this case, sent you out to Australia to answer questions about this matter if you are not in a position to inform us. Have you been sent here because of what you don't know?

A.   I can't tell you that I do know what I don't know, can I now, Mr. Turnbull?

Q.   I will start that again, I am sorry, you can't tell me what you don't know?

A.   Hmmm.

Q.   What I am asking is were you selected for this job because you are not in a position to answer these questions?

A.   I don't know why I was selected for this job.

Q.   Who selected you?

A.   I suppose the Attorney-General did since
            he is the plaintiff.

Q.   That was very gallant of him, wasn't it?

A.   I don't think I can comment on that.

Justice Powell was looking puzzled, and intervened to
see if he could make sense of this increasingly curious
evidence.

His Honor   I wonder, Sir Robert, if the position is
             this, and you may confirm or deny it: it
             was proposed, I assume, that you should
             answer the interrogatories on behalf of
             the British Government?

A.   Correct.

Q.   May I take it that you perused the in-
             terrogatories, what they were all about?

A.   I read them with care.

Q.   And you caused certain inquiries to be
             made within those departments of the
             Government which you thought were ap-
             propriate?

A.   Where I needed to do so, yes.

Q.   And you caused the answers to those in-
             quiries to be placed before the Treasury
             Solicitor for his advice as to how the
             interrogatories should be answered?

A.   It would no doubt be he who had to
             make the inquiries.

Q.   May I take it that a draft of the answers
             to interrogatories was placed before you
             for your consideration?

A.   Certainly.

Q.   And that you consulted with either the
             Treasury Solicitor or some of the officers

> in his establishment as to whether it was proper that these things be answered in the form in which they were or suggested alterations where you believed they were desirable or necessary, is that a correct assumption?

A.   That would be correct.

Q.   Am I correct in assuming that where matters of legal form were involved you acted on the advice of the Treasury Solicitor?

A.   Yes, you are correct.

Q.   And where matters which were not within your personal knowledge were concerned you acted on the information conveyed to you by officers?

A.   Right.

Q.   And where matters were within your personal knowledge you vouched for them yourself?

A.   Correct.

Q.   And in answering the interrogatories you believed they were correct and sufficient answers in the form in which they were ultimately put before the court?

A.   That is right your Honor.

His Honor   That is the best I can do, Mr. Turnbull. I don't know that gets you very far, or whether you wish to pursue it further.

The judge had not got much further, but he had established at least that Armstrong was prepared to take full responsibility for what were appearing to be increasingly unsatisfactory answers. He may not have known it, but Justice Powell was offering him a way out. In the Equity Division of the Supreme Court, most evidence is given on affidavit.[3] Justice Powell knew that most affidavits

---

3. An affidavit is a statement of evidence made by a witness and sworn on oath to be true.

are written by lawyers who take a little more license with their clients' evidence than they ought to and then give them to their clients and tell them "Sign it." In the real world, the judge knew it was not fair to hold a person entirely responsible for his lawyer's wording. But this witness seemed determined to insist that it was all his own work. In his efforts to explain the extraordinary "advice" given by the Attorney-General not to stop *Their Trade is Treachery* Armstrong suggested that the Government did not know the precise identity of the source of Pincher's inside information. I tested him on this explanation.

Tuesday November 18, 1986

Q.   Surely in the Security Service, Sir Robert, there is "a need to know" principle is there not?

A.   Very certainly, sir.

Q.   Certain sorts of information have limited access to known individuals?

A.   Yes.

Q.   If that information pops up in a book or in a public domain, it is not terribly difficult to narrow the sources of information down to a few people is it?

A.   It was narrowed down to quite a number of people, quite quickly.

Q.   How many?

A.   Three, I think.

Q.   Three?

A.   But to take it further, it was more difficult.

Q.   Prior to publication you, through the analysis, were made to ascertain with some degree of certainty that at least one out of three individuals had been Pincher's source?

A.   I was advised that the analyst suggested that the source might have been any one or any number of three suspects.

Q.   That is what I meant, at least one. Did you approach any of those three prior to publication to ask them whether they had been the source?

A.   I did not do so.

Q.   Were they approached by members of the Service?

A.   Not so far as I know.

Q.   It [MI5] seemed hardly the diligent guardian of the nation's secrets. Sir Robert, you ascertained one or more of three individuals and you have taken no steps to interview them?

A.   Those concerned would want to be very concerned of their grounds before making that serious charge. They would want to be able to ensure what they said was sustainable.

Q.   Sir Robert. I am sure you would agree, in a security investigation, that if one reached the view fairly quickly that the information had come from one or more of three people, what possible harm could there have been, in approaching one of them and saying to him, "Look, Pincher's got a whole lot of material about Hollis. Did you give it to him?" What possible harm could be caused by that?

A.   So far as I know it was not done, Mr. Turnbull.

Q.   I put it to you that it was not done because the Government did not mind that the book was published.

A.   That is not true as I have already said.

Q.   Sir Robert, you have told us that when
        you got the manuscripts analyzed, you
        were faced with a lack of evidence suf-
        ficient to bring an action to restrain the
        breach of confidence. No basis to restrain
        publication of the book. You analyzed it
        down to three people and you did not
        even take the fundamental step that any
        police constable would know to take to
        go and ask them whether they provided
        the information?

A.   That was not done, no.

Q.   Indeed. That is a pretty sorry commen-
        tary on your concern about protecting
        the nation's secrets, is it not?

A.   It was not for me to conduct those in-
        quiries but it still was not done.

Q.   It is a pretty sorry commentary on the
        Security Service's interest in protecting
        those secrets that those steps were not
        taken is it not?

A.   I wish it had been done.

Q.   Why did you not cause it to be done?

A.   I don't remember why I did not cause it
        to be done. I don't think it occurred to
        me, I'm afraid."

I could sense a growing feeling of unreality in the
court. The whole courtroom was astonished by these
answers. Either Armstrong, the Attorney-General and
MI5 were collectively so incompetent as to be unfit to
hold their offices, or the witness was lying. Here we had
an Attorney-General whose knowledge of the law of confidential information appeared so poor as to disentitle
him to practice law at all, a Cabinet Secretary who didn't
think of asking the three possible "sources" whether they
were responsible in order to narrow it down and a Security

Service whose officers failed to perform the most basic investigative procedures.

Q.   Sir Robert, I am putting to you now that you ensured that nothing was done that could possibly stop the publication of *Their Trade is Treachery*. You did everything in your power to assist its smooth passage onto the bookstand.

A.   That is absolutely untrue and false.

Q.   You knew before publication that a small number of officers, former officers, were the suspects of the information yet neither you nor the Security Service ever thought of going to interview any of them?

A.   That would not necessarily have stopped the publication would it?

Q.   Please answer the question. You did not even think of going to interview them did you?

A.   I didn't.

Q.   And neither did the Security Service?

A.   I cannot answer for the Security Service who did not do so as I understand it.

Q.   A deficiency in your legal armory as you told us earlier was a lack of certainty as to the source and yet you took no steps to ascertain the source prior to publication?

A.   As I say, there was an analysis put in hand as soon as the book became available. That analysis, because of the length and the detailed nature of the book, took a very considerable time.

Q.   Do you believe it to be a part of your job to assist in the protection of the nation's secrets?

A. I believe so.

Q. You were derelict in your duty in respect of *Their Trade is Treachery?*

A. I don't accept that.

Q. You failed in your duty to protect the nation's secrets?

A. It is not for me to decide publication of a book.

Q. You did nothing to assist the suppression of *Their Trade is Treachery* at all, did you?

A. Advice was given to the Attorney-General as to the nature of the damage that would be caused and he took his decision.

Q. You are assisting in the suppression of this book?

A. I did not tell the Attorney-General that he must do this or that.

Q. You are assisting in the suppression of this book are you not?

A. The Attorney-General sought an injunction and here I am to answer to the court.

Q. Lending your assistance to this enterprise?

A. If that is the way you would like to put it, yes.

Q. But you did nothing to assist the suppression of *Their Trade is Treachery* even though you told us earlier that it was your personal view that it should have been stopped?

A. I was presented with a situation in which the Attorney-General concluded that there was no basis for restraint.

The Attorney-General was now not just a skirt to hide behind, but a scapegoat. Sir Robert's language, in the midst of his embarrassment, had changed dramatically.

He was "presented" with the *fait accompli* of the Attorney's decision. A germ of an idea started to form in my mind. If Armstrong was not telling the truth about Havers' role, then we should ensure Havers is properly humiliated over his ludicrous advice. If Havers is a man of some pride, he will insist that Armstrong set the record straight.

The judge brought me back to earth as he ruefully closed the day's proceedings with an oblique reference to the Court of Appeal where Simos was taking us the next day.

His Honor   Whether or not we continue tomorrow is in your hands and those greater than I. I adjourn until not before 2 p.m. tomorrow.

CHAPTER 6

GREENGRASS AND I WENT for a long walk on the evening of the 18th. He had read the Pincher-Wright letters. I had not had time to do so. He was very excited and didn't want to talk to me inside.

"The letters are complete proof of Victor's involvement."

I was still a little stunned by Greengrass' information about Rothschild. A respected, seventy-year-old Peer of the Realm, Pillar of the City, bearer of banking's greatest name, this man had been party to Wright divulging the whole Hollis scandal and had then channelled half of the proceeds to Wright. It would not take an imaginative prosecutor to work out half a dozen serious charges with which to prosecute Rothschild. It was crazy.

Following Greengrass' revelation of Rothschild's role, I had asked Peter about it and he had replied, "I don't want to get Victor involved. He was very good to me." Wright's affection for Rothschild was almost filial. Rothschild had been the only member of the establishment who had welcomed Wright and made him feel an equal.

"It's an operation." I repeated. "It's a deniable operation. Pincher was the safe way of letting the Hollis story out without making an official statement. It was a typical unattributable leak."

"That's funny, that's what the CIA think." It was my turn to be puzzled. "The CIA, are they involved too?" Paul appeared satisfied to have surprised me. "I explained the whole Pincher/Wright/Rothschild story to a friend of mine in CIA Counter-Espionage. He had exactly the same reaction."

"Well, I must be right." Paul shook his head. "A lot of the hacks think you are drawing a very long bow with this conspiracy theory. It seems too far-fetched." We were on our way home now, up the hill from Rose Bay and the harbor lights. When we got back in, Lucy was still up and I asked her and Paul to argue out the conspiracy theory with me.

"OK, Point 1: Once Andrew Boyle's book about Blunt comes out and Blunt is exposed, everyone is speculating about the fifth man. Who's the next mole? Arthur Martin is talking about Hollis to Jonathan Aitken. It is only a matter of time before Hollis is exposed."

"Yes, that's right." said Lucy. "We've got the letter from Aitken to Thatcher saying it's about time the Hollis affair is brought into the open."

"Point 2: Thatcher is new in office. Whatever has happened to MI5 in the past is certainly not her fault. She can suffer no damage by cleaning out the Augean stables with a full public statement and assurance that nothing like that will happen in the future. That essentially is what Aitken recommended."

"But that's where you are so wrong." Greengrass interjected. "That's what Australians would do, or Americans. The British aren't like that. They are dedicated to secrecy, for its own sake."

"But what about the lobby system?" asked Lucy. "The only thing the British are obsessed about is not being responsible. They don't mind leaking stuff into the public domain as long as the leaker cannot be identified.

Greengrass appeared somewhat persuaded. "OK, press on with the theory."

"Point 3: Rothschild's involvement. Why would he risk all he had earned in his life unless he knew he was acting with authority, albeit covert authority. He was a spook[1] once, wasn't he? That's how those blokes think."

"That's a long bow. Your theory is entirely dependent on making assumptions about Rothschild. You need to get an admission from Rothschild. What does Wright say?" Lucy was skeptically practical.

"We haven't properly debriefed him on Rothschild yet. I've been trying to go through Armstrong's affidavits with him. You're right. We need to get Peter to cough the lot on Rothschild. We then need to make the allegation about Rothschild public. We need to stir up the Opposition in London with calls to prosecute Rothschild. The Government will have to respond by saying they are going to investigate. Rothschild might defend himself by telling the truth."

"If the conspiracy is the truth," Lucy added.

"Well if it isn't, they should bloody well charge him." I replied. "Anyway, I think we need to get the Labor Party involved. This Havers business is rubbish. I simply do not believe that he told Thatcher there was no legal basis for seeking an injunction to restrain *Their Trade is Treachery*. He's either the worst lawyer God ever put breath into, or he's taking responsibility for something he didn't do. Kinnock should have a go at him. How do we get onto Kinnock?"[2]

---

1. Slang for an intelligence operative. Rothschild had worked for both MI5 and MI6.
2. Neil Kinnock was and is the leader of the British Labor Party and since Labor has the second largest number of members of Parliament after the Conservatives, he is also the Leader of the Opposition in the House of Commons. He is a charming, eloquent and moderate democratic socialist. To date he has made very little impact on Margaret Thatcher's dominance of English politics because of the unacceptably radical platform of the Labor Party which among other things supports the unilateral withdrawal of all nuclear weapons

"David Leigh's the man. He knows Kinnock and Patricia Hewitt well." said Greengrass, referring to Neil Kinnock's Australian-born press secretary.

Leigh was closely connected with the Labor Party and was the most politically committed of the journalists covering the case, so Greengrass and I had nicknamed him Comrade Leigh. (The moustachioed and well built correspondent for the *Guardian,* Richard Norton-Taylor, was nicknamed "the Major," but that referred to his appearance rather than any militaristic inclinations.)

The next morning, Wednesday November 19, found us in the Court of Appeal. The British Government had sought special leave to appeal against Justice Powell's order that they provide discovery of documents relating to the publication of *Their Trade is Treachery, A Matter of Trust* and a number of other books which had previously published information in *Spycatcher.* As I had made plain to Armstrong the previous day, a key part of our case was that not only had almost all of the information in *Spycatcher* been previously published, but much of it had been previously published with the covert authorization of the British Government. In particular we wanted to prove that Chapman Pincher's *Their Trade is Treachery* had been unofficially authorized. The Government did not want to provide us with these documents and sought to challenge Justice.

Powell's order for production by arguing that the only relevant issue in the case was whether Wright had been officially authorized by the Government to write his book. This ignored our contention that the Pincher and West books had been covertly authorized.

The Government had no automatic right of appeal, but had to obtain the special leave of the Court of Appeal. I knew that if they succeeded in obtaining special leave,

---

from British soil. As Leader of the Opposition he is the alternative Prime Minister.

the trial would be interrupted and would not conclude until the following year. Armstrong would go home and the whole momentum of the the cross-examination would be lost as the case became embroiled in a complex miasma of technical legal argument in the Court of Appeal. The most distasteful and cynical part of the Government's conduct was that they could, and should, have challenged Justice Powell's order months before. They waited until the last moment in order to cause the maximum disruption to the trial.

Their purpose in bringing the application for special leave was cynical. They realized as well as I did, that my clients were simply not in a position to match the unlimited treasury of the British Government. A long, tedious expensive excursus into abstruse interlocutory points would exhaust Wright and Heinemann's resources. Already, back in Britain, a number of key directors of Heinemann were opposed to the case. More delay, more expense and the faint hearts would carry the day and persuade Paul Hamlyn to throw in the towel.

Simos rose to explain his arguments to the Court of Appeal. It consisted of Sir Laurence Street, the Chief Justice, Michael Kirby, the president of the Court of Appeal, and Michael McHugh. All three were distinguished judges, and all three were men who had been, in different ways, something of mentors. Ten years before when I was writing a column about legal affairs for the *Bulletin* I came to know Street and Kirby. Street was Chief Justice then, and Kirby was the first chairman of the Australian Law Reform Commission. Kirby had acquired a reputation as a legal radical, which says more about the stiff and reactionary world of the legal profession than it does about Kirby's rather mild reformist philosophy. Street is a conservative man. His father and grandfather were Chief Justices of New South Wales before him. Street had served in the navy during the second world war, and was unlikely, I thought, to have much sympathy for Wright. Kirby, on the other hand, comes from humbler stock. Nonetheless both came to like me, and both wrote references for me in 1977 when I won a Rhodes Scholarship. I came to know McHugh later, he was in the same set of Barristers Chambers I shared when I practiced at the Bar from 1980 to 1982.

Kirby and McHugh were both regarded as being much less conservative than the Chief Justice. Kirby had been a protégé of that great radical lawyer, Justice Lionel Murphy.[3] It was Murphy who promoted the young and unknown Kirby to the post of chairman of the Australian Law Reform Commission. Kirby successfully combined his talent for hard work and publicity to make himself a national figure. McHugh had been a powerful advocate at the bar. He had a photographic memory and could remember verbatim passages from leading cases, quoting the page and paragraph number for his references. He was married to a left-wing Labor member of the House of Representatives, Jeannette McHugh. I had reason to expect Kirby and McHugh would be, at least, sympathetic. I had no such expectations from Street. He was bred in the establishment and an Anglophile. He is the Lieutenant-Governor of New South Wales, and fills in for the Governor[4] when he is out of State residing in great

3. Lionel Murphy had been Attorney General in the radical Whitlam Labor Government in Australia from 1972 until 1975 when he was appointed to the High Court. Murphy was very influenced by the radical and socially aware members of the United States Supreme Court, particularly under the Chief Justiceship of Earl Warren. His career ended in 1987 when he died of cancer following two dreadful years in which he was charged with trying to influence proceedings in a lower court. He was finally acquitted, but the ordeal broke him and he died within months of his vindication.
4. A Governor of an Australian State, like his federal counterpart the Governor-General, is a stand-in for the monarch and is therefore a well-paid figurehead without any real executive or constitutional power. The head of Government of an Australian State is called a Premier and his federal counterpart is called the Prime Minister of Australia.

splendor at Government House. This is not to say that Sir Laurence Street is an arch-Tory. He is far too intelligent for that, but he is comfortable with and respectful of the authority of the Crown, unlike many Australians who share a cantankerous and skeptical distrust of authority in all its forms.

The Chief Justice quickly fulfilled my expectations. He gave me the distinct impression that he was in favor of granting special leave to appeal. This would have brought the trial to a grinding halt. I could not sense the inclinations of his two colleagues, but I could tell from the satisfied smiles on the faces of my opponents that they at least felt they were going to succeed.

When I rose to address the Court I was dizzy and overcome with anxiety. I had had so little sleep for what seemed so long and now it seemed these British, who for one moment I hated with a passion, were going to stop me just as I was starting to get to the truth. And these three judges were going to let them do it, just because they thought there was an interesting question of law. They didn't care that the British had waited until the last moment to argue this point. I gripped the lectern and focussed on the Bench, and coldly and with a vicious passion that was met with startled blinks from the judges, stated my position:

Wednesday, November 19, 1986

Mr. Turnbull   The trial has started, the battlelines have been drawn, my old and sick client is in Sydney at considerable expense to himself. My client, the publisher's, resources are derisory compared to those of the other side. It is plain, that here, if there ever was one, is a client with a long pocket determined to avoid the continued cross-examination of Sir Robert Armstrong down in Court 8D.

Street CJ	Let me just point out to you that what has triggered this off is your application for discovery. It is your desire to have this wide-ranging sweep through the plaintiff's documents.
Mr. Turnbull	With respect it is not a wide-ranging sweep, with the greatest of respect.
Street CJ	Well it is a sweep.
Mr. Turnbull	It is not a sweep. If your Honors considered that this application had any merit whatsoever that would make your Honors consider granting leave so that the result would be that my old client will be kept out of his rights for one day longer, then I will waive my right to discover these documents. I submit I am entitled to have them, but my clients cannot survive more delay, they cannot survive more expense. We have been driven from interlocutory hearing to interlocutory hearing.

The case dragged on for a few more minutes, but I had said all of importance I had to say. I had flung down the gauntlet. They could grant Simos special leave, but that wouldn't stop the trial. I would do without the documents, and I would keep battering Armstrong until he told me the truth. The argument ended, the judges left the bench for a few minutes. They came back and Street announced the application had been dismissed. We had won another battle, but the war was far from ended. I stood outside the Court of Appeal and, alone in a corner and shaking, lit a cigarette. I was smoking far too much. I shouldn't be smoking at all. Bugger these people, they were trying to drive me mad.

Exhausted though I may have been, I was not the unhappiest man in court. Sir Robert looked appalled. This could never happen in England. He had been told that Justice Powell was a one-off eccentric, and that in the Court of Appeal order would be restored. But now, his ordeal would continue. Theo Simos was putting a brave face on it when the trial resumed before Justice Powell at 2:00 p.m.

Mr. Simos	May I inform your Honor, if your Honor already does not know of the fate of our application in the Court of Appeal. It was refused, your Honor.
His Honor	It was refused. There goes my peerage.
Mr. Simos	As your Honor is being jocular, perhaps I can be too. Since I began appearing before your Honor, your Honor is having a far better run in the Court of Appeal.
His Honor	That is very kind of you, Mr. Simos. You must stay and come more often.

It was apparent to everyone who had seen the manuscript of *Spycatcher* that very little of it indeed had not been previously published, mainly by Chapman Pincher and Nigel West. This defense of "public domain" was a key part of our case and the Government had sought to meet it by arguing that when a former MI5 officer ("an insider") like Peter Wright published something that a journalist ("an outsider") like Chapman Pincher had previously published, additional harm was done to national security because the insider spoke with enhanced authority. In short more people were likely to believe Wright than Pincher.

This proposition simply flew in the face of the facts, at least as far as Wright was concerned. Peter's obsession with Hollis' guilt had been derided by most respected commentators. He was seen as an embittered old man whose hatred for Hollis and resentment of his old superiors had seriously tainted his objectivity. Writers like Phillip Knightley and Hugo Young had poured scorn on

Wright long before his book was published. Still Sir Robert's task was to argue that Wright's book would have a hitherto unheard-of credibility.

Wednesday, November 19, 1986

Q. Let us go back to the outsider/insider dichotomy because it is pretty important. If you were writing a history of the intelligence service, and one had full and free access and so forth, one would undoubtedly want to look at the documents and talk to a number of former officers and possibly serving officers, would one not?

A. I would think so.

Q. And there would be very few histories regarded as authoritative for any period of history which are based on one participant's recollection solely. That is correct, is it not?

A. Yes.

Q. So if you wanted to get an accurate history of the Second World War, one would not simply pluck one retired General's memoirs off the shelf and read that?

A. Not for the history of the whole war certainly.

Q. Nor, indeed, let us be honest, Sir Robert, for the history of a particular campaign?

A. Probably not.

Q. Because cross-referencing is very important in the work of history, is it not?

A. I have never written it. I am sure it is so.

Q.   What I am putting to you, Sir Robert, is that in fact the work of Nigel West or Chapman Pincher, who had access to a number of sources at M15 and a number of documents from M15, is more authoritative and has a better provenance than a personal memoir of one man, if he is what we call an insider, will carry great authority because he is an insider.."[5]

I made little progress with Sir Robert on this score and moved onto another type of detriment he claimed Britain would suffer if the book was published. This was the argument that M15's status would be diminished in the eyes of other, friendly intelligence agencies. We argued that this was particularly specious since the most important intelligence relationship Britain had was with the United States which I knew, from *extremely* reliable sources, collected more than 85 percent of western intelligence material. The CIA (and the other American intelligence agencies) had for some years allowed former agents to write books about their work as long as they had been vetted first. Moreover material which was already in the public domain or which was out of date was never objected to. In fact the CIA performed precisely the sort of negotiated blue-pencilling exercise which we had asked the British to undertake, and which they had refused. It was quickly apparent that Armstrong knew nothing about the American manuscript clearance policy. I suggested to him that all I was asking his Government to do, was to take a similar blue-pencilling approach to *Spycatcher*. He still insisted the Americans might think less

5. Three years later, in 1988, when Peter Wright gave a different version of his role in the plot against Harold Wilson, Armstrong was quick to write to *The Times* and say that this had destroyed Wright's credibility.

of M15, if it adopted the same approach as the Americans. I asked him to explain this. He answered:

Wednesday, November 19, 1986

A.　　Because I don't believe they would necessarily be perfectly logical in the matter as you are rightly seeking to be.

Q.　　You say the American Central Intelligence Agency lacks the same logic which you have seen from me this afternoon in court?

A.　　Not everybody behaves with equal logic.

Q.　　So the American Central Intelligence Agency is run by illogical men?

A.　　That is not what I said.

Q.　　Is it your experience that the policy of the Central Intelligence Agency has been illogical?

A.　　I don't think that it has always had perfect logic.

Q.　　By and large would you agree that the Central Intelligence Agency is run in a logical fashion?

A.　　I don't know enough about it to say whether by and large. I expect so.

So Armstrong had given a sworn affidavit saying that he believed the CIA would think less of MI5 if it offered to blue-pencil *Spycatcher*. His only reason for this view was that he feared the CIA would react illogically, although he did agree that, by and large, it was run in a logical fashion. He was even prepared to compare MI5's "leakiness" favorably with that of the CIA.

Q.　　Does MI5 think less of the Central Intelligence Agency because of its manuscript clearance policy?

A. I think that it would be thought that the CIA is apt to be more leaky than some other intelligence agencies and that this policy would be part of it.

Q. The people who brought us Philby, Burgess, Bettaney and McLean say that the CIA is apt to be more leaky?

A. I think you could match that list of spies in America very easily.

Q. So you say the CIA is more penetrated by Soviet agents than MI5?

A. I haven't said that.

Q. You say it is leakier?

A. I said I think more information comes out of the CIA than out of the Security Services without authority.

One previous publication upon which our public domain case relied was a television interview with Peter Wright broadcast in 1984 on the "World in Action" program in Britain. This program had been produced by Paul Greengrass and John Ware and in it, Wright for the first time openly stated his case against Hollis. No effort was made to stop the broadcast of the program. The explanation for this failure to stop it was, to say the least, unsatisfactory.

Wednesday, November 19, 1986

Q. Sir Robert, in 1984 there was a television program broadcast by Granada Television in England featuring an interview with Peter Wright called "The Spy That Never Was." When did you first learn that program was in the course of preparation?

A.   We gathered from an article in *The Times* shortly before—we learnt about it probably some days before. We did not know much about the contents until there was an article in *The Times* I think on the day when the program was due to come out.

Q.   I put it to you that the Security Service became aware of the preparation of that program some months before it was broadcast.

A.   I don't know about "months." Weeks, possibly.

Q.   No steps were taken to stop it?

A.   No.

Q.   Why?

A.   It was not possible to say whether it was likely to be damaging, and nothing was known about the contents of the program.

Q.   Do you regret not having taken steps to ascertain whether the program contained information which Wright had gathered during his years in the Service?

A.   Perhaps more should have been done to try to find out whether it would have been possible to do so, I don't know.

Q.   Well, anyway, you knew the story was coming up on Granada Television and you were concerned, were you not, at the time, that Mr. Wright might say something about his life in the Service?

A.   We didn't know what he was going to say, but we assumed that he was going to propose that there should be a further inquiry.

Q.   Did you assume that he would comply in all relevant respects with the obligations which you say were owed by him to the British government?

A. We had no grounds for making any other assumption.

Q. So you assumed that this man whom you believed to have spilled the beans to Chapman Pincher, you believed that he would go on television and comply in the strictest possible way with the provisions of the Official Secrets Act, as you saw it?

A. We didn't know what he would do.

Q. You assumed that he wouldn't do anything that would give you cause for complaint?

A. We didn't have any reason to assume that he would.

Q. You didn't therefore have any reason to make any inquiry?

A. Until we saw the article in *The Times*, to which I have already referred.

Q. Did that shock you when you saw that?

A. It was something of a shock, yes.

Q. What time do you get in your office in the morning?

A. It is not just a matter of me. It is a question of lot of other people.

Q. People generally start work at 9 o'clock at Whitehall, do they?

A. That sort of time.

Q. Most of them would have read *The Times* by the time they got in?

A. I should think.

Q. There was plenty of time to get Mr. Nursaw to swear a brief affidavit and get an injunction against Granada Television?[6]

---

6. Nursaw had been the official from the Attorney-General's office in London whose two-page affidavit had been successful in getting

A.	If the Attorney-General so decided it, yes.
Q.	Why didn't the Attorney-General so decide?
A.	I don't know the answer to that, but I suspect because there simply wasn't time to get the act together.
Q.	Really. Not enough time for Mr. Bailey, the Treasurer Solicitor's office to draft up an affidavit?
A.	To get a decision in the time available which at that stage was very short.
Q.	So here we have Mr. Wright revealing information—you now know he was going to reveal information which you say is damaging to national security—and you cannot get a decision out of the Attorney-General quickly enough to get an injunction?
A.	I think that must have been the explanation.
Q.	Of course you could have gone off to court and got an interim injunction and then negotiated with the television company just like you did with Mr. West, couldn't you?
A.	With the Attorney-General's agreement, yes.
Q.	How zealous is the Attorney-General in his defense of the nation's secrets, Sir Robert?
A.	I think he is properly zealous.
Q.	But not hastily zealous?
A.	At the time of this instance, the time was very short.

an injunction to stop Nigel West's book *"A Matter of Trust"* in 1982. It was the stark contrast between the approach to this book and other publications that gave the lie to Armstrong's whole claim of a consistent Government attitude to such publications.

Q.   Very short. The program was going to air at 8 o'clock at night, or 8:30 at night?

A.   I don't remember the time.

Q.   Even the sleepiest man in the Attorney-General's office would have read *The Times* by 9 o'clock, wouldn't he?

A.   I suspect so.

Q.   So he had eleven and a half hours to swear a one-page affidavit, annex it to a summons and get an injunction. Do you believe that the Attorney-General is worthy of criticism for this failure to make a decision quickly?

A.   I don't know where the responsibility lies.

Q.   Has any inquiry been made as to where the guilty men are?

A.   Not by me.

Q.   Has there been an inquiry made as to who slipped up?

A.   I don't know.

Q.   If there hasn't been one, do you think there should be one?

A.   I will try to find out but I don't think I shall be able to do it in the course of these proceedings.

Q.   If in fact this eleven-hour period was insufficient time to get a one-page affidavit and summons done in the Attorney-General's office, there is surely a considerable inefficiency in the Department of Law Officers in London?

A.   I think it is a question of getting a decision rather than putting the decision to effect once it has been made. I am sure the Attorney-General's division or the Solicitor's Department could draw up an affidavit of the kind required at the speed required.

Q.   What if there was an article in *The Times* tomorrow morning at 9 o'clock which said that at 8:30 tonight on television we are going to show you all the blueprints for the latest cruise missile. Do you think the Attorney-General would be able to gird his loins and make a decision whether to seek an injunction?

A.   I hope so, certainly.

Q.   But it is a real risk in England?

A.   It happened on this occasion.

Q.   You see, Sir Robert, I put to you that far from being concerned about this program, far from wanting to stop it, you were so little concerned about it that you knowingly allowed it to go to air without any thought of seeking a restraint?

A.   I think thought was given to seeking a restraint but I do not think the decision was taken in the necessary time scale.

Q.   Were any written minutes created indicating this consideration of seeking restraint?

A.   I should think the space of time was too small for that.

Q.   Were there any communications with the Prime Minister or the Security Service made by you concerning that program during the day?

A.   There were no communications with the Prime Minister, but then the decision was not for her, the decision would be with the Attorney-General.

Q.   Did you discuss it with the Attorney-General?

A.   I did not myself do so.

Q.   Did the Security Service discuss it with the Attorney-General?

A.   I think they may have discussed it with his officers, but I don't know for sure.

Q.   Were the Security Service opposed to the program being allowed to go to air?

A.   They told the Attorney-General that they were of the opinion that the program should not go to air.

Q.   Did the Attorney-General recognizing the grave concern of MI5 cause Granada Television to be contacted about the program?

A.   I don't know.

Q.   It is hardly indicative of great concern about detriment [to national security], is it?

A.   I can understand that point of view.

Subsequent evidence in the English *Spycatcher* case in December 1987 demonstrated that Armstrong's evidence here was false. In fact MI5 had known about Wright's television interview months before it went to air. The producer of the program, John Ware, had gone to considerable lengths to persuade MI5 to allow another former officer, Alec McDonald, to give an interview rebutting Wright's allegations against Hollis. Was Armstrong lying, or had MI5 been "economical" with the truth when it briefed him prior to his giving evidence?

We returned from Court that Wednesday afternoon and immediately sat down to go through some curious correspondence. During and after Pincher's writing of *Their Trade is Treachery* and the revised paperback edition, Pincher and Wright had corresponded with each other. They used childish codenames (Peter Wright was "Phillip" and Chapman Pincher "Henry") and sent their letters to accommodation addresses. These letters basically consisted of Pincher picking Wright's brains. Wright on his part provided more and more detail to Pincher. The correspondence made frequent reference to "Victor" and the fact that the money was being paid to Wright through the "V-Channel." It confirmed Rothschild's deep involvement in the publication of *Their Trade is Treachery* and made it impossible for him to deny it.

Wright and Pincher had agreed to destroy their correspondence, but Wright was too much of an old intelligence man to destroy such valuable documents. He hid them for many years until in late 1985 he handed them over to his former solicitors. Wright's short-term memory was then very bad and by the time I became involved in the case he had completely forgotten what had happened to them. The former solicitors failed either to tell me of their existence, or hand them over to me after their retainers were terminated, apparently because they were still owed money by Heinemann and Wright. Then, out of the blue, a large carton of papers, including the correspondence, arrived at my office on the second day of the trial. It was a godsend and doubly appreciated for being unexpected.

Pincher boasted of his superb contacts, particularly with Michael Havers. He wrote to Wright on January 27, 1983:

Dear Philip,

Your letter of 9.1 has just arrived. I can see no reason why we should change our postal arrangements. I am sure that we are in no danger.

On New Years day I was shooting with Havers, the Attorney-General, who is very friendly and told me about West's book. *[A Matter of Trust]* It is an extraordinary story and I urge you to have nothing whatever to do with West or with anything associated with him.

For reasons I do not understand Martin agreed to see West. Havers told me that they met six times and on each occasion Martin told West secret information. In addition he showed him secret documents which should not have been in his possession. West then wrote his book and in it not only quoted Martin by name but quoted from the documents saying they were secret! West is so stupid and naive that he then sent Martin a copy of the script for his comments. Martin was terrified and immediately took the book to the office in an effort to get himself out of the mess. The office informed Havers who then issued an injunction to have the offending parts removed for had the book been published the Government would have had no option but to prosecute both Martin and West. West had included several names including yours. He was required to remove but still kept you in as Peter W.

[Pincher then expresses some salty views about Mr. West's character]

Havers told me that he is still considering whether to prosecute Martin but says he cannot do that without prosecuting West who has been adopted as a Tory candidate! Mrs. T is furious with him. (West). . . I can assure you that there is no intention whatever of taking action against me, which means you too. I lunched with Dickie Franks[7] recently and he told me that they had my book weeks in advance and came to the conclusion that they would rather I did it than anyone else. They had heard that West, Duncan Campbell, Penrose etc. were on the trail and preferred my authorship. Further I have been functioning for some months as a specialist adviser (paid) to the Parliamentary Defense Committee and have just been appointed chief adviser on an inquiry into positive vetting. I am also elected to an MOD Committee to study censorship problems arising out of the Falklands affair. So I do not think we are unpopular.

---

7. Head of MI6.

Pincher was relentless in his requests for more information from Wright, all the time offering the prospects of more money for his stud farm. In one memorable phrase he wrote on March 4, 1983: "The great thing is to have the meat and then we can make and market the rissole."

The full file of letters is voluminous, but throughout it Pincher refers, sometimes more obliquely, to the arrangements with Rothschild over the money. On January 7, 1981 he writes "Five is on its way through the V-channel." Wright was complaining about the delays in receiving funds and on January 20, 1981 Pincher wrote, "Our mutual friend has just confirmed that the deposit for the mares is on its way to you." On March 13, 1981: "I have talked with our intermediary and he will see what he can do re your Swiss venture, but rather regards himself as having completed his contribution." On May 24, 1981: "The Ks you request immediately available. Held up only on advice our mutual friend." On June 4, 1981: "After consultation with your adviser your Ks for the horses already sold are on the way to you. No more may be expected for three months when your adviser may have organized a new arrangement." On July 22, 1981: "I am appalled to hear that you have not received your stallion proceeds. I set this in motion a month ago and the failure is due to the mechanics at our mutual friend's end. Am doing all I can to expedite. Will see him." On July 28, 1981: "Have seen our friend who promises to pull out all stops. No problems my end re: stallion Ks. Hope now with you."

Apart from pumping Wright for more and more information which he could include in the paperback edition of *Their Trade is Treachery* and later in *Too Secret Too Long* Pincher even solicited suggestions from Wright concerning censorship. Pincher then used them as part of his submissions to the various governmental committees he had been co-opted to. As I read this I could not imagine anything more bizarre. Pincher, the man who has exposed Hollis, is not prosecuted or shunned. No, he is appointed a paid adviser to government on matters of censorship. Pincher then proceeds to supplement his own ideas by consulting Peter Wright!

Pincher's generous Christian spirit shone out, however, in two letters in particular. In a letter of March 13, 1981, referring to Harold Wilson, he wrote: "HW's health problem is real and organic—cancer of the bowel. Suspect he will not last long. Anything further usable if he goes? May be seeing Angleton soon. Meanwhile must soft pedal on HW [Harold Wilson] and K [Lord Kagan, a friend of Wilson]." Pincher, the experienced journalist, knows that it is not possible to libel the dead and wants to be ready with the first and foulest bucket of slime to sling over Wilson's corpse. As in many things, Pincher was wrong in predicting so early a demise for Lord Wilson of Rievaulx.

Wilson was not the only "dead" man Pincher had in his sights. On August 18, 1981 he wrote: "That horrible little bastard Will Owen has died, so anything extra about him can now be printed. Any RHH [Roger Hollis] connections?"

The correspondence demonstrated beyond a shadow of a doubt that both Pincher and Rothschild were deeply involved in the financial arrangements with Wright. These were profoundly serious matters: they amounted to bribing a man to reveal official secrets. I could not believe either Pincher or Rothschild would take such risks without some form of clearance.

Paul and I decided we had to confront Peter and wring the truth out of him once and for all. Paul spoke to him and Lois alone, for about half an hour, and then I came in.

"Malcolm I simply don't want to get Victor involved. He is an old man, it could kill him."

I am afraid I was fairly brutal with Peter. "Well you may have to choose between him and yourself Peter. If you don't tell the truth about Rothschild, I think you'll lose the case."

"Do I have to tell the court everything?" the old man pleaded.

"Yes, Peter, you cannot tell the court anything but the truth, and you can't leave things out. If you do, they will cross-examine you the way I have been cross-examining Armstrong, and they will destroy you."

The conversation went on in this vein for some time. Finally Wright went silent and nursed his whisky glass for a full minute. He took a deep swig of his drink and held the empty glass up as if for a toast. An almost theatrical tone of resolve took over his old man's voice sad and weary like one who knows the dreadful consequences of what he was about to say.

"Oh well, poor dear Victor," he intoned, deliberately replacing the glass down on the desk. "Throw him to the wolves!"

The next day was Thursday November 20. Late on Wednesday night after our session with Wright and having perused the "Henry-Phillip" correspondence, I rang Theo Simos and told him I would be asking Armstrong about what he knew of Havers' contacts with Pincher. Perhaps Sir Robert might care to make some inquiries. Theo was unresponsive, noted what I said and bade me good night.

CHAPTER 7

THE NEXT MORNING, true to my word I proceeded to explore Sir Robert's knowledge of the world of Chapman Pincher.

Thursday, November 20, 1986

Mr. Turnbull Sir Robert, yesterday you were talking about Mr. Chapman Pincher amongst other things. Do you consider that Mr. Pincher has a good reputation for accuracy?

A. He has had a good reputation for accuracies and good sources.

Q. And he is generally regarded, is he not, as having access to good sources in the intelligence world?

A. I think that is true.

Q. Indeed, in 1982 and 1983 Mr. Pincher was a specialist adviser to the Parliamentary Defense Committee, was he not?

A. I believe so.

Q. He was also asked to serve on a Ministry of the Defense Committee considering censorship problems arising out of the Falklands War?

A.	Yes, he was.
Q.	It would be fair to say, would it not, that following the publication of *Their Trade is Treachery* his career was hardly blighted by any official shunning of him?
A.	Not so far as I know.

Chapman Pincher's best contact in the intelligence world at that time was none other than Sir Arthur Franks, head of MI6 from 1978 to 1982. When I asked Sir Robert whether Sir Arthur had been head of MI6 he declined to answer. Theo Simos objected and we were bogged down in a legal argument about whether Sir Robert should be forced to acknowledge that Britain had an intelligence service called MI6. While this argument was going on, David Hooper and Lucy rummaged back through the transcript.

Mr. Turnbull	If I might submit, your Honor, Sir Robert has already admitted the existence of MI6. At p. 78 of the transcript:
Q.	Who is Sir Dick Goldsmith-White?
A.	He was the Director-General of the Security Service some years ago.
Q.	And also MI6, was he not?
A.	He had other jobs, yes.
Q	And also MI6, was he not?
A.	He was also head of that other organization, yes."
His Honor	We have had a great debate for no purpose. You have got your answer, you got it last night, Mr. Turnbull. The existence of the organization may be admitted. The nature and extent of its activities may not be.

Mr. Turnbull	I have no desire to get to the nature and extent at this stage.
Q.	Sir Robert, Sir Arthur Franks was like Sir Dick Goldsmith-White who also was head of that organization, was he not?
A.	I acknowledge the existence of MI6 at the time Sir Dick White was head of it. I do not wish to go any further than that.

So MI6 did exist, but only until Sir Dick retired in 1969!

We turned back to *Their Trade is Treachery*. We knew from Pincher's letters to Wright that Pincher had lunched with Sir Arthur Franks, the recently retired head of MI6, in January 1983. This fact alone was astonishing. Here was a journalist who, according to Sir Robert, had caused considerable damage to national security by publishing the Hollis story. Yet only eighteen months later he is lunching with the former head of MI6. He had not been hounded by lawyers or excoriated in Parliament. Instead he is laden with official duties and lunched by influential spymasters.

Q.	Is it one of the rules of the intelligence services that all contact with journalists should be reported to the head of the service or those responsible to the head of the service?
A.	I believe it is a rule that they should be reported to the appropriate place in the service, not necessarily the head.
Q.	If the head of a particular service, be it MI5 or another organization, had a contact with a journalist, he would pass that on to you, would he not?
A.	Not necessarily.
Q.	Who would he pass it on to?

A.   If he passed it on to anybody, he might pass it on to the Secretary of the State to whom he was answering to. In the case of MI5, the Home Secretary.[1]

Q.   In the case of other places, the Foreign Secretary?[2]

A.   Yes.

Q.   Let me ask you this. Have you received from the Foreign Secretary a report of Sir Arthur Franks meeting with Chapman Pincher in January 1983?

A.   I have not received such a report from the Foreign Secretary. I was aware that there had been a meeting at that time.

Q.   Are you aware of what Sir Arthur said to Mr. Pincher?

A.   I am not aware of what Sir Arthur said to Mr. Pincher. I was in summary aware of what Mr. Pincher said to Sir Arthur.

Q.   Who caused you to be given a report of that meeting?

A.   I speak from recollection, but I think Sir Arthur himself.

Q.   So Sir Arthur told you what Pincher said but not what he [Sir Arthur] said?

A.   As far as I recollect he told me briefly how he had such a meeting and the information that he had learned at it.

Q.   So what did Sir Arthur say Pincher had said?

A.   He did not say, he did not give quotations from what he had said, as far as I remember, but he indicated that he said his indications were that Mr. Pincher was preparing another book.

---

1. The cabinet minister responsible, among other things, for police and internal security.
2. The British equivalent of the Secretary of State.

Q.   And that is *Too Secret Too Long?*

A.   I suppose so.

Q.   That book was not published until, when, 1984?

A.   Some time.

Q.   Armed with this information did you take any steps to ascertain whether the second book would contain information obtained in breach of what you would say the confidential duties owed by officers to the Crown?

A.   Either Mr. Pincher or the publishers were requested to provide a copy of the book and refused to do so.

Q.   You were unsuccessful on this occasion in obtaining an advance copy?

A.   I think we may have seen a review copy a couple of days in advance.

Q.   You did not get six weeks' warning as you did with *Their Trade is Treachery,* is that right?

A.   That's right.

Q.   Did you have reason to believe from what Sir Arthur Franks told you about his January meeting with Pincher that there would be information in the book obtained by Pincher from confidential intelligence sources?

A.   The indication as far as I remember was that the book might cover very much the same ground as was covered in the earlier book.

Q.   But Pincher told Franks he had additional information, did he not?

A.   I don't recall that.

Q.   Did Pincher say "I am just rehashing the first book"?

A.   I do not recall that in the report I received from Sir Arthur.

Q.   But it would be a reasonable surmise, would it not, that Mr. Pincher would be intending to put in the second book additional information which had not been in the first book?

A.   If he could get it, yes.

Q.   So you had every reason to believe in the normal course of events that Pincher was up to his old tricks and was going to publish some more secrets to the world at large?

A.   We had every reason to believe that Mr. Pincher was going to produce another book and it might contain additional information.

Q.   Obtained in breach of confidence?

A.   Obtained—it was impossible to say how.

Q.   Mr. Pincher did not tell Sir Arthur Franks the book was about landscape gardening, did he?

A.   I don't know what Mr. Pincher would have had in mind but there had been other books and other material out between *Their Trade is Treachery* and *Too Secret Too Long*.

Q.   When Sir Arthur reported to you about this meeting with Chapman Pincher did Sir Arthur tell you what he believed the nature of the second book would be?

A.   He said he thought that it would cover very much the same sort of ground as the first.

Q.   It would be dealing with the intelligence services, Soviet penetration of them and so on?

A.   All that matter which was in *Their Trade is Treachery.*

Q.   That sort of matter?

A.   Yes.

Q.   Indeed, your expectations were satisfied when the book came out, were they not?

A.   If that is the way to put it, yes.

Q.   So the book when published conformed in terms of its general subject matter with the description given in January 1983 by Sir Arthur Franks?

A.   Yes.

Q.   Did the book contain confidential information obtained by Pincher previously unpublished?

A.   I cannot answer that question. I'm afraid, I don't know.

Q.   Was any analysis done of the book in the same way as analysis was done of *Their Trade is Treachery?*

A.   I am sure that an analysis was done, but I don't remember seeing the detail of it.

Q.   You did not see the detail of it. Was the general substance of it discussed with you?

A.   I heard that the general substance of it was that there was very little that was new in it.

Q.   So basically it was information which was already in the public domain, is that what you are saying?

A.   It was the mixture as before, roughly speaking.

Q.   Did the report say that there was any information in the book previously unpublished and which it was believed Pincher had obtained from former officers or serving officers of the Service or other intelligence organizations?

A.   I cannot remember the exact detail but I should think it said nothing of any real significance, or words to that effect.

Q.   Did Sir Arthur Franks when he related this conversation to you tell you what he said to Pincher?

A.   No.

Q.   Did you ask him?

A.   No.

Q.   That wasn't very curious of you, was it?

A.   It was mainly a listening occasion.

Q.   Chapman Pincher is fond of monologues over lunch?

A.   I never had lunch with him, so I don't know.

Q.   On what occasions have you met him?

A.   I met him at some evening reception.

Q.   What did you discuss with him then?

A.   I cannot remember anything of any significance.

Q.   And likewise you are positive that you did not ask him what he said to Pincher?

A.   I assumed that he would have confined himself to observations which noted what Pincher said and would not have made any admissions, or other observations of that kind.

Q.   You see, in your evidence, if I may be somewhat blunt, uncustomarily blunt, you have endeavored to push off responsibility for the decision about *Their Trade is Treachery* on the Attorney-General. You have consistently said it was his decision and not a matter you can comment on and so forth?

A.   I am not trying to push off responsibility. It just is not my responsibility to decide whether to proceed in a matter of that kind.

Q.   If you were not intimately involved personally in the decisions concerning *Their Trade is Treachery* why would Sir Arthur Franks come to you and not the Attorney-General to talk about his lunch with Pincher?

A.   I am one of a number of people involved in these matters.

Q.   Why did he come to you?

A.   I don't know.

Q.   You did not say: Dicky, why are you coming to see me, you should see Michael Havers. Did you say that?

A.   No, I don't remember saying that.

Q.   You did not say: you have come to the wrong place, go and see the Foreign Secretary?

A.   For all I know Sir Arthur may have told other people.

Q.   So you think he went up and down the length and breadth of Whitehall chattering about Chapman Pincher's lunch conversations?[3]

A.   I don't know what he did.

Q.   He is a man who is by the very nature of his position and experience discreet, is he not?

A.   He may have told people in the Security Service.

3. Whitehall is a famous avenue which runs from Trafalgar Square to the Houses of Parliament and it is lined with the imposing buildings which house the great departments of the British State.

Q.   I put it to you that he told you and you alone?

A.   I don't think that is right.

Q.   Who else did he tell?

A.   I don't know.

Q.   Did he tell you he was going to tell anyone else?

A.   I would have assumed that he would do so.

Q.   Did he tell you he was going to tell anyone else?

A.   I don't remember.

Q.   So you assumed and accepted that you were the appropriate recipient of this information?

A.   I assumed that I was an appropriate recipient and I assumed that other people equally appropriate would also receive it.

Q.   Did you pass on that information to anyone else?

A.   I can't remember.

Q.   Sir Robert, you were the Government's man principally involved in the decisions about *Their Trade is Treachery*, were you not?

A.   I was one, as I think I said earlier, I was one of a number of people involved in advising, by no means the only one.

Q.   The final decision not to do anything about *Their Trade is Treachery* was taken by you and the Prime Minister and not the Attorney-General, is that not right?

A.   That is absolutely untrue.

Q.   You expressed your view that the book should not be stopped, did you not?

A.	No.
Q.	Did you express a view that it should be stopped?
A.	No, I was told that there was no basis for a restraint, or whatever the words used.
Q.	Did you express a view that it ought not be published?
A.	I expressed a view that it would be preferable that it should not be published at some stage, yes.
Q.	Did you write a written report or minute concerning your conversation with Sir Arthur Franks?
A.	I don't think so.
Q.	Did you tell the Prime Minister about your conversation with Arthur Franks?
A.	I may well have told her we learned there was another book on its way.
Q.	But you took no steps to ascertain what was going to be in the book?
A.	As I told you, we did take steps and we were not able to obtain a copy.
Q.	There were other steps you could have taken?
A.	I don't know what other steps you would have expected us to take.
Q.	You could have done what you did before and obtain a copy of the book from the printers; that is what happened before?
A.	We sought to obtain a copy and did not do so on this occasion, at least until the review copies or something like that.

The conspiracy theory became more and more plausible. Pincher has lunch with Sir Arthur. Does Sir Arthur report this to his old office, MI6, or the Foreign Secretary? Does he report it to the Attorney-General, Sir Michael Havers, who Sir Robert insists is the man who decides whether to stop books of that kind. No, he goes to Sir Robert. But Sir Robert doesn't know why. The man with the Rolls Royce mind seems to have vast gaps in his knowledge. For a first-class intellectual he seems remarkably lacking in curiosity. His assessment of *Too Secret Too Long*, the second book Pincher wrote about Hollis in October 1984, is not a fair one. Far from being a rehash of *Their Trade is Treachery*, *Too Secret Too Long* is a much longer book, almost three times the length with considerably more inside information. Moreover at the time of the Pincher-Franks lunch, Pincher was corresponding with Wright about them cooperating on a second book to be called "The Atlantic Connection" about Soviet penetration on both sides of the Atlantic. Was Pincher clearing that one in advance with his old friend from MI6? However, I had to press on, there were other mysteries with which to tax Sir Robert.

As I promised the night before, I then turned to Rothschild. As I mentioned his name, the atmosphere turned to ice. We were treading on sensitive ground.

Thursday, November 20, 1986

Q.	Do you know Lord Victor Rothschild?
A.	I know Lord Rothschild.
Q.	He is a friend of yours, is he not?
A.	I know him.
Q.	He is a friend of yours, is he not?
A.	He has been a colleague of mine.
Q.	You worked with him closely during the Heath Government, did you not?
A.	I was his principal private secretary. He was the head of the Central Policies Review staff.

Q.   Otherwise known as "the think-tank"?

A.   The think-tank.

Q.   In that time you became particularly close to him, did you not?

A.   No.

Q.   You would call him—even now you speak to him on an average of once a week, would you not?

A.   Nothing like that.

Q.   Once a month?

A.   Once? No. Once every six months maybe.

Q.   I put it to you that you have said to a journalist employed by Granada Television at the time you were interviewed by them that you spoke to Victor Rothschild about once a week?

A.   When he was in the the think-tank maybe; not nowadays.

Q.   Victor Rothschild in the course of his duties under the Heath Government and in the course of your duties under the Heath Government, you would both discuss intelligence matters, would you not?

A.   With each other?

Q.   Yes?

A.   I do not recollect discussing with Lord Rothschild any matter concerning intelligence, save one.

Q.   I see. Did that relate to the publication of *Their Trade is Treachery?*

A.   No, the dates are wrong for that.

Q.   Victor Rothschild is a man, who I think has written it even in his own books, a man who has had a personal involvement in intelligence affairs, has he not?

A.   Yes.

Q.   Indeed he has been a trusted confidant of Conservative governments both now and in years past on matters relating to intelligence, has he not?

A.   I think that would be an overstatement of his relationship with the Government on intelligence matters.

Q.   Could you possibly rephrase it so that it is an accurate statement, neither over nor under?

A.   He has occasionally made views known to government.

Q.   On intelligence matters?

A.   On intelligence matters.

Q.   And he is a man that has even when he has not had official office considerable access and trust reposed in him by the Government and government officials, has he not?

A.   He was head of the think-tank for four years and many people came to trust and respect him in that period, yes.

Q.   And they continue to trust and respect him, do they not?

A.   I am sure that they do continue to trust and respect him, yes.

Q.   Across the wide range of the administrative side, i.e. the non-political side of the Government of Britain?

A.   Usually on matters . . . well, he was chairman of a Royal Commission on Betting and Gaming. He has been an occasional source of informal advice on matters scientific and technical with which he was familiar.

Q. He is a man who today, even today, still has access in the sense of contact to and confidence from senior officials involved in British intelligence, is that not right?

A. I think that these contacts and that confidence is much attenuated.

Q. But they still exist?

A. I should think they still exist.

Q. So he is, if not a complete insider nowadays, he is not entirely an outsider?

A. I think that for these purposes he would be regarded as an outsider now.

Q. In the British establishment of which you are a most distinguished part there are people like Victor Rothschild who may not be in the Government but still have considerable contact with government and considerable confidence placed in them by government?

A. Yes, I think that is fair.

Q. Victor Rothschild is one of those people?

A. He certainly has been. He is now getting on in years and has not been very well and is rather more remote from these things.

Q. Did Victor Rothschild discuss the publication of *Their Trade is Treachery* with you prior to its publication?

A. No.

Q. Are you sure of that?

A. I am sure of that.

Q. Have you received any reports from the Security Service concerning Victor Rothschild's role in the publication of *Their Trade is Treachery?*

A.   I would not wish to answer these questions in open court since any information I have on these matters is confidential.

Armstrong was no more forthcoming in closed session than in open session. However I knew from Greengrass that the information he had received about Rothschild's role in the *Their Trade is Treachery* affair had come from the Central Intelligence Agency. As something of an insurance policy Greengrass had fully briefed his contacts in the CIA about the Rothschild/Pincher/Wright affair some time earlier. Suspecting yet another covert leak, the CIA had formally asked MI5 for an explanation. This embarrassing request had put the matter "officially" on Armstrong's desk. When the court reopened from the confidential session, we turned to another key issue in the case: Mrs. Thatcher's truthfulness to the House of Commons. Following the publication of *Their Trade is Treachery*, Mrs. Thatcher had made a statement to the House of Commons. In that statement she denied that Hollis had been a Russian agent and said that a series of inquiries had cleared him. Wright had taken exception to a number of passages in her statement, but above all he objected to this paragraph:

> The case for investigating Sir Roger Hollis was based on certain leads that suggested but did not prove that there had been a Russian intelligence service agent at a relatively senior level in British counter-intelligence in the last years of the War. None of those leads identified Sir Roger Hollis or pointed specifically or solely in his direction. Each of them could also be taken as pointing to Philby or Blunt.

Wright insisted this was quite false. His book demonstrated that the case for investigating Hollis was made up of *postwar* events. Indeed it was only when it was clear that apparent leaks of information to the Russians could *not* be laid at the door of Philby and Burgess and Blunt that it was decided to investigate Hollis. During this part of the cross-examination, I slipped into error.

Thursday, November 20, 1986

Q.	May I take you to page three of your third affidavit, Sir Roger?
Mr. Simos	Sir Robert.
Q.	I am very sorry for that.
Witness	Perhaps we should say that every time you say "Sir Roger" you mean Sir Robert unless you say otherwise.
Q.	Yes absolutely. If you can think of someone particularly odious you can address me by that name.
Witness	I can't remember what the recording angel's name was.[4]

A curious crack. Too close to home to be entirely jocular. Armstrong was looking more and more uncomfortable. I was now quite convinced that his evidence about the Attorney-General's role was false. How long would it be persevered with? Even if, as he later claimed, Armstrong had originally believed his evidence was truthful, he must by now have started to wonder whether he had been mislead by those responsible for preparing him for this ordeal. Like a man adrift in a stormy sea, he needed a life-line: Havers must corroborate his evidence. But Havers could not do that without casting himself adrift.

---

4. According to Christian belief, the recording angel keeps a celestial register of all of our sinful acts, omitting not a one, so that when we come to judgment nothing is overlooked.

Q.	You would agree, however, that none of the leads which formed the basis for investigating Sir Roger Hollis could have been leads which related to events after Blunt left MI5 or Philby left MI6, which we call "the other organization."
A.	Right. I would agree that none of the leads discussed in that paragraph which were the leads as you say which were the basis for investigating could be leads which pointed to Blunt after 1945 or Philby after 1951 or 1952 or whenever it was.

Armstrong struggled valiantly to avoid admitting that Thatcher's statement was contradicted by the "true" allegations in *Spycatcher*. But it was, as Justice Powell pointed out, "self-demonstating.' " Wright had made it quite plain in *Spycatcher* that the basis for investigating Hollis were post-war leads which could not be laid at the door of either Blunt or Philby. Thatcher had stated the contrary. Unless *Spycatcher* is complete fantasy from cover to cover, which it assuredly is not, then the Thatcher statement about Hollis is very much at odds with the evidence. In his book Wright relates how the decision to investigate Hollis arose from the long series of post-war operations which failed. These could not have been due to Philby or Blunt. Mrs. Thatcher's statement probably allayed public concern about MI5, but its contradiction by *Spycatcher* raises the issue of how fully she has been briefed by MI5 about the molehunts.

After court that Thursday evening, we asked Peter whether he thought Thatcher knew she was telling a lie.

"Oh, heavens no," he chuckled. "She has just said what MI5 told her. They don't argue the toss with politicians. We just tell them what to say and the poor beggars have to say it."

"But the politicians get the blame if it turns out to be false." I protested.

"Well, of course, that's their job, isn't it?" Peter replied as though it was the most obvious thing in the world.

CHAPTER 8

We returned from court on Thursday evening feeling somewhat triumphant. The evidence about Pincher's lunch with Franks added color to the consipracy theory. As we walked through the park back to the office, even the skeptical Lucy was starting to think it was a little fishy.

"Well if Pincher wasn't actually authorized to publish *Their Trade is Treachery*, he certainly seems to have had a blessed existence afterwards, getting all those cushy government jobs and lunching with Dickie Franks."

"The only thing he's missed out on is a seat in the House of Lords," muttered Greengrass.

Our travels to and from court had become much more comfortable. In my preparations I had overlooked the huge quantity of books and folders we needed to cart to and from the Supreme Court each day. It was a pleasant walk, through Hyde Park, but with each of our party laden down with at least two big bags of books and folders it was very hot work in the November sun.

So we acquired a tall version of a supermarket shopping cart. I had seen other lawyers with them in the past, but had never troubled to buy one. We could load all our material onto it. Generally Colin Winter, a young English law student who was helping in the office, acted as pusher, but occasionally I took charge, demonstrating the non-hierarchical nature of the defense team. The cart became somewhat of an international television star. Television, or other, cameras are not allowed in the court so the only pictures the television reporters could take to illustrate their commentaries were of the various lawyers and witnesses going to and from the court. To many British eyes it was bad enough that I wasn't robed, but to see me pushing a large chrome supermarket cart was too much.

We had no doubt whatsoever that Armstrong was not telling us the truth about the way in which *Their Trade is Treachery* had been allowed to be published. But there was only one man who could give the lie, and that was the Attorney-General, Sir Michael Havers. There were two obvious ways to force this admission out of Havers. The first was to ensure the English press continued to give exceptional prominence to the *Their Trade is Treachery* issue. The second was to arrange for Havers to be questioned in Parliament by the Leader of the Labor Opposition, Mr. Neil Kinnock.

David Leigh accompanied us back from court that afternoon and later in the evening telephoned Charles Clarke who was Kinnock's private secretary. Leigh had been in close touch with Dale Campbell-Savours, the Labor MP who had repeated some of Wright's allegations in the House of Commons in July 1986. Campbell-Savours, however, lacked the political clout for a serious attack on the Government. Unless and until Kinnock took up the cudgels, the matter would have remained of fringe interest at least at the political level.

I spoke to Clarke for about half an hour, explaining to him the significance of Armstrong's evidence. Finally he agreed that Kinnock would call me back. David Leigh, Paul Greengrass and I waited in the office for Kinnock's call. At that time of year London was about eleven hours behind Sydney.

The Opposition leader was skeptical at first. He had no affection for Wright, who after all was a right-winger who had entertained grave suspicions about the loyalty of many of British Labor's greatest leaders. Nonetheless he quickly recognized that if Armstrong was telling the truth, the Attorney-General must be either a legal imbecile or a man prepared falsely to represent his own opinion in order to add legal color to what was a shabby political decision.

"But are you sure that Havers couldn't have simply been rather muddled. He's a very fine fellow, but his best friend wouldn't claim he was the brightest Attorney-General."

"No one," I insisted, "is that thick. Ask any of your own lawyers. A first year law student would have been able to get an injunction. Armstrong is not telling the truth. Havers may not be Perry Mason, but he isn't that dim." I thought for a moment, perhaps there was something about Havers I didn't know. "Just assuming he knew nothing about law, he must have a whole department full of bright lawyers. No, Neil, Armstrong is not telling the truth and you should nail him."

"Yes, that's true," said Kinnock, "he wouldn't have made this decision himself, assuming he made it at all."

"Okay, so therefore he couldn't have made it. Now the average person neither knows nor cares what the law is on injunctions, so in order to flush out this lie you have to humiliate Havers. You have to accuse him of legal incompetence, until all his friends in the Temple are laughing at him.[1] No matter how mediocre a lawyer he may really be, he *is* the first law officer and he must have some pride."

---

1. The Inner and Middle Temples are two "Inns of Courts," ancient societies whose splendid medieval buildings still house most of London's barristers.

Kinnock sounded quite alarmed. "But the real villain is the PM, not Michael. He's sick you know. So's Rothschild for that matter. They are both old men, this business could kill them."

I was quite surprised at this touch of humanity. It was so unlike a politician to be concerned about the health of his opponents. I didn't know what to say, so I made a joke.

"Oh well, Comrade, everyone has to make sacrifices for the revolution. Why not start with Havers and Rothschild?"

I heard a gasp at the other end. "Well, I hope that it won't come to that. If, as you say, the Cabinet Secretary is not telling the truth, then it should be a matter of real concern for the Opposition. After all, he must be doing this on Thatcher's instructions. I'll see what I can do. Would you make sure we have copies of the transcripts of Armstrong's evidence? I need to be sure of my facts before we move in the House."

I had little doubt that my conversation with Kinnock was being taped. The calls to England were being monitored by the Government Communication Headquarters in Cheltenham. International calls travel by way of satellite and are most vulnerable to electronic eavesdropping. Calls to Canberra were by and large conveyed by microwave links, again very vulnerable to eavesdropping. Local calls in Sydney went through the usual wired Telecom network and could not be recorded without the active cooperation of Telecom. My informants advised me that neither Australian nor British intelligence had bothered to record these conversations as the risk of public exposure was too great.

Kinnock has been criticized for discussing the case with me. Indeed, some days later he was vigorously attacked in the House of Commons for "treacherous" conduct. One particularly hysterical member of Parliament compared his conduct with discussing British naval strategy with General Galtieri during the Falklands War!

This criticism demonstrates the unusual state of parliamentary democracy in Britain. At that stage the Prime Minister's principal advisor and head of the Civil Service was being accused of perjury in an Australian court. His evidence, if believed, meant that the Attorney-General was either monumentally incompetent or was prepared to prostitute the stature of his great office to lend a little legal color to what was an otherwise pragmatic and political decision.

There was no alternative. On the one hand you could conclude that the Attorney was either a fool or knave; on the other you concluded that Armstrong was not telling the truth. Either alternative was of profound political concern. Had the position been reversed and this evidence been given by an Australian Cabinet Secretary in an English court, I have no doubt whatsoever that the Australian Parliament would have compelled a full and frank answer from the Government of the day. In England, however, Mrs. Thatcher was able to resist any demands for an explanation. It is a tribute to her total dominance of English politics that she seems quite unresponsive to the normal democratic requirements of Westminster democracy.

Students of political science have been told for many years how superior is the Westminster system of parliamentary democracy to the presidential system in the United States or France. They are told that English prime ministers are directly answerable to Parliament. Yet throughout this affair when the integrity of her Attorney-General and her Cabinet Secretary were put into serious doubt, she managed to avoid giving any explanation to Parliament.

Later that day, English time, Kinnock rose to ask a question of the Prime Minister. It was precisely in the form we had discussed.

Mr. Kinnock: May I ask the Prime Minister a question about the conduct of the Attorney-General? Is she aware that in court in Australia, Sir Robert Armstrong, has testified that officers of the Crown had photocopies of Mr. Chapman Pincher's book several weeks before it was published in 1981? He has said in court that "of course" the book contains a substantial amount of information from former officers of MI5 that in Sir Robert's view, "could certainly prejudice national security, including current and future operations." Is the Prime Minister aware that Sir Robert has further testified that the decision of the Attorney-General in 1981 was that there was: "no basis on which an injunction could be launched" to prevent the publication of Mr. Pincher's book? Is it not obvious that any Government who had foreknowledge that information prejudicial to national security was to be published would have absolutely no difficulty obtaining an injunction against its publication? Can the Prime Minister tell us precisely why she accepted that decision not to seek an injunction to prevent publication of Mr. Chapman Pincher's book, which was obviously prejudicial to national security?

The Prime Minister: Proceedings continue in the Supreme Court of New South Wales. Particularly as the Government are the Plaintiff in the case in Australia, it would be inappropriate for me to comment on the case [*Interruption*] or on matters in issue in the proceedings so long as those continue. With regard to some previous books, there are questions on the Order Paper for written answer, I believe to the Attorney-General, who will of course, answer in his own way.

Friday, November 21, began with Theo Simos seeking leave to make further amendments to his statement of claim. He was hoping that these fine alterations might cause Justice Powell to review his decision to order the British to provide discovery of documents. I was suitably unsympathetic and told the court so: "It is an intolerable burden upon a party in litigation of this kind to be constantly dealing with amendments to pleadings and technical arguments of an exquisite nature that distract one from the task of ascertaining the facts the subject of the case."

Nonetheless I agreed to the amendments upon Simos' assurance that they were not some clever way of changing the issues in the case. Sir Robert returned to the witness box and we began the fourth day of the trial, and the third day of his cross-examination.

I returned to the issue of why the British Government had refused to particularize the allegedly damaging material in Wright's book. I referred Sir Robert to a letter published in a magazine by Catherine Massiter which described a number of branches of MI5. He told me there had been no prosecution following its publication, and when I asked him whether he objected to Wright referring to those branches, he replied:

Friday, November 21, 1986

A.	Our case rests, as I understand it on the general breach of the duty of confidentiality.
Q.	Your affidavits are a long argument about why this book should not be published, is that so?
A.	Why books of this kind should not be published.
Q.	So you would agree with me that your affidavits are general propositions about books of this kind rather than particularly directed at this book?
A.	They are propositions about the damage likely or possibly to be done by books of this type published by former members of the Security Service.

Q.   Your affidavits are simply a general state-
       ment about the general proposition of
       former MI5 officers writing books about
       their work, are they not?

A.   Primarily, yes.

Q.   In preparing your affidavits you have had
       no regard to the particular information
       in Mr. Wright's book?

A.   Some regard was had to that in deciding
       whether to bring these proceedings.

Q.   But no regard was had by you in pre-
       paring your affidavit?

A.   I was not addressing the particular mat-
       ters.

Armstrong's admissions were subsequently fatal for his
case. He based his case on the broad proposition that no
former MI5 officer should ever write about his work,
regardless of the content of what he had written. Yet
this all-or-nothing prohibition had never been applied to
anyone before. Indeed the Cathy Massiter affair seemed,
by Armstrong's canon, a worse breach of security than
Spycatcher.

Cathy Massiter had been an officer of MI5 from 1970
until 1984. After leaving university she became a librar-
ian. Bored, she was directed by her university appoint-
ments officer to MI5. Her work in MI5 involved her in
eavesdropping on trade unionists, left-wing members of
the Labor Party and officers of the National Council for
Civil Liberties, including its general secretary, Patricia
Hewitt, now press secretary to the English Opposition
Leader, Neil Kinnock. Not surprisingly, she found this
work distasteful. She felt it was more directed at sup-
pressing political dissent than protecting the realm from
subversion. So, in 1985 she provided interviews and other
information to Claudia Milne and Dennis Wolfe who

produced a television documentary for England's Channel 4 television network.

The program, entitled "MI5's Official Secrets," was an up-to-date, first-hand account of how MI5 broke the law. Together with another, unnamed, former MI5 officer she demonstrated that MI5 had systematically abused its position and sought information about persons who could not, on the wildest and most paranoid view, be regarded as dangerous subversives menacing the Constitution.

Britain's commercial television companies are strictly regulated. Indeed the Independent Broadcasting Authority, a government agency, owns the transmitters. The television companies are really just production houses which supply an agreed number of hours of programming in return for the advertising revenue earned during the period of transmission. The IBA has to vet all the programs and when it viewed the Massiter Program it decided that the show could not go to air. The producers forwarded a copy of both the program and the script to the Prime Minister's office where it was viewed by Armstrong and MI5.

Armstrong admitted that the MI5 opinion was that the program contained up-to-date material about the Service which was only a year old. According to him, MI5 considered its broadcast would be "damaging." Yet no effort was made to stop it going to air. Logically the Massiter program was more damaging than *Spycatcher*, since the information in it was much more current. Armstrong explained the failure to stop the program by recalling that it had been shown to some members of Parliament and hence the material "was already virtually out."

The real reason for not stopping Massiter was political. In her interview she alleged that MI5 conducted widespread telephone tapping and bugging of left-wing Labor MPs, civil libertarians and trade unionists. Her unnamed former colleague alleged that she had been instructed to eavesdrop on unionists' telephone calls and to take particular note of their "bottom line" in upcoming pay negotiations. Such information was of no value to anyone but the employers. Massiter had participated in these exercises; her allegations were first-hand. She was accusing MI5 of fighting, not the cold war, but rather the class war, and of fighting it on the side of the bosses and reaction.

The rights or wrongs of the mole-hunts of the 1950s were not really capable of generating much political heat thirty years later, but Massiter's allegations were, and so a shrewd political decision was made to let Massiter's fastball go through to the catcher.

Now Armstrong could not admit to this. He had to find a non-political reason for allowing Massiter to go to air which distinguished her position from that of Wright. He first suggested that her program was already in the public domain, but retreated from that when it was put to him that a private showing to MPs hardly compared with all the extensive prior publication of the material in *Spycatcher*. (In late 1987 the former MI6 officer, Anthony Cavendish, privately published a memoir of his intelligence experiences and distributed about 300 copies to his friends, mainly members of the establishment. The Government took no objection on the grounds that he did not publish his memoirs to the public at large.)

Armstrong then suggested Wright's work was a comprehensive account of his whole life with MI5. I told him I thought that was a lie. *Spycatcher* was far from being comprehensive. Wright had deliberately kept out of it anything he thought was sensitive. I went back to the attack.

Friday, November 21, 1986

Q. You know that the book is not a full account of his life in the Service, nor is it a comprehensive one. That is so, isn't it?

A.	It covers many of the details of his life in the Service.
Q.	It says nothing about his work in Northern Ireland, the substance of it?
A.	I believe not.
Q.	That was an important part of his work in the Service, wasn't it?
A.	I believe so.
Q.	So how do you reconcile that with your earlier statement that Mr. Wright's book was a comprehensive account of his life in the Service?
A.	I have said to you Mr. Turnbull that if comprehensive is to mean every episode, every element of service is described in detail, then I withdraw the word "comprehensive."
Q.	I put to you that Mr. Wright has gone to great pains to ensure that there is nothing in his book of sufficient currency to prejudice any operations of MI5?
A.	He may well have sought to do that, but his judgment is not the only judgment which is relevant to these matters.
Q.	But you are unable to point to any particular piece of information in the book the publication of which would prejudice the current operations of MI5?
A.	We have not been discussing particular allegations.

Armstrong agreed, however, that a considerable amount of analysis had been performed on Wright's manuscript. But why, then, could he not point to particular parts of the manuscript as causing particular damage? His answer was, yet again, quite disingenuous:

A.   It is very difficult to make a damage as-
              sessment of that kind before a book is
              published.

I pressed Armstrong on the process of analysis that
had been performed on *Their Trade is Treachery*. He had
previously told the court that before *Their Trade is Treachery* was published there had been an assessment of the
damage that would be caused by its publication. I then
asked him whether there had been a further assessment
of the damage caused by *Their Trade is Treachery* in the
light of the events following its publication. Incredibly
Armstrong replied that he had not seen any such report.

Q.   So deep was the concern about the dam-
              age done by Mr. Pincher's book that the
              Security Service did not even write a re-
              port about it?

A.   They may have written a report. I haven't
              seen it.

Q.   Did you ask for it?

A.   I have no views of the Security Service
              on the report on the matter and I haven't
              asked for the report. I haven't asked for
              the report or whether there was a formal
              report.

The Government's case became more and more un-
believable. Here was Armstrong ten thousand miles from
the safe harbor of Whitehall endeavoring to ban a book
on the grounds that it would cause terrible damage to
the work of MI5. Only five years before, *Their Trade is
Treachery* had been published with much the same contents
as could be found in *Spycatcher*. It was perfectly obvious
to anyone with one whit of intelligence that part of my
case would be that *Spycatcher* would cause no harm since

Their Trade is Treachery had apparently not caused any. Yet Armstrong didn't bother to inquire of MI5 whether *Their Trade is Treachery* had *actually* caused any damage. For a man supposedly a master of detail, his preparation for cross-examination appeared to be woefully inadequate. Or perhaps great care had been taken not to tell him about these things.

I then moved to explore, yet again, the scope of what I had alleged to be Armstrong's lie about the *Their Trade is Treachery* affair. He had claimed that the Attorney-General had advised that there was no legal basis to move against Pincher or his publisher. Yet he agreed that even as a layman he knew that if a publisher received information he knew to be provided in breach of confidence, the publisher could be restrained from publishing it. Why then, did he accept this unusual advice from the Attorney? It was clear Pincher had received confidential information from someone. He boasted of it in the preface to the book.

Q. You believed the book should not be published. You knew that a right of action lay against a publisher and or an author in those circumstances, and I put it to you that when the Attorney said that he considered there was no basis to restrain the author and the publisher you were surprised?

A. No, I was not surprised, I was resigned, although I was not surprised.

Q. But the Attorney's expressed basis for his decision was inconsistent with what you understood the law to be, was it not?

A. It is not for me to query the Attorney-General's view of what action he should take within the law.

Those who seek to defend the integrity of Robert Armstrong should ask themselves whether these were the answers of a man who was merely confused. Armstrong was sticking like glue to his story about the Attorney making the decision not to injunct *Their Trade is Treachery.* Indeed he was sheltering behind the Attorney's skirts. That wasn't an unreasonable position. Armstrong was making it quite clear that he found the Attorney's advice somewhat unusual, as indeed it was. But, after all, how could he question the legal opinion of the first law officer of the Crown? In short, Armstrong was not denying that Havers was a fool, but he was the Attorney-General and Sir Robert had to go along with his advice.

A good cross-examination has to be methodical. After closing one avenue of escape, you then move on to close another. Armstrong's original statement that Havers had advised there was no basis to stop *Their Trade is Treachery* was found in his answer to Interrogatory 150, so I asked him who had discussed the draft of this answer with him before he signed it. At first he claimed not to remember, but he finally admitted that it was either or both of Mr. John Bailey, the Treasury solicitor, or Mr. David Hogg, his assistant. Both of these gentlemen were in court during Armstrong's ordeal. Armstrong said that they told him the answer was correct, and that this accorded with his own recollection. Despite my frequent invitations neither Bailey (now Sir John) nor Hogg entered the witness box to explain their role in preparing this false evidence. (It would have been possible for me to subpoena both men to give evidence, but if I had called them they would have been my witnesses and I would have been bound by their answers. Better to let the judge draw the obvious conclusions from their not having been called by the British Government.)

Armstrong did not wish to dissociate himself from Bailey, however:

Friday, November 21, 1986

Q.	Who gave the answers to you to sign?
A.	I suppose that the Treasury Solicitor would have done so.
Q.	Is the Treasury Solicitor in court?
A.	He is.
Q.	Mr. John Bailey sitting over there next to the trolley?
A.	Mr. John Bailey is the Treasury Solicitor.
Q.	He was the Treasury Solicitor when you signed these answers to interrogatories, was he not?
A.	Yes he was.
Q.	He is not a man one is likely to forget meeting?
A.	I am interested to hear you take that view.
Q.	I am putting that as a question. Is he forgettable, Mr. John Bailey.
A.	I don't know.
Q.	Would you like to forget him?
A.	No, no, no . . . he is a good colleague.

As we were proceeding to shut off avenues of escape, I established that Armstrong had not discussed his answer to the interrogatories with Sir Michael Havers. Indeed he said that the answer had been provided to him to sign by Bailey or his assistant Hogg. For a moment I thought Armstrong was going to escape culpability by pinning all the blame on the Treasury Solicitor.

Q.	So the answer was not one based solely on the assurance of Mr. Bailey or Mr. Hogg, it was also based on your own recollection.
A.	It accorded with my recollection, yes.

Q.	And if you had been asked to answer that question without the careful assistance of Messrs. Hogg and Bailey, you would have answered it in the same terms. That is correct, is it not?
A.	I would certainly have taken advice before answering question 150.
Q.	But you would have answered it in the same terms, would you not?
A.	I cannot tell you what terms I would have answered it in. This is the answer I have given.
Q.	You would have answered it in substantially the same terms?
A.	I should think substantially the same terms.

I then showed Armstrong a piece of paper with the name of a man I suspected of having been the source of *Their Trade is Treachery* manuscript. Simos objected, claiming it was all irrelevant. Justice Powell had been unusually quiet and reflective and the objection stirred him to share his thoughts with the courtroom.

His Honor	I don't know about that. I must say in the light of what little I know of what the Attorney is said to have known and what the Attorney's advisors are said to have known in England in March of 1981, I am puzzled as to why somebody did not hotfoot it up to the Strand[2] not only to get an ex parte injunction, but to get an Anton Piller[3] order that would impound

---

2. The Royal Courts of Justice are located in the Strand, just before it becomes Fleet Street.
3. Named after the case in which it was first given, an Anton Piller order enables the successful applicant to seize the articles or docu-

every copy of the book and the manuscript. I am just puzzled. I find it very difficult at the moment to think of a reason why it was not done and, if there were no legitimate reasons why it was not done, no legal reasons why it could not be done.

I would find myself pushed further and further towards the view that the Government knew exactly what was being done and it was not going to take a step to stop it and, if that be so, it is no great step towards saying that the Government authorized the book to be published.

On Thursday Mrs. Thatcher had said the Attorney-General would answer questions about *Their Trade is Treachery* "in his own way." Friday, November 21 showed the good Sir Michael to be as informative as his leader:

Mr. Campbell Savours asked the Attorney-General on what basis he reached his decision that there were no legal grounds to proceed against Mr. Chapman Pincher for breach of confidence in respect of his book, *Their Trade is Treachery.*

The Attorney-General: It would be inappropriate for me to comment on matters at issue in the proceedings concerning the Peter Wright case in Australia, while those proceedings continue.

The weekend intervened and on Monday, November 26, the trial began again with Armstrong still in the box. The tension of the lengthy cross-examination was becoming palpable. Armstrong seemed to have shrunk. He

ments named by the judge. It is particularly important when a Court is concerned that evidence may be destroyed and spirited away before trial.

flinched at the questions. It was a ghastly experience for him. I must have seemed like a moderately well-educated thug, the judge was treating Armstrong like an ordinary witness (something which would not happen in England) and worst of all a claque of English journalists were jammed into the press box all chuckling and sneering as he staggered through his answers.

I felt a growing warmth for Armstrong. There is a basic thrill of the hunt as you harry a witness, but I could not help feeling that I was destroying a man for no good reason. Why on earth was he persisting with this evidence? To what end. I found myself alone with Armstrong riding in the elevator up to the eighth floor of the courts building.

"I hope you don't feel any of this is personal, Sir Robert. It's all part of the job you know," I feebly observed.

The doors of the elevator opened. Armstrong smiled. "Don't worry about me, Mr. Turnbull, I'm just the fall guy."

Armstrong's courtesy was undiminished by the pressure he was placed under. I recall one particularly torrid afternoon, when the court adjourned for a few minutes. The court attendant, a Mrs. Thoms, discreetly refilled Sir Robert's glass of water. "Thank you, Mrs. Thoms, you are very kind," he said. Few witnesses would have bothered to thank her, and even fewer would have bothered to find out her name.

I tried to persuade Theo Simos that if only Armstrong and I could spend a few hours together we could settle the case. He, quite properly, rejected such an unusual approach. Nonetheless he was putting on a brave front. One night I was having a rather rowdy dinner at Kinsella's restaurant with Lucy, Hooper, Greengrass and some of the journalists. Armstrong entered with the British Consul and his wife. We called him over. "Come and have a drink with us, Sir Robert." He declined the offer of a drink, but politely shook hands with everyone. He is a gentleman, but sadly, he had not been given a gentleman's job in court No. 8D.

Despite the mounting pressure in the House of Commons and in the English press, Armstrong stuck to his story about the Attorney's role in the *Their Trade is Treachery* affair.

November 24, 1986

> Q.   Sir Robert, last week I asked you a great many questions about *Their Trade is Treachery*. Have you or any of those advising you sought any clarification about the reasoning behind that decision not to seek an injunction?
>
> A.   No, I have no more to say on that.
>
> Q.   Have you sought any clarification on it?
>
> A.   No.
>
> Q.   You are content for this to remain somewhat of a legal mystery, are you?
>
> A.   I have given you the explanation which I believe to be the correct one.

Despite all that, Armstrong could still rise to a little joke. On Monday afternoon we were discussing the case of George Blake, an MI6 agent convicted and jailed of spying for Russia in 1960. He had been in charge of Operation Gold, or the Berlin Tunnel Operation. It involved burrowing underneath the Berlin Wall across East Berlin and underneath the principal East Berlin telephone exchange. There special technology was used to eavesdrop on Communist communications. He blew the whole operation to the Russians who let it run for a while and then seized the equipment.

November 24, 1986

Q.	Blake in fact set up the Berlin Tunnel intelligence operation, did he not?
A.	He was involved in it, I believe. I don't know in exactly what detail.
Q.	He was an insider as far as the tunnel was concerned.
A.	Yes.
His Honor	I thought only I was allowed to make jokes.
Mr. Turnbull	It is a quarter past three, Your Honor has been quiet all afternoon.
Witness	I guess that's as near as you get to the real mole.
His Honor	Two strikes and I am out.
Mr. Turnbull	If I keep on being your straight man, Sir Robert, people are going to suspect collusion.

CHAPTER 9

IT WAS IRONIC THAT earlier, before the trial, I had endeavored to settle the case through the intermediation of Jonathan Aitken MP. It was not until the trial was under way that I learned that Jonathan had, from one perspective, been responsible for starting the whole thing.

After Thatcher's exposure of Blunt in the House of Commons on November 21, 1979, it was inevitable that sooner or later somebody would reveal to the press that Roger Hollis had himself been investigated. Thatcher had just been elected and Jonathan was an ambitious backbencher anxious both to impress his leader, and, quite properly, to avoid a security scandal erupting that would embarrass the new leader.

He wrote a Private and Confidential letter to Thatcher on January 31, 1980. In the letter he summarized the material about Hollis which he understood to be circulating at the time. Hollis had been investigated in the mid-seventies and according to Jonathan's letter was alleged to be a spy, as was his deputy Graham Mitchell. Most important, he added that the material alleged:

That Hollis and Mitchell between them recruited other unidentified Soviet Agents into the Security Services. It follows from this that our Security Services may still be severely penetrated today.

He went on to outline the dangers which lay in an uncontrolled exposure of these allegations. He made six recommendations:

1) The paramount need is to set up a major independent inquiry into all these allegations, headed by a High Court Judge or Service Chief sitting in secret, supported by his own independent staff drawn from outside the ranks of the Security Services.

2) As a first step for this inquiry, Graham Mitchell, who unlike Hollis, is still alive and living in retirement, must be interrogated in depth and if necessary offered immunity in return for his cooperation.

3) With or without Mitchell's cooperation all members of the Security Services recruited in the time of Hollis and Mitchell should be re-vetted on a much stricter basis.

4) All files relating to the alleged treachery of Hollis and Mitchell should be reopened and comprehensively reviewed, and the officers and former officers engaged on that investigation should be asked to cooperate with that review as part of the independent inquiry.

5) As certain judgments and disclosures made in your own speech to the House of Commons on November 21, 1979 may well be seen in a more critical light in the event of the Hollis story becoming known, I think it might be wise to prepare a House of Commons statement of great frankness to defuse all such potential criticisms. If you did not know of the Hollis story when you took the decision to go public on Blunt then I believe you should say so even though this would inevitably amount to a serious indictment of the Security Services.[1]

1. In 1979 Sir Anthony Blunt was director of the Courtauld Institute,

6)   Any such statement should include the announcement of a major reform of the Security Services.
The objective of such a reform would be once
and for all to close the chapter on past treacheries
and penetrations and to restore confidence in the
Security Services. One option to be considered
would be the uniting of MI5 and MI6 into a single
Security Service with a new outside Director General drawn from the Armed Forces.

The key recommendation was for Thatcher to get the
Hollis story into the public domain before someone else
did. Aitken was not a mere busybody. He had a long-
standing interest in intelligence matters, although he had
never actually worked for British intelligence. He had
struck up a friendship with a clerk at the House of
Commons, Arthur Martin. Formerly Wright's mole-hunt-
ing companion at MI5, Martin, like Wright, harbored a
deep and bitter conviction that Hollis was a Russian spy
and that the establishment had covered up his treachery.
Two years later he was the source for Nigel West's *A
Matter of Trust*.

I tendered the letter on Tuesday, November 25 and
asked Armstrong about the circumstances in which it had
been received. He agreed that he had been aware there
was some journalistic investigation directed at the issue
of whether there were other moles to be discovered. He
denied however that *Their Trade is Treachery* had been

Surveyor of the Queen's Pictures and a world authority on fine art.
He had worked in MI5 during the Second World War. In 1963 he
also confessed to having been a KGB agent. His confession was kept
secret, he was given immunity from prosecution and he was allowed
to retain all his positions. However a journalist called Andrew Boyle
in 1979 wrote a book called "Climate of Treason" which exposed
Blunt, but did not name him. Thatcher was obliged to make a
statement in the House of Commons which officially exposed Blunt,
but made no reference to Hollis. Blunt was disgraced, stripped of
his knighthood and died shortly thereafter.

allowed to be published in response to the suggestion in Aitken's letter or otherwise.

Tuesday, November 25, 1986

Q. Sir Robert, if you and the Prime Minister decided that a particular piece of information should be put in the public domain, there are two routes open to you for putting it there, are there not?

A. Would you like to identify the two that you have in mind?

Q. I put to you that one of them is an official attributable statement and the other one is an unattributable statement, otherwise known as an inspired leak; that is so, is it not?

A. Certainly the second is not unknown.

Q. So you would agree with me then that there are at least two time-honored methods in Whitehall of getting information into the public domain. One is an official statement and the other is an unofficial inspired disclosure, that is so, is it not?

A. Yes.

Q. When you in your capacity as the principal security adviser for the Prime Minister considered Mr. Aitken's proposals did you give consideration to whether the disclosure should be by way of an official statement as suggested by Mr. Aitken or by way of an inspired leak?

A. I don't think that was ever considered, no.

Nonetheless he agreed that *Their Trade is Treachery* did assure its readers that while there had been Soviet penetration of MI5 in the past, the intelligence services were now "clean."

Q.   I put it to you that the most important objective the Government had and you had particularly at that time was to reassure the public that whatever may have happened in the past, there was no present Russian penetration problem with the intelligence services.

A.   If there was such concern, that would obviously be the object.

The rest of that day was concerned with tendering a great many examples of intelligence information being published with either explicit or implicit consent. It ranged from official publications, such as reports of the Security Commission, to the writings of Duncan Campbell in the *New Statesman.* Each of these publications when together demonstrated two things. First that there was nothing new in Wright's book. Second that the Government had over the years allowed so much information about intelligence services to be published that it was simply nonsense to say they were fighting for a principle of confidentiality. That principle had been abandoned long ago.

As recently as the week before the trial began a new book on Blunt had been published with dozens of direct attributed quotes from former intelligence officers. The Treasury Solicitor had advised the publishers of *Conspiracy of Silence* that he did not propose to seek an injunction. Why not? Armstrong said that it was because the information disclosed was insufficiently damaging. So a qualitative assessment had been made. Why had not one been made of *Spycatcher?*

Or take Kim Philby.[2] His memoirs were allowed to be published. He had signed the Official Secrets Act, he had

2. Possibly the most famous double agent of all time, Philby had

sworn to be silent. Yet he could publish. Why do former intelligence officers get preferred treatment if they work for the KGB? A great part of Armstrong's argument was that it was hard to determine whether information about intelligence would be harmful, therefore nothing should be published at all. But the Security Commission report following the conviction of Geoffrey Prime for passing the secrets of GCHQ to the Russians went into considerably more detail on a number of intelligence issues than did *Spycatcher*.[3] Armstrong could offer no satisfactory reasons for the inconsistencies.

Armstrong refused to admit the existence of MI6, yet details of its premises, its training camp, its senior personnel and its overseas listening posts were all published in an academic work, *Ties That Bind*, that contained more raw information about intelligence activities by the Western countries than Peter Wright could ever remember.

Justice Powell looked increasingly askance as the mountain of books and newspaper articles piled up on his bench. Finally he could not resist a bitter jest: "I do not want to stop you Mr. Turnbull, but please remember Mr. Turnbull that in thirteen years, eleven months and fourteen days I reach the statutory age of judicial senility."[4]

The action had however largely moved to London at this stage. The Government were fighting back on the propaganda front and had leaked to the Whitehall cor-

---

been well on the way to becoming head of MI6 when he became suspect following the defection of Guy Burgess and Donald McLean to Russia in May 1951. He finally defected to Russia himself in January 1963.

3. GCHQ, the Government Communications Headquarters, is Britain's equivalent of the National Security Agency. It is responsible for monitoring international telecommunications particularly those emanating to and from the Eastern bloc. It operates from sprawling headquarters at Cheltenham south of London.

4. Australian judges are obliged to retire at 70.

respondent of *The Times* the fact that Wright had received a share of the royalties from *Their Trade is Treachery.* Wright had never said otherwise and indeed had admitted as much in his answers to the Government's interrogatories. He had not however made any public statement on the matter as we considered it more appropriate that he make a full statement when he gave evidence later in the trial and could put everything in context.

The Times' revelation was potentially very dangerous for us. Our whole strategy against Havers was dependent on the Labor Party attacking him, and Thatcher, in the Commons. Kinnock was rightly suspicious of being used by us and he would be even less likely to help if Wright was perceived as a greedy old man, rather than a genuine (if a little misguided) patriot.

The Times' story was not the only aspect of the Government's counterattack. On the previous Friday the Prime Minister's deputy press secretary, Jim Coe, started attacking Kinnock for his questions about Havers. Coe, in unattributable lobby briefings, went so far as to accuse Kinnock of breaking the usual bipartisan approach to security matters, even though Kinnock's questions clearly had nothing to do with security, but a great deal to do with whether the Attorney-General was incompetent, or whether the Cabinet Secretary was lying. Coe went further and said that ministers were of the view that Kinnock could not be trusted with security information traditionally provided to Opposition leaders. He said that Kinnock was unfit to be Prime Minister. This was all duly reported as having emanated from "Cabinet sources."

Coe went a little bit too far for his mistress's own good, however. He let it be known that Havers had been responsible for the whole Wright case. This was not lost on experienced observers of the Prime Minister. Plainly Havers was being prepared for the role of scapegoat. Havers, however, had the key to his own salvation. He simply had to pluck up the courage to threaten to resign unless the evidence in Sydney was corrected. This, I believe he did on Wednesday, November 26.

We could not afford to let Wright lose any more public support and so we decided that Wright should answer his critics. I arranged a press conference at 5:00 p.m. after court on Tuesday, November 25.

Peter was nervous about the press conference and so was I. He certainly could not answer any questions and anything he said was certain to be used to cross-examine him with later. Peter read a prepared statement which for the first time disclosed the substance of the *Their Trade is Treachery* conspiracy.

> I have been preparing for my appearance in court next week and preparing a full disclosure of the circumstances of the publication of *Their Trade is Treachery.*
>
> However the Government has selectively leaked parts of my evidence to the Whitehall correspondent of *The Times* in an effort to discredit me in advance. Accordingly I have no choice but to make a public statement which will of necessity contain information which will be part of my testimony.
>
> In the summer of 1980 I received a letter and a first class air ticket from Lord Rothschild inviting me to come to London to discuss the impact of the Blunt disclosures in 1979, disclosures with which I was not involved in any way. This approach came totally out of the blue.
>
> When I arrived Lord Rothschild explained that he had recently met Mrs. Thatcher and that she was inexperienced in intelligence matters. We discussed the Hollis affair as we had many times before.
>
> I expressed concern that the true facts of the Hollis case be placed in front of her, and showed Lord Rothschild a paper I had begun to write on the subject. I asked him if he would be prepared to use his influence to place the documents in Mrs. Thatcher's hands.

Lord Rothschild said this approach would not work as Mrs. Thatcher would feel obliged to refer any official approach direct to MI5. He told me that the best way to procure a proper investigation of the Hollis affair was to write a book.

He told me that the book would have to be written by someone else and he suggested Harry Pincher. He telephoned Mr. Pincher and shortly afterwards he appeared. I had the distinct impression this meeting had been prearranged.

I was terrified of getting into trouble. Lord Rothschild assured me it was going to be all right. He told me that he would arrange for his Swiss banking facilities to pay me half the royalties from the book.

He knew I was in financial difficulties and I was grateful for his assistance. Mr. Pincher told *The Times* that he was not involved with these payments. I can prove and will prove in court this is not true.

I knew Lord Rothschild to be an intimate confidant of successive heads of British intelligence establishments. I could not conceive of him embarking on such a project without knowing it had the sanction, albeit unofficial, of the authorities.

I sensed I was being drawn into an authorized but deniable operation which would enable the Hollis affair and other MI5 scandals to be placed in the public domain as the result of an apparently inspired leak.

All I know about Lord Rothschild and the ease with which *Their Trade is Treachery* was published leads me to the inescapable conclusion that the powers that be approved of the book.

The allegation about Rothschild had really intensified the political debate in London. The Opposition called for Rothschild to be prosecuted, while the newspapers called on him to give an explanation. *The Daily Telegraph* summed up the general attitude of the press in its editorial on November 27.

However well intentioned his motives, Lord Rothschild owes a public explanation of his role in bringing together Mr. Peter Wright and Mr. Chapman Pincher to enable Pincher to write his book *Their Trade is Treachery*. Since Lord Rothschild in the past, as far as we are aware, has never acted without some public interest in mind, it seems legitimate to demand what public interest was at stake in contriving an airing for Wright's thesis that there were traitors in high places at MI5.

The Telegraph editorialist was even prepared to demand an explanation from the Prime Minister.

. . . the Prime Minister must take a vigorous counter-offensive against her critics, by making the fullest possible statement about the affair. It will simply not do to take refuge indefinitely in claims of national security.

The drama of the political developments was not lost on the London directors of Heinemann. The increasingly agitated Brian Perman rang me in a great panic late one night. His voice was filled with horror. "Malcolm, Malcolm," he wailed, "you're going to bring down the Government. It's all getting terribly political, we can't be seen to be attacking the Government." I am afraid I was less than sympathetic. "I've got the Cabinet Secretary in the box and I am accusing him of committing perjury. Now if you would like me to apologize tomorrow and retract it all, we could probably arrange to lose the case by Friday lunchtime."

We intensified the pressure by releasing to the press and thence to the Labor Opposition one of Pincher's letters to Wright in which he refers to having been shooting with Havers on New Year's Day 1982. Campbell

Savours read portions of the letter into the Hansard.[5] The calls intensified: Prosecute Rothschild for introducing Wright to Pincher, prosecute Havers for talking to Pincher, prosecute Pincher, prosecute West, prosecute Martin for talking to West, prosecute Franks for talking to Pincher. As we watched it all unfold from the safe distance of Sydney it all looked very satisfactory. The more you stir a turd, so it is said, the more it stinks, and this particular one was starting to stink to the heavens. Havers would not be able to stay silent for much longer. I was only concerned that I be able to keep Armstrong in the witness box long enough.

In that regard I was mightily assisted by yet another fight about discovery of documents which took up Wednesday and Thursday of that week. In compliance with Justice Powell's orders the British had supplied a list of documents which they now objected to producing. They had a new argument this time, however. They claimed they were the subject of public interest immunity on the grounds that any documents relating to national security had to be privileged from production.

A preliminary issue was whether the judge should look at them first before he made up his mind. On Wednesday, November 26, Simos told the judge that if the judge decided he had to inspect the documents before ruling on the privilege claim, they would be made available to him. Powell was obviously irritated by these interlocutory arguments constantly interrupting the progress of the trial, particularly when the Government could and should have raised them long before.

He nearly exploded however the following morning, Thursday, November 27, when Simos told him that over-night his instructions had changed and now if he did

5. Hansard is the official record of the Parliamentary Debates, the equivalent of the Congressional Record.

decide he needed to first inspect the documents the Government would take him to the Court of Appeal. In short they had made a complete turnaround.

Thursday, November 27, 1986

His Honor	Mr. Simos, I hope you will forgive me if I appear to exhibit a degree of pique in what I am about to say.
Mr. Simos	If your Honor pleases.
His Honor	Yours, if I may say, is the only head above the sandbags at the moment.
Mr. Simos	I am grateful that it is, your Honor.
His Honor	I regret to say that I find myself placed in what I can only describe as an intolerable situation. I am quite unable to predict from one day to the next what is the attitude of the plaintiff in this case; what submissions will be persevered with and what course is to be taken. The situation I am placed in is, I believe, intolerable.
Mr. Simos	We regret that your Honor feels that.
His Honor	And more to the point, if I may say so, since I am paid to sit here anyway it appears to me that if it is to be a continuing pattern of this case the defendants are to be placed in an intolerable situation and one in which I fear they will be subjected to grave injustice.
Mr. Simos	Nothing is further from our mind, your Honor.
His Honor	I now urge you to retreat under the sandbags.
Mr. Simos	If your Honor pleases.

The Tory counterattack that had begun with the leak of the fact that Wright had received money for his contribution to *Their Trade is Treachery* continued in the House of Commons. In Prime Minister's question time on November 25 Thatcher claimed that Kinnock was breaking the bipartisan approach to security matters. Kinnock responded vigorously:

> The Government who put the Cabinet Secretary in a very exposed position that ensures that attention is drawn to disclosures that are harmful to national security are not in a position to lecture. I put it to you Mr. Speaker that the only question that I have raised or would raise is one relating to the decisions of the Attorney-General. The explanation of those decisions which I have asked for has no implications for the national security of my country whatsoever.

However the Tories got much more mileage out of the revelation that Kinnock had been speaking to me. Nonetheless our strategy of using the House of Commons to extract the truth about *Their Trade is Treachery* finally succeeded during Prime Minister's question time on Thursday, November 27.

> *Mr. Kinnock:* Will the Prime Minister tell us, whether the decision not to impede publication of Mr. Pincher's book in 1981 was taken personally by the Attorney-General and whether the decision to put Sir Robert Armstrong in court in Australia was taken personally by the Attorney-General.
>
> *The Prime Minister:* As I said to the House last Thursday, it would be inappropriate for me (HON MEMBERS: "Answer") to comment on matters which may arise in the proceedings concerning the Peter Wright case in Australia while those proceedings continue. On the general question of security matters I shall follow the precedent set by previous Prime Ministers and, I

understand, set out in Erskine May of not commenting on Security matters.[6]

Mr. Kinnock: This is a specific question about the decisions and responsibilities inside the Government that has no implication whatsoever for matters of national security. Although it does not raise questions about national security it raises questions about the competence and integrity of the Government. Will the Prime Minister give a straight answer to a straight question? Did the Attorney-General personally take either or both of those decisions? In these matters, has the Attorney-General been a fool or a fall guy?

The Prime Minister: The Right Hon. Gentleman's question is totally unworthy. [HON MEMBERS: "Answer"] On the general question of security I shall follow the precedent set by previous Prime Ministers and I understand upheld in Erskine May of not commenting on security matters.

Mr. Kinnock: The Prime Minister must then now explain what is the implication for national security of telling us whether it was an individual member of her government who personally—not nominally and formally, but personally—took a decision that has a direct effect on the integrity of national security in this country.

The Prime Minister: The Government as the Right Hon. Gentleman knows, are indivisible. [Interruption] The decisions are decisions of the Government and not of particular Ministers. If he wishes to table a motion of censure he is fully entitled to do so.

This answer was relayed to me within minutes of being given. The game was not well and truly up. Armstrong's evidence had consistently been that the decision not to injunct Pincher was taken by the Attorney-General personally, acting in his special independent capacity, not as

6. "Erskine May" is the name of the standard British text on parliamentary procedure and practice.

part of the Government. Thatcher under the most pressure she had ever experienced in the House had let loose a little chink of truth. It was now impossible for Armstrong to dissemble any further. I knew that the morrow, Friday, November 28, would see some interesting answers from the Cabinet Secretary.

CHAPTER 10

THE CASE RESUMED ON Friday November 28, with Simos changing course yet again. No doubt in response to Justice Powell's "pique" of the previous day he announced that the Government would not challenge the judge's decision to inspect the documents himself. Justice Powell said he would do this over the weekend.

I wished to take Armstrong to some confidential matters and so the court was closed. Much of what Armstrong said in that confidential cross-examination remains confidential and cannot be disclosed, but the questioning quickly turned to the *Their Trade is Treachery* affair.

Friday, November 28, 1986

Q. I ask you about this one question. You said about *Their Trade is Treachery* that it was a decision of the Attorney-General himself and not of the Government collectively. Do you have any reason to revise that answer now?

A. I should wish to say that I am afraid I did mislead the court in that matter and that matter only and that since I gave those answers I have been advised that the answer to Interrogatory No. 150 was correct in so far as the plaintiff was the Crown. The conclusion that there was no basis for restraint was a view reached by legal advisers after consultation among all the legal advisers concerned and it was a unanimous view. I was aware of the view that was reached. I am afraid I assumed from what I was told that it had been referred to the Attorney personally. I now understand that it was not referred to the Attorney personally.

In a way the impact of this admission was more devastating in the confidential hearing than it would have been in open court. Only the judge, his associate, the court attendants and the lawyers and advisers on each side were present. Everyone knew the significance of what had been said. Even though all of us on the defense team had been convinced Armstrong's original answers were false, we were still a little stunned as we absorbed the consequence of Armstrong's about-face. The British lawyers looked grim-faced straight ahead. Simos looked down at the bar table; Armstrong was resigned. He was indeed the fall guy. The judge looked rather smug as though he was thinking to himself that he had been right all along when he expressed the view that the Attorney-General could not be so ignorant as to have given such wrong-headed advice.

The story that then emerged became more and more improbable with every answer. Armstrong admitted that the change in evidence followed a call from the Cabinet Office early that morning (i.e., after the exchange in the House of Commons on the 27th) which relayed the news that Havers was "unhappy with the answers" which Armstrong had given.

Armstrong had previously identified the Treasury Solicitor, John Bailey, and his deputy, David Hogg, as having been responsible for drafting the answers to the Interrogatories. He insisted that in drafting the answer to Interrogatory 150 they had consulted the Attorney-General's Department. Yet the answer was incorrect and now confessedly so.

I probed a little further and asked from whom this legal advice was received, if it had not come from Havers. It was like pulling teeth. Armstrong did not remember the names of the legal advisers, he was slow to recall to whom the advice had been given, but under persistent questioning he admitted there was a meeting at which Thatcher, himself, Whitelaw and the Director General of MI5 were present. But he couldn't recall who had given the advice.

Friday, November 28, 1986

Q.	Right, that advice was given not by the Solicitor-General, not by the Attorney-General, not by the Treasury Solicitor but by some anonymous lawyers whose names you can't remember and whose position in the hierarchy hardly indicates that they were people of first-class calibre, that is so, isn't it?
A.	I don't think that follows at all. I have said that I am not informed about who they were. I have been informed that the advice was reached after consultation among the legal advisers concerned. I am not able I'm afraid to advise you who those were because I can't find out. There are no documents to show it.
Q.	Do you only tell the truth when there are documents likely to demonstrate it?
A.	I have tried to tell the truth throughout, Mr. Turnbull. I'm sorry that I was misled in this case, that I misled myself in this case. I assumed that when it said the legal advisers concerned it included the Attorney, but I was wrong.

Q.	Sir Robert, why was the Attorney-General left out of the decision-making process in respect of *Their Trade is Treachery?*
A.	I don't know why he was not brought into the process by which that conclusion was reached.
Q.	He wasn't part of the conspiracy, was he?
A.	He was not part of the conspiracy.
Q.	And you were?
A.	I was not part of the conspiracy either.
Q.	Sir Michael Havers has refused to carry the can for this hasn't he?
A.	Sir Michael Havers has said that he made it clear that he was not personally responsible for a decision not to restrain the publication.
Q.	Is Sir Michael Havers going to resign this week?
A.	I have no knowledge about Sir Michael Havers' intentions in that respect.

The cross-examination finished at about 3:30 p.m. and it was agreed that as soon as a transcript was ready we would meet with the judge in chambers and agree on an edited version, free of confidential matters, which could be made available to the press that night. My opponents were opposed to such a hasty release of the admissions made by Armstrong, but the judge recognized the enormity of the confessions made and by 6:30 we had edited versions of the transcript ready and we distributed them to the press in my office.

It was not an easy exercise. Bill Caldwell, the barrister assisting Simos, became quite heated with Greengrass and me as we waited outside the judge's chambers for the editing session. "Don't think you'll get away with talking to the Labor Party, Turnbull," he growled. "MI5 will pull your security clearance if you are so indiscreet about their bugging my phone," I sweetly replied. The banter became increasingly heated. Finally Greengrass pulled me aside. "Is it contempt of court to smack a barrister one in the chops?" he asked. On balance I told him I thought it probably was.

The press corps devoured the transcript of Armstrong's humiliation with almost carnivorous glee. Brian Barron, for BBC Television, had London ready on the phone when the transcript arrived. He took about a minute to flick through it, said "Righto, I'm ready to go live now." He then summarized the evidence, entirely ad lib for about ten minutes. Alex Kirby from BBC Radio was equally professional. Greengrass was delighted as the hacks filed their stories. He rubbed his hands and said with a wicked grin, "This will throw a little more kerosene on the fire, won't it."

At this point I imagined the Kinnock assault on the Prime Minister would be unstoppable. But it faltered. Kinnock took off on a trip to America and allowed the Tories to pursue him for the terrible crime of having spoken with me. Without his powerful eloquence all the steam went out of the Labor attack. His colleagues were simply not able to withstand the counterattack.

I could never understand why Kinnock was subject to criticism for having spoken with me. I asked Jonathan Aitken about it and he said that in Australia or America no one would think less of Kinnock for making inquiries as widely as he liked, but in England people were different.

The Prime Minister and her colleagues exemplified the way in which modern Conservatives have little regard for the traditions their predecessors stood for. Here was the Cabinet Secretary misleading a court in Sydney. The representative of the British Government is telling falsehoods on oath and has been doing so for ten days. The Opposition leader casts his net wide and finds out the facts. Given that the Government is refusing to answer any questions he talks to me, among other persons. His pressure on the Government results in the lie being corrected.

In truth Kinnock did Britain a great service. Perhaps Mrs. Thatcher believed that the case should be won at all costs, regardless of whether perjury was committed in the process. There was no doubt I was using Kinnock, in the sense that his questions assisted my endeavors to extract the truth from Armstrong, but naively perhaps, I believed that Governments should conduct litigation on a higher moral level than private citizens often did. I could not believe that the Conservative Party, supposedly the defenders of Britain's traditions, would prefer to win the case on the basis of perjured evidence, than to tell the truth and lose.

Ironically, at the same time another conservative administration, of Ronald Reagan, in the United States was being brought to account for its program of illegal assistance to the Nicaraguan Contras. But in America, at least the legislators were able to get a little closer to the truth. In Mrs. Thatcher's Britain, that would never happen.

There were some amusing aspects to the Tory onslaught against Kinnock. One of the principal yah-booers was a young and undistinguished barrister by the name of Richard Saladin Hickmet. His second name was not the result of an old English family commemorating Richard the Lionheart's doughty opponent. Mr. Hickmet was a first-generation Englishman, his father having been born in Turkey. This learned gentleman intervened frequently in the debates. On November 18 he expressed the opinion that the Government should not answer questions about the case since it could be the subject of an appeal to the Privy Council! That was wishful thinking since appeals to the Privy Council had been abolished from Australia many years before.

His confusion persisted however. On November 27 he seemed to be under the misapprehension that the proceedings were taking place in South Africa. Perhaps this was another Freudian slip . . . no doubt judges in South Africa would be more respectful of cabinet secretaries.

Nonetheless the case was developing a real head of steam in English politics. The newspapers were largely supportive. *The Sunday Times* on November 23 was particularly scathing:

> . . . Mrs. Thatcher dispatched her most senior civil servant to the other side of the world to blunder ever deeper into the morass of a futile cover-up. At home, Whitehall has been able to rely on pliable judges—notably Sir John Donaldson, the Master of the Rolls—to block publication of Mr. Wright's material. What is extraordinary is that it seriously expected the same deference from an Australian court. Assuming the government loses the Australian case, it will unleash a flood of further revelations on the misdeeds of British intelligence. It is ludicrous that such material will be available everywhere but in Britain, where it will presumably circulate in samizdat, as if Britain were a province of Brezhnev's Russia.

The political furor in England had succeeded in flushing Havers out, but we had no such luck with Rothschild. Our strategy was that newspapers and Labor MPs would call for an explanation of his role in introducing Wright to Pincher and then funneling the funds to Wright. If he had done this off his own bat, it would not be difficult to frame a few serious criminal charges against him. However Rothschild stayed mute. He wrote to Iain Walker of the *Daily Mail* in these terms:

> The purpose of this letter is just to confirm what I said to you yesterday, namely, that I shall not consider

making any statement until after the Australian trial,
and any Appeal that there may be, are concluded.

The trial resumed in Sydney with the evidence of the
Australian Cabinet Secretary, Michael Codd. His affidavit
had been read together with Armstrong's on the first day
of the trial, and now it was my turn to cross-examine
him upon it.

Codd was a much more taciturn man than his English
counterpart. He was not interested in playing verbal games
with the cross-examiner. He adopted the best possible
tactics for a witness: keep the answers short and don't
argue with the cross-examiner, don't volunteer anything
and don't lose your temper.

Nonetheless Codd had to admit that his objection to
the book was really an objection in principle.

Monday, December 1, 1986

> Q. Do you say to the court that every par-
> agraph in the chapters objected to by the
> British Government would, if published,
> be detrimental to the national security of
> Australia?
>
> A. No. I have said that the manuscript as a
> whole is a matter that was at issue, as I
> understand it, in these hearings and that
> is what has been examined by me.
>
> Q. Did the Australian Security Intelligence
> Organization tell you that every para-
> graph in this book was as objectionable
> as every other one?
>
> A. I have already explained that the book
> or the manuscript has not been examined
> paragraph by paragraph, nor any attempt
> made to judge whether any particular part
> of it should or should not be suppressed.

Q.   And why have you not done that?

A.   Because it is not our role to do that. That
                  is a matter going to authorization which,
                  as I said, is properly for the British Gov-
                  ernment and it's former employee.

Codd was therefore not exercising any independent judgment as to the contents of *Spycatcher*. The Australian Government was simply taking the line that if Britain failed to authorize a former intelligence officer to write his memoirs, Australia would support the general proposition that publication was not permitted without authority.

Codd, however, was no better prepared than Armstrong. Like Sir Robert he argued in his affidavit that friendly foreign intelligence agencies might think less of Australian agencies if Wright was allowed to publish his book in Australia. The reasoning went that a foreign agency would see the Australian courts were liberal in their approach to such memoirs and would then withhold information from ASIO. Yet his knowledge of CIA practices was nonexistent.

Q.   Mr. Codd, are you familiar with the CIA's
                  manuscript clearance policy?

A.   No I am not.

In his affidavit Codd had quoted from the Royal Commission report of Mr. Justice Hope. Hope had inquired into the various Australian intelligence agencies and had uncovered a lot of malpractices and inefficiencies. His report had received considerable bipartisan support. It had been held up as the sort of review the intelligence services of Britain were long overdue for.

Codd quoted two paragraphs dealing with foreign intelligence agencies:

Foreign Liaison

449   Effective internal security is a highly specialized and expensive undertaking. Recognizing that, ASIO maintains, and has maintained, active liaison both here and abroad with the internal security and intelligence services of several friendly nations. It does so for these reasons:

(a) To ensure that it has taken full advantage of advanced techniques and methodologies available to friendly services with common goals.

(b) To take advantage of the information available to other intelligence and security services on security threats, intelligence about the operations of espionage services and agents, and about terrorism and terrorists.

(c) To ensure that ASIO keeps up to date with international security developments of interest to Australia.

450   In my view these liaison relationships contribute significantly to ASIO's overall efficiency. They can help to minimize the costs involved in accomplishing its internal security mission. I find that the Australian liaison efforts of these friendly services are in the national interest.

Codd went on to say in his affidavit that he agreed with the views expressed by Hope. What he did not say was that Hope had seriously qualified these opinions in the next three paragraphs of his report.

451   I would only add three points.

452   The first is that ASIO must take special care to ensure that any information that passes to other services is carefully scrutinized and checked, not only for accuracy, but also as to whether it should properly be passed to a third country.

453   Secondly, ASIO should be careful to ensure that its relationship with any foreign intelligence service is in harmony with the principles of legality and propriety I have already mentioned. Therefore ASIO must take

care to see that its liaison arrangements accord with the foreign policies of the government of the day and that liaison does not assist any service which does not sufficiently respect civil rights and freedom.

454   Thirdly ASIO should not be uncritical of information obtained from foreign liaison services. It should not be automatically accepted as correct merely because it has been so supplied and because to check it is difficult.

Codd knew that a large part of our case was that *Spycatcher* contained extensive evidence of criminal activities on the part of MI5. To paraphrase Justice Hope, we were arguing that MI5 was a service "which does not sufficiently respect civil rights and freedom." Even the judge was surprised at the way Hope's report had been selectively quoted by Codd. I asked Codd whether he agreed that the Australian people should be made aware that a foreign intelligence agency with whom ASIO liaised was systematically infringing civil liberties. Codd declined to give any meaningful answer, until the judge intervened.

Monday, December 1, 1986

His Honor   Mr. Codd, you will forgive me again if I interrupt, and I do so only because of a matter that appears to have attracted a great deal of attention in the Press over the weekend. I do not ask you to confirm or deny whether or not our security agencies liaise with the security agencies of General Pinochet's regime in Chile . . . If the truth of the matter be, first, that we did liaise with the security services of Chile and, second, that only half of the stories one reads about the activities of the security and other forces within Chile are true, surely to heaven you do not suggest that the Australian Government would wish to prevent the Australian people being told about them.

A.	I do not intend to suggest that. I think the relevant piece of the Hope report which one would need to look carefully at is the words "which does not sufficiently respect civil rights and freedom."
His Honor	I can appreciate that, but who is to be the judge—you or the Australian people? It is as simple as that, isn't it?
A.	(No response)

The judge had characteristically put his finger on the very heart of the issue. How can a democracy tolerate a situation where a vast intelligence apparatus is completely above the law, not because the law does not apply to it, but simply because it is so secret that nobody is ever in a position to know what it does?

Codd became less dogmatic in his answers as the examination progressed. I felt we were developing a civil libertarian for a moment or two.

Q.	If the facts disclosed that Mr. Wright's book contained evidence of MI5 failing to live up to these standards of legality and propriety that Mr. Justice Hope has referred to, would you agree with me that that is information which the Australian people are entitled to know in the light of Australia's stated relationship with Britain?
A.	I guess the answer to that is yes, but not necessarily through the publication of a book in these terms. If there is established illegal activity then it would be important for Australia's agencies to know about it and to assess its implications and for the Australian people to be aware of it.
Q.	But if the Australian agencies were not aware of it, for instance, because Britain

had not told them or the Australian agencies did not wish to make it public for reasons of their own concerns about secrecy, it is nonetheless appropriate, would you not agree with me, in a democratic society, that this information be placed before the people so that they can assess the virtues of the relationship with Britain?

A. I can only answer for the Australian Government. I believe if there were a situation where illegal activity were proven in the operations of one of its agencies, the Australian Government would be intent on ensuring that that was made known to the public.

Codd was difficult to shake. His proposition was either good or bad. He argued that unauthorized memoirs were a bad thing generally and he would not be drawn into particulars. It was a somewhat lacklustre performance. When he explained that if an Australian court allowed the book to be published, ASIO would lose confidence in MI5 even though the publication had been allowed in Australia, in exasperation, the judge aptly described Codd's evidence as "complete and utter moonshine."

Like Armstrong, Codd was long on generality but very short on details. It was the same old waffle. In the absence of having any particular incidents to tax him with, there was not a lot of point in my debating him, particularly since he seemed quicker on his feet than Armstrong. He was finished in an hour and half, and the next witness was one of mine, the Honorable Edward Gough Whitlam QC.

Whitlam is a living legend, and looks it. His full head of white hair, his six-foot-five-inch bearing and his enormous bulk certainly give him the appearance of a statesman. He was Prime Minister of Australia for only three years, 1972 to 1975, during which stormy period he initiated more reforms than the country had seen in the previous twenty years. He was sacked by the Governor-General and the ensuing fracas polarized the country in a way it had not been since the mid-sixties. Half the country would walk over hot coals for him, and the other half would have cheerfully murdered him without offering the victim even a local anesthetic.

The intervening years had seen him become a much-loved elder statesman. He compares so favorably with his drab successor, the Liberal Malcolm Fraser, that even his enemies have come to admire him. But I had not asked him to give evidence because of his good humor and erudition. It was Whitlam's government which for the first time really asserted the independence of Australia. His Liberal predecessors had been proud to be "British to the bootstraps."[1] While he had not been prepared to go so far as to press for an Australian republic, he had insisted that Queen Elizabeth be styled "Queen of Australia" when in Australia and he had abolished appeals to the British Privy Council from the Australian Federal Courts.

The court was packed with standing room only when Whitlam arrived. Unlike Armstrong and Codd who seemed to shrink in the witness box, Whitlam expanded to almost spill out of it. He detailed his distinguished career in politics and diplomacy (he had been Australia's Ambassador to UNESCO after he left politics). We then turned to matters of importance.

Monday, December 1, 1986

Q.   Have you had experience involving the secret intelligence organizations of Australia?

1. Particularly Sir Robert Menzies, Prime Minister from 1949 until 1964.

A.   Yes, I was largely responsible for them and I settled the terms of Reference of Mr. Justice Hope's Royal Commission and I countersigned the Commission.

Q.   Mr. Whitlam, can you tell his Honor the country with whom Australia has its major intelligence-sharing relationship?

A.   Throughout my period in public life, the United States of America.

Q.   Can you give his Honor a view of the comparative importance of the relationship with the United Kingdom in that regard?

A.   Smaller and diminishing.

Q.   Could you give his Honor any reasons for this diminishing scale?

A.   The diminution of the power of the United Kingdom and its withdrawal from the Pacific.

Whitlam pointed to a significant fallacy in the British Government's argument. If it was so important that Australia should preserve the secrets of MI5 and Britain the secrets of ASIO, why had there not been a convention or treaty between the two countries? Such a convention would be debated in both Parliaments and if accepted would become the law. He highlighted the essential inappropriateness of a court being drawn into what was really a political issue.

I had provided a copy of the transcript of Cathy Massiter's television interview to Whitlam. In that she described how MI5 had bugged the telephone of Patricia Hewitt, the Australian-born Press Secretary to British Opposition Leader Neil Kinnock, when she had been General Secretary of the National Council for Civil Liberties.

A.	I knew some of the persons involved there, one in particular, Mr. Neil Kinnock's secretary. I have known her all her life. I went to school with her mother.
Q.	Miss Patricia Hewitt.
A.	Yes, Sir Lennox Hewitt's daughter. I have known her mother since I went to school with her in Canberra in 1930. I have known her father since they were married in 1941. I have known her and her sisters and brother her whole life. I have known her in Britain and followed her activities. I think it is monstrous that persons should be paid for monitoring her activities in the Civil Liberties organization in Britain.
Q.	You do not therefore regard her as a person likely to be plotting the violent overthrow of the British Government?
A.	I never felt myself at risk in her company.

Whitlam stressed that Australia's intelligence agencies were not free to break the law and that Australia should be most careful of cooperating with or condoning foreign intelligence agencies which break international law, as MI5 had been shown to have done.

A.	It is quite essential for a country of the location and size of Australia to abide by international agreements and to promote respect for them. Might may be right for superpowers, or former superpowers. It could never be right for a country located and endowed as Australia is.

He went further and argued that it was important that Australia be seen to be prepared to expose the sort of criminality *Spycatcher* revealed.

A.   I think it is very much to Australia's advantage that [these allegations] should be published and that at the same time it should be known that Australian Governments in the last fourteen years have not condoned those activities which are in breach of Australian domestic laws or international law as accepted by Australia.

                      Many of the countries whose premises are being bugged in the days with which the book deals and whose premises Australia attempted to bug in those days are not being bugged by Australia now because it would be in breach of the law which applies in Australia for that to be done.

                      I believe that the fact that this did happen and that Australia has learned and that Australia does not condone such illicit and undercover activities by a country which it has been so closely associated as the UK, would be very much to the advantage of this country.

Whitlam's performance was more than a little theatrical. The old politician revelled in the limelight. During the luncheon adjournment, while he was still giving his evidence in chief, we slipped out of the court building to walk up Macquarie Street where Whitlam had an appointment. A posse of photographers and television cameramen spotted us and within a few minutes we were facing a phalanx of lenses. Whitlam lost interest in our discussion, drew himself up to his full height, sucked in his belly, stuck out his chest and strode down the street like an ancient Shakespearian actor.

I hung back while the adoring mob trailed after him. You can take the man out of politics, but, so it seems, you cannot take the politics out of the man.

Whitlam retired from the witness box after Simos attempted to cross-examine him. I sympathized with him; it was hard enough getting Whitlam to answer my questions . . . and he was my witness. Theo didn't stand a chance. What should we do now, asked the judge. "Let's have another swing at Sir Robert," I am alleged to have remarked. Thankfully the transcript does not record such a disrespectful remark, and my memory is somewhat dimmed.

So for the first time since his humiliating admission the previous Friday, Sir Robert returned to the witness box. I proceeded to probe the revised version of events Sir Robert had now shared with us.

Monday, December 1, 1986

Q.   Sir Robert, why was the Attorney-General kept out of this decision?

A.   I don't think it was really correct to describe it as a decision. As I, again, tried to suggest on Friday, I think it was a kind of—it was a conclusion to which all those who were consulted came, that there was no basis for proceeding to try to restrain publication, and that being the general view and general conclusion, there was no proposition to put to the Attorney-General, there was no suggestion that he should take action.

This was Sir Humphrey Appleby at his best.[2] He distinguishes between "a decision" and "a conclusion," the latter being the best description of what occurred. It

---

2. Sir Humphrey Appleby is the Cabinet Secretary in the popular British television series "Yes Prime Minister" which parodies the workings of No. 10 Downing Street with such wit and accuracy that the scripts have become texts for students of political science.

seemed Sir Robert was trying to suggest a sort of osmotic consciousness which crystallized into reality without any of those involved actually deciding they wanted it to. Government by levitation.

He still insisted however that the basis for this "conclusion" was that certain lawyers advised that an injunction could not be obtained without revealing the source of the manuscript. I endeavored to discover who perpetrated this arrant nonsense.

Q. Sir Robert I want to put to you that you received advice in this matter from only one lawyer, and that was Bernard Sheldon, the legal adviser to MI5?

A. What was reported to me was the conclusion after discussion among a number of legal advisors.

Q. But he was one of them?

A. The legal advisor to the Security Service was one of them.

Q. Who were the others?

A. Oh, I am afraid I can't tell you that. There was formal discussion with a number of others, but I don't know who they were because I wasn't a party to them and there was no record.

Sir Robert went on to tell me that he could not recall speaking to any of these mysterious lawyers nor did the Prime Minister or the Home Secretary speak to them. The Director-General of MI5 may have spoken to his own legal advisor, but he was not sure.

Q. Accepting that the weight one gives to a lawyer's opinion depends in part upon his experience and reputation and what you know of him, why did you place so much weight on the advice from these lawyers,

	only one of whom you knew the identity of?
A.	I had placed weight on—I think this would be true for others too—the weight was placed on what was a general view after consultation among a number of lawyers and what seemed even to the layman an inherently reasonable view to take. Now you might take a different view, but that was how it seemed at the time.

Armstrong's latest version was even less believable than the first. The Prime Minister, the Home Secretary, the Cabinet Secretary and the Director-General of MI5 are all opposed to the publication of *Their Trade is Treachery*. They receive advice from a group of lawyers so eminent, so persuasive, that nobody can remember their names. Despite the fact that Pincher boasts in the book of having obtained information in breach of the Official Secrets Act, the advice is that no action can be brought for an injunction. In the face of this improbable advice they do not seek a second opinion from the Attorney-General. They do not ask for counsel from a distinguished QC. No, they cop it sweet as though this preposterous advice had been written in the heavens in letters of fire.

As we wended our way home from court on December 1, London began to stir on the morning of the same day. The Government was busy with its smear campaign against Kinnock, suggesting that his criticism of Havers and Armstrong and his discussions with me demonstrated that he could not be trusted on matters of national security. It is perhaps an indication of Mrs. Thatcher's dominance of Britain and the uncritical nature of the conservative press that so ludicrous a campaign could be got under way. It was helped by Kinnock being in America explaining the Labor Party's defense policy which involves removing all nuclear weapons from British soil. But it was nonetheless a great lie.

The press were full of obviously inspired leaks concerning the attitude of Sir Michael Havers. He had made
it plain that he was profoundly displeased with the Prime
Minister's attitude to the case. However, doubtless with
a tongue firmly planted in his cheek, he told the House
of Commons later that afternoon: "I have had the most
wonderful and loyal support from the Prime Minister,
for which I am extremely grateful." Mr. John Morris was
unable to persuade the Speaker that the matter deserved
a debate on the adjournment. With Kinnock away in
America, the Labor attack over the *Spycatcher* case lost
all momentum. Incredibly the battle in England started
to swing around to the Government's favor.

CHAPTER 11

TUESDAY, DECEMBER 2, 1986 began with Justice Powell providing his judgment on the production of documents question. He had, he said, read the documents produced by the Government and he produced a schedule referring to each document which indicated whether it ought to be produced and whether it should be edited if it was. The documents related to the circumstances in which *Their Trade is Treachery, Too Secret Too Long, A Matter of Trust,* The Massiter television interview and the Wright television interview had been published. Powell's associate distributed copies of his judgment, carefully removing the schedule from the copies given to the press, and the court adjourned while everyone read it.

It was a good, sensible decision. Powell had obviously invested many hours in carefully editing each document so that only the material relevant to the case would be produced to me. It was craftsmanlike. But it was not satisfactory to the Government.

This decision posed a tactical conundrum for us. The press in London had been suggesting, no doubt on the basis of Government leaks, that if the Government were ultimately forced to produce the documents, it would chuck the whole case. The Prime Minister, more in sorrow than in anger, could say that while she abhorred Wright's breach of trust, nonetheless she could not countenance so dangerous a precedent as the production of internal MI5 documents and in the circumstances, therefore, the case had to be dropped.

If I had believed these leaks, which were widely reported, I would have fought the discovery question to the death. But I did not believe them. I felt I now had the measure of Mrs. Thatcher. I had been mistaken about her determination and now I had learned, as had many others, that she fights to the finish, and then some.

Simos' first step would be to seek leave to appeal to the Court of Appeal. On the face of it he ought to get leave. He was now raising a general issue of principle; should internal intelligence agency documents ever be produced for discovery? There was precedent for both sides of that argument and I had no doubt the Court of Appeal would want to hear a full argument on it. My best point, however, was that Simos should have raised this public interest immunity argument back in October. Had he done so then, this preliminary question which was inevitably going to arise, would have been sorted out before the trial began. It was just another example of the way the British abused the legal system to cause the maximum disruption to the trial. I resolved then to fight the leave application as hard as I could, on that issue, and if I lost then quickly to do a deal. There was no point allowing the discovery question to go the full distance; by the time the Court of Appeal had heard a full argument on it and the case had then gone to the High Court it could be six months before we got back to Justice Powell and finished the trial.

After we had studied Justice Powell's judgment on the documents, the court reconvened and Sir Robert returned for what was his last spell in the witness box. The frustrating feature of the Government's case had been its failure to get down to particulars. Armstrong's affidavits were no more than a chronicle of general observations of the sorts of damage that could be caused by books written by former intelligence officers. Armstrong's affidavits did not address the issue of whether this particular book, *Spycatcher*, actually caused any of the kinds of damage. During a confidential session I had endeavored to tease some detail out of Armstrong and I had taken him to particular passages in the book and asked him for his specific comments. His answers were so unhelpful that I discussed the matter with Simos who agreed with me that if we chose not to raise particular passages with Armstrong, that would not be counted against us. Just to make sure Armstrong understood what was happening I gave him one last chance to descend from his high plateau of generality.

Tuesday, December 2, 1986

Q.   Your affidavits do not particularize particular passages or sections of the book and relate them to particular sorts of objection, do they?

A.   No, they don't. There is a general description of the kind of objections that would apply.

Q.   Given that it may well be that his Honor would have to consider a blue-pencilling job, do you wish to give his Honor particular details of particular passages in the book to which you object for particular reasons?

A.   No. I don't wish to do that, Mr. Turnbull. I rest on the case that has been made in my affidavits on the general breach of duty of confidentiality and the detriment that is done by publication by an insider or former insider. Whether material is material in the public domain or other channels or whether it is not.

The next witness was William Henry Schaap. Bill Schaap
is an American lawyer who has practiced extensively in
military law and over the last fifteen years or so been an
advisor to many former CIA officers who have sought to
publish books about their life in the Agency. Schaap is
a lean volpine-looking man with a villainous moustache.
It was Hooper who found him for us in the United States
and certainly his credentials were outstanding. However,
when he arrived in Sydney I was told by Greengrass,
whose excellent contacts in the CIA were no doubt keeping him well informed, that Schaap had been associated
with a publication called *Covert Action* which had disclosed
the names of some CIA officers in place in foreign countries. Following the disclosure of their names one of them
had been assassinated.

Schaap I must confess is a highly intelligent and charming man. He insisted that he had not been associated
with *Covert Action* at the time it exposed the agents in
place and I have no reason to doubt him.

He told the court that before 1967 there had been
very few significant revelations about the CIA's work.
However in the late sixties and early seventies there was
an increasing flood of disclosures culminating in the book
by Victor Marchetti and John D. Marks, *CIA and the Cult
of Intelligence*. That book was the subject of court action
and finally an appeals court made 168 deletions to the
text. The book is full of detail about CIA operations,
many of them relatively current. After Marchetti and
Marks, Phillip Agee wrote his work *Inside the Company*.
It was not vetted by the CIA as it had been published
in the United Kingdom and subsequently republished in
the USA. Following these exposés Congress got into the
act with committees of both the Senate (under Frank
Church) and the House of Representatives (under Representative Pike) inquiring into the CIA's illegal activities.
Following these Congressional investigations which exposed even more malpractice on the part of the CIA,
both the Senate and the House of Representatives estab-

lished permanent Select Committees on Intelligence which have jointly exercized oversight responsibilities since.

In 1977 the CIA established a Publication Review Board which consists of the Deputy Director of Public Affairs and representatives from the five directorates of the CIA. The CIA General Counsel's office acts as legal advisor and coordinator to the Board. Schaap tendered schedules showing the many hundreds of books, articles and speeches which had been approved for publication by the Publication Review Board since 1977. Many were by very distinguished former officers. Former Director-General Admiral Stansfield Turner was the author of over forty articles, books and speeches, all of which were approved. The obligation on CIA officers to submit their writings for clearance is contained in the standard secrecy agreement signed by each officer when he joins the CIA.

The Publication Review Board, Schaap testified, "has not been overly concerned with the release of details of its operations, provided that they do not expose personnel currently under cover or operations currently under way, nor endanger former agents whose role with the CIA has never been exposed. Subject to these restrictions the theory and the philosophy has been one generally of greater rather than lesser openness, even with regard to technical information."

One of Armstrong's principal arguments was that the publication of *Spycatcher* would cause the CIA to think less of MI5, particularly if information concerning Wright's work with the Americans were published. Schaap poured scorn on this argument pointing to numerous officially cleared books which discussed at length CIA operations with the British.

Schaap concluded his testimony with this assessment of Armstrong's evidence:

> I have read those portions of the testimony and affidavits of Armstrong which suggest that the CIA would be extremely concerned with the publication of a book

such as that in issue herein, a conclusion I find un-
tenable. The CIA, on its own, has approved the publication of books with information at least as intriguing
as that in the book in issue herein, and with considerable, indeed voluminous details about personnel, operations, technology, and all aspects of intelligence
work. The only restrictions which have been applied
consistently to the release of information relate to the
endangering of personnel still under cover and the
exposure of operations still under way. Virtually all
details have been released about countless old operations, and, as I have been informed that the information in the book in issue herein is virtually all ten
to twenty years old, I cannot see how, under the
standards applied in the United States, such a book
would be suppressed, in whole or in part.

Perhaps the best corroboration of Schaap's testimony
was that Simos chose not to cross-examine him. He did
however reserve the right to call his own American witness
to contradict Schaap, but never did. So MI5 with all its
boasted closeness to the CIA was unable to persuade the
Americans to provide a witness to contradict or even
qualify the opinions expressed by Schaap. That only served
to confirm that if a CIA officer had given evidence, he
would have had to agree with Schaap.

The judge was rummaging through the long lists of
officially cleared publications Schaap had provided until
one struck his fancy.

Tuesday, December 2, 1986

His Honor   Before we pass on to another topic, I am
                intrigued by at least one of the titles that
                appears to have been submitted. I am not
                sure how it gets into the intelligence world.
                It is Mr. Mullens' *I Was Idi Amin's Bas-
                ketball Czar.* That does not seem to be
                terribly secret.

Mr. Turnbull   Do you know anything about that book?

Witness   Yes I have read the article and heard
               Mullen speak. He was a CIA agent in
               Uganda during the time Idi Amin was in
               power. His major problem was to keep
               General Amin happy. General Amin liked
               to play basketball, but he was a very bad
               basketball player so Mullen as an expe-
               rienced CIA officer was detailed the job
               of playing basketball with him every day
               and trying to improve his skill.

Schaap rattled through his testimony at breakneck speed
and the shorthand writers were regularly making pained
signals to me which I correctly interpreted as requests to
ask Schaap to slow down. The judge finally intervened.

His Honor   Mr. Schaap I wonder if I might just in-
               terpose for a moment. If I may say so,
               your method of speech is like a Gatling
               gun with hiccups and the court Reporter
               is struggling to keep up. I wonder if you
               could help us by just slowing down a little
               bit?

Witness   I am sorry, I am a lifetime New Yorker
               and it is a problem we all have.

Schaap also exploded Armstrong's distinction between
insiders and outsiders. Sir Robert had argued that even
if a journalist had published something about MI5 additional grave damage was done if a former MI5 officer
republished it.

Witness   The problem with the insider/outsider
               distinction is that it somehow assumes all
               former intelligence officers tell the truth
               when they write their books. I know for
               a fact that cannot possibly be true because
               there are many books by former intelli-

gence officers which disagree with each other and one of them has to be lying, even if I don't know which one. A good example is Kermit Roosevelt's *Countercoup* and Bill Eveland's *Ropes of Sand* where they each dispute each other's description of what happened in Iran in 1953, overthrowing Mossadegh, yet both of these books have been cleared for publication.

Some of the most respected writers on intelligence are outsiders, journalists who specialized in the field for many, many years whose writings were considered much more authoritative. Moreover, frequently when the CIA disagrees with something that a former employee has published, even something they have cleared, they deny it. They will say Agee is lying about that, Marchetti is lying about that in some sort of press release, stressing again that the fact they cleared something for publication did not mean they were authenticating anything in it.

Also in the United States, there is a tradition of journalists specializing in intelligence matters, as in defense matters and so on, who go on to have not only high reputations in those areas but generally from what we see in the papers, far greater access to sources than any disgruntled former employee would hope to have. Nobody in the CIA will talk to Phillip Agee and give him any information to help him write an article, but they talk to journalists from the major papers all the time.

The conservative elements of the press in England now endeavored to defuse the embarrassments in Sydney by representing the whole trial as an exercise in "Pom-bashing."[1] The *Daily Express* headlined its main *Spycatcher* story on December 2 as "Roll up and bash a Pom!" The former editor of *The Times*, Sir William Rees-Mogg, added his own childish observations to the case as he wrote in *The Independent:* "I do not know why so many Australians have chips in [sic] their shoulders; Gallipoli seems to me to be a long time ago, and Botany Bay an even more remote piece of history. Yet the atmosphere of the court seems to be seething with class resentment, as though Phillips [I assume Rees-Mogg means Powell here] and Turnbull were citizens sans-culottes relishing sending M. Le Comte d'Armstrong to the guillotine."

However, possibly the best contribution to the English side of proceedings was an after dinner speech given in Selby, Yorkshire by one of Mrs. Thatcher's parliamentary private secretaries, Mr. Michael Alison. He said that at No. 10 Sir Robert was being described as "a wally among the wallabies" and that the whole case was either Gilbert and Sullivan or a re-run of the two Ronnies. Mr. Alison promptly denied ever having uttered such sentiments, but few were convinced and the *Express* and *Telegraph* both ran it on the front page.

The Guardian provided a measured assessment of the mess so far:

> Was there a better way? Of course. A practical politician, with a leery eye for what makes a stinking row might well have shrugged as Mr. Wright readied his manuscript. Poor old Peter. Good fellow in his time. But driven by this curious thing about poor Roger Hollis. It's all old stuff, you know. Even Pincher had it. Can't see what the fuss is about myself, but shouldn't get too upset. Anything to coin a slightly

1. A "pom" is Australian slang for an Englishman. Its origins are obscure but it is probably derived from "pomegranite," which was in turn rhyming slang for immigrant.

dubious penny, what? Ask Heath and Wilson if you want a proper quote.

But no. In the looking glass world of Whitehall, where even vitriolic political briefings are off the record, no-one paused to weigh the odds. That is the humiliating fact of this incompetence for Mrs. Thatcher's administration. Not that they look conniving, silly asses. Loyally and wonderfully, of course, various backbenchers are making efforts to redress the balance. Mr. Kinnock's phone log seems an oddly open book. The normal checks that any MP with his head screwed on straight makes before sounding off are somehow portrayed as sinister. But, when all the din of loyalty wanes, even the most vociferous Conservatives ought to have a word with their whips. If a highly experienced Tory government can't contrive the basic competence of putting two and two together, then it sets the most fundamental question mark over its political nous.

The Daily Telegraph was of similar mind as to the Government's incompetence, but predictably critical of the Labor Party:

As Mr. Gough Whitlam left the witness box in Sydney yesterday, the court looked at its watches and noted that there remained 55 minutes of play before stumps were drawn for the day. Mr. Malcolm Turnbull, the defense counsel, stepped forward in the fashion of Mr. Chris Broad, returning to the crease after tea with a century already behind him: "We could have another swing at Sir Robert" he said hopefully. To mix metaphors a little further, the Cabinet Secretary now resembles a bull so extensively adorned with banderillas that even the most sadistic spectator yearns to see him decently dispatched. Poor Sir Robert. It is difficult to see how the dignity, the natural gravitas, of the highest civil servant in the land can ever recover from the sort of public humiliation to which he has been exposed in Australia.

The principal damage to the Government's standing with the British electorate from the affair lies in the ridicule to which Britian has been exposed by it. The British people are a little tired of being ridiculed abroad, however familiar the sensation has become. They can hardly think well of a Government which stage-manages such a farce on the other side of the globe.

But fortunately for Mrs. Thatcher, the Labor Party can usually be counted upon to act in a fashion that restores the appearance of competence to Conservatism, and Mr. Kinnock has not disappointed this time. His telephone calls to Mr. Turnbull must appear in the eyes of Australians—and the rest of the world— as an attempt to derive paltry party political advantage from a case in which, however incompetently, the British Government was seeking to defend a wholly legitimate national interest . . . The overwhelming majority of the British public understand and support the principle that intelligence officers should not be able at will to disclose details of their past or present activities. The Government's legal difficulties in Australia stem from the inconsistency and whimsicality with which this principle has been enforced in the recent past. The tatters of Government dignity may or may not be perceived to demand that the case in Sydney should be seen through to its inglorious conclusion before losses are cut. Thereafter, the secret of happiness is to ensure that all members of the intelligence services sign cast-iron security contracts which are rigidly enforced.

The Daily Telegraph's editorialist overlooked the fact that it was no part of Wright's case that all restrictions on intelligence memoirs should be lifted. He sought no more than a discerning and discriminating approach such as that which the CIA adopted.

Wednesday afternoon, December 3, saw the emergence of a new dirty trick in London. Mr. Richard Hickmet, by now confident the trial was occurring in Sydney and not Capetown, tabled a motion alleging that Paul Greengrass had been briefing Neil Kinnock's office on information heard in the confidential sessions. This was picked up by the *London Standard* in a page 1 splash. Greengrass had been admitted to the confidential sessions and had gone so far as to sign a deed of covenant binding him to keep secret forever anything he heard there. In fact there was very little interesting or useful said by Sir Robert, or anyone else, in confidential sessions. The Managing Director of William Heinemann in London, Brian Perman, was particularly panicked. He rang me late on Wednesday night in Sydney and said that Heinemann were planning to issue a press statement in London dissociating themselves from Greengrass.

I was furious. This was precisely the sort of panicking weakness which had the potential of losing the case. "Don't you understand Perman, this is a smear? Greengrass has passed nothing to Kinnock which is confidential, nor have I. Nothing has been said in the bloody confidential sessions anyway." Perman was unmoved. "We are very worried that we will be seen as working for the Labor Party, we have to be non-political." "Good God man," I replied, "Greengrass is a bloody Thatcherite. Just because he's got long hair and a moustache doesn't mean he's a Trotskyite. You must not issue any statement at all. Keep your head down and leave it to me. I'll handle this in my own way. Just shut up." The conversation rather deteriorated after that. I recall telling Perman that he represented the culmination of years of English decadence and that he should be shot or perhaps mercifully gassed. Finally, more out of terror than anything else, Perman confirmed that he would leave the matter to me.

The rather out of control conversation had a humorous ending. Lucy was so appalled by the violence of my remarks that she rang him back and tendered an apology.

"Doesn't he mean what he said to me?" Perman asked. "Oh, yes he means all of it, Brian, it is just that he's sorry about expressing himself so bluntly." Perman was in many ways the meat in the sandwich. Other members of the Heinemann board, including the chief executive of its parent company, Ian Irvine, were having grave reservations about the conduct of the case.

But this is what happens when you engage cut-price lawyers, you can't control them like you can those large law firms with their big fees. Worse still from Heinemann's point of view, even if they did tell me to stop the case I would not stop, since I was also representing Peter Wright and he was determined to fight the case to the bitter end.

The next day I challenged the Government to make its allegations in open court. "This past week has seen a despicable smear campaign against Mr. Wright, myself and now Mr. Greengrass. Mr. Greengrass has considerable knowledge of intelligence matters and has provided an enormous amount of research material. He has undertaken to the court and to the British Government that he will not reveal any information learned by him in confidential session. He has not provided any such information to any person, other than those entitled to receive it. Those responsible for this campaign are plainly endeavoring to pervert the course of justice. They are cowardly and despicable people whose conduct disentitles them to any respect from those who believe in the impartial administration of justice."

On Tuesday the trial adjourned until the following Friday, December 5, to allow Simos to make his application to the Court of Appeal for leave to appeal from Justice Powell's ruling on the discovery of documents. The application was heard on Thursday, December 4, by Chief Justice Laurence Street, Justice Michael Kirby and Justice Harold Glass. Michael McHugh, who had been the third member of the bench on the previous occasion was not present, and I feared his replacement would adopt a more conservative approach. I was right. I chronicled the way in which the Government had dribbled out its interlocutory objections one at a time and in a way calculated to cause the maximum delay and disruption to the trial. But these arguments fell on deaf ears. The Court of Appeal granted Simos leave to appeal and fixed the hearing date for the following Thursday, December 11. I knew then that I had to do a deal. If I won the following Thursday, as I expected to, the Court of Appeal would probably not release its judgment until the new year, and then the Government would appeal to the High Court of Australia and it would be six months before we got back to the trial. I felt we were winning the trial and I did not want to lose any momentum.

Wednesday, December 3, also saw a debate in the House of Commons initiated by the Alliance leader, Dr. David Owen; the purpose of which was to establish a parliamentary intelligence committee designed to exercise a degree of oversight on intelligence matters. Owen excoriated Wright, but argued that Britain should fall into line with most other Western countries in making its intelligence agencies accountable. Douglas Hurd, Home Secretary, used his speech as an opportunity to attack the still absent Kinnock for having dared to discuss the case with me. It was perhaps a little optimistic to expect the debate would be about anything other than the Wright case and few of the speakers canvassed any of the issues of parliamentary accountability. Mr. Gerald Kaufman, a Labor frontbencher, made a cogent analysis of the Wright case to date. His peroration summarized the political issue as it had developed in England:

> Will the Prime Minister say why, after Sir Robert Armstrong failed to tell the truth about the Attorney-General's role in relation to *Their Trade is Treachery* she allowed that untruth to remain on the record for

11 days, although she knew that it was an untruth? She knew it was an untruth because she was present at the meeting that decided not to proceed against Mr. Pincher's book and the Attorney General was not. Therefore she knew that Sir Robert had not told the truth when he said that the Attorney-General was not involved in that decision. Why did the Prime Minister not take the tiniest step to put that untruth right? Would she ever have put it right if the Attorney General had not gone to her and told her that he had had enough. Would she have allowed that untruth to remain on the record?

Roy Jenkins saw in Sir Robert's predicament a warning to other civil servants:

Sir Robert Armstrong, as the Prime Minister must now know well, should never have been sent to Australia, but it is not only he. Private secretaries and press officers are treated like junior officers, constantly called upon to go over the top in desperate partisan assaults not made more attractive by the fact that the primary orders are to safeguard the political life of their colonel-in-chief, the Prime Minister. My advice to the substantial number of notable civil servants who worked with or for me is "Do not get too close to this Prime Minister. She is an upas tree—the branches may look splendid, but contact can be deadly."

Only Jonathan Aitken of the Tories was supportive of more parliamentary oversight. He described the Government's conduct of the Wright case as a shambles and went on:

The Government's tactics of which I have already been critical remind me of an old strip cartoon in Punch. It begins with a rather unpleasant wasp invading a family picnic. The next picture shows the father seizing an umbrella and striking out in all directions. With a

hail of inaccurate blows, he breaks the china, tramples
the food, smashes the bottles and injures his children.
As the wasp buzzes away, he stands among the mayhem
and destruction that he has created saying, "At least
that will teach the wasp a lesson."

But Mrs. Thatcher was not present in the House during
the debate, nor was Sir Michael Havers and neither were
prepared then, or indeed today, to vouchsafe any explanation for the extraordinary events surrounding *Their
Trade is Treachery.*

Lord Rothschild burst into print on Thursday, December 4, but sadly not for the purpose of detailing his role
in the *Their Trade is Treachery* affair. He wrote a letter
addressed to "The Editor and Readers" of the *Daily
Telegraph* which called on the Government to confirm
that MI5 had "unequivocal, repeat unequivocal" evidence
that he was not and never had been a Soviet agent.

The Prime Minister was apparently taken a little by
surprise by this outburst and it was not until Friday,
December 5, that she issued a one-line clearance of the
elderly peer. "I am advised that we have no evidence
that he ever was a Soviet agent." The clearance of Rothschild was a cause of great relief to Peter Wright. Peter
had been appalled at the smears against Rothschild. He
perhaps more than anyone believed implicitly in Rothschild's integrity and loyalty and, a little too uncritically
I fancy, worshiped him as his mentor in all things to do
with intelligence.

The hearing in Sydney before Justice Powell resumed
momentarily on Friday, December 5. I repeated my challenge to the British to make their allegations about Greengrass in open court. Simos did not rise to the challenge.
The court adjourned until Monday when Wright would
go into the witness box for the first time.

The old man was very anxious about giving evidence.
Old age and diabetes had made him forgetful, particularly

if put under pressure. He had first-class memory, but he often needed time to think before he could be sure he was being accurate. "I am worried they will make a fool of me, Malcolm," he complained. I had saved a lot of time by preparing a thirty-page affidavit for Peter which contained all his evidence in chief. Much of it related to the contents of the book and therefore would have to be edited before it could be published. I reassured him over a whisky at the office. "Don't worry, just take it very slowly. If you need time, ask for it, we have all the time in the world. I don't care if it takes three weeks for you to get the answers straight. Don't let Simos dictate the pace of the cross-examination. Answer at your speed and in your own words. If he's bullying you, complain about it." Peter cheered up at this. "I know a bit about interrogation, Malcolm. I interrogated Blunt for hundreds of hours."

Meanwhile I concentrated on the question of documents. There was only one document I really wanted. It was referred to obliquely in the confidential list of documents as "a synopsis" sent from MI6 to MI5 on December 16, 1980. This suggested that Pincher had provided a synopsis of *Their Trade is Treachery* for informal vetting by MI6 and MI5 only weeks after he got back from Tasmania at the end of November 1980. If this was so, then the Government had wind of the book for at least six weeks before Armstrong had said they had. It created another inconsistency with Armstrong's evidence and added to the evidence which suggested *Their Trade is Treachery* was unofficially authorized.

The press were aware of the synopsis, although not because of any leaks from me. During the Court of Appeal hearing on Thursday, December 4, I referred obliquely to the synopsis by reference to the number it had in the list of documents. Mr. Justice Glass innocently observed: "Oh, the synopsis," and then it did not take much before the more perceptive journalists gathered the nature of this document that I had somewhat theatrically described as "the whale in the bay." I felt that Simos could not refuse to produce the synopsis, since unless it had been actually written by MI6, it was presumably written by Pincher, and I failed to see how his writings could be covered by crown privilege.

So the weekend arrived with much of the spice gone from the trial. Only Wright was left and then it was time for submissions, and then it would be over. As we prepared Peter for the ordeal of the witness box our exhaustion was distracted by some more madness emanating from the British Government. In a breathless piece the *Mail on Sunday* revealed that MI5 was busy reorganizing its agents and moving over twenty-five staff in anticipation of the secret documents which had been produced to Justice Powell being leaked. How anyone would seriously imagine that documents concerning the publication of a few books would contain operational information of this magnitude is hard to credit. But the *Mail* went even further in its welcome home message to Sir Robert. Headlined "Brave Sir Robert fought for us all," *The Mail* observed:

It should be an occasion for national celebration that Sir Robert Armstrong is back with us again—alive and well. Though it's far from clear who he was protecting and why, the fact is that he stepped ashore upon a foreign field to fight the good fight on behalf of us all. Viciously assailed by native tribesmen, he held up high, however tattered it eventually became, the flag of this country.

Sir Robert is indeed the stuff upon which the Empire was made—Gordon of Khartoum, Clive of India, Lawrence of Arabia—what mighty names and what mighty deeds they commemorate. Welcome to this pantheon of heroes, Armstrong of Sydney.

CHAPTER 12

IT WAS THE WEEKEND of December 6 and 7 that I received an unusual telephone call from Brian Barron, the BBC's correspondent. "Malcolm, I have just had confirmed to me from a most senior and reliable Foreign Office source that Sir Robert has confirmed in closed session that Oleg Gordievsky cleared Hollis when he defected in 1985." Gordievsky had been the KGB Head of Station in London and I had asked Armstrong in open court whether Gordievsky had said anything about Hollis. Armstrong declined to answer any questions about that in open court and the matter was pursued in camera.

Barron's call was most disturbing. It was clear that somebody on the Government side was endeavoring to leak confidential evidence, or what purported to be confidential evidence, as a means of discrediting Wright's thesis about Hollis. I called Ivor Roberts, the Foreign Office press officer who had accompanied Armstrong to Sydney to manage the hacks.

The phone rang in his hotel room and Roberts answered. "Hello Ivor, it's Oleg Gordi-bloody-evsky here. You miserable bastard, I'll have you done for contempt leaking confidential evidence like that." I had no reason to believe Ivor would have been responsible for such a leak. The standards of the Foreign Office are *far* too high for such *disgraceful* conduct as spreading misinformation. Nonetheless he was closest to hand and if anyone could find out the culprit, Ivor could. I felt that a violently worded accusation might focus his attention on the task of unmasking the leaker. Ivor was horrified. "Oh, who's that, what do you mean, who are you." I toned down a little. "It's Malcolm Turnbull, Ivor. I've just had a very interesting little telephone call from Brian Barron about Oleg Gordievsky and the confidential sessions . . ." I explained the tale to Roberts. He was highly agitated. "He's obviously gone mad, he's hallucinating." I offered a solution. "Well, Ivor, you give him a ring and tell him to stop hallucinating or you might find yourself receiving a summons for contempt. After you and your chums in London have spent the last week accusing me and Greengrass of leaking confidential evidence, I don't propose to let you get away with it."

About twenty minutes later Barron rang up in high dudgeon. "Look here, Malcolm, I don't think you should have done that. Roberts thinks I told you he was my source."

"Well, was he?"

"You know I can't reveal a source."

"Well if you think Ivor thinks I think he is the source then I can only say if the cap fits, he should wear it. If it doesn't fit him, then he better find the person it does fit, because I propose to issue a summons for contempt against him. If he's not guilty no doubt you will spring into the witness box, exonerate him and in passing implicate the real villain."

"Anyway, as it is, Roberts says if I run the story he'll have the FO onto the BBC in London. You've absolutely blown the whole thing."

"All's fair in love and war, Brian. I still might decide to summons you. Will you reveal your source or go to jail like an honorable journalist?"

"I won't reveal my source, ever."

I decided not to pursue the matter. Whoever was responsible, it underlined the cynicism with which the Government was approaching the litigation.

When the hearing resumed on Monday, December 8, Justice Powell was seething over the *Mail on Sunday* piece.

> In the light of this statement I wish to make it quite clear first that although as I recorded on Monday last, the documents in question were delivered to me at my home on Saturday 29th and Sunday 30th November last for inspection by me, they were on the evening of each day returned to the custody of the plaintiff or its officers.
>
> Secondly, that the documents have not been in my possession since the evening of 30th November last and thirdly that at no time has any member of my staff had access to the documents or any of them.
>
> If, therefore, the item in question is to be read or understood as suggesting that the documents in question have been or are likely to be leaked, I make it abundantly clear that that has not been, nor will it be, as a result of any action on the part of my staff or myself.

Peter limped to the witness box, and began to read from his affidavit. Great slabs of it had been edited from the publicly available version, and his evidence had a curiously disjointed air.

He began by describing how he became involved with MI5. He was working for the Royal Naval Scientific Service at the time.

> 5. In 1950 Sir Frederick Brundrett had established a committee to advise MI5 on scientific matters and the membership was myself and others. The Committee met once a month. Brundrett told me that he had told Sillitoe [Sir Percy Sillitoe, Director-General of MI5] he did not need an eminent scientist with an

FRS to assist the service with scientific matters. He had said you need a young man with a good war, who is a problem solver, as opposed to an analytical theorist. Brundrett set up the committee and proposed me.

6. Brundrett asked me to talk to the people at MI5 and MI6 and establish what sort of problems existed and then write him a paper about it. The basic problem was that there was no application or understanding of science other than what the post office provided. There was also a pretty elementary chemical laboratory for detecting secret writing and developing secret inks. It was almost a schoolboy operation.

7. I agreed with [deletion] that we should explore a number of projects which related to the development of new eavesdropping techniques. I undertook to do some of it in my spare time for no reward. From about 1952 I worked at Marconi's Great Baddow Laboratory at Essex as an officer of the RNSS on a naval contract concerning a special radar system for detecting submarine snorkels.

8. In 1952 as related in the chapters 2–4 [of *Spycatcher*] the CIA and State Department brought me the SATYR microphone which had been found by the Americans in the Great Seal in the ambassador's office in Moscow. They asked me to work out how it operated as notwithstanding their vast resources they had been unable to get it to work properly. It took me twelve weeks to work out how it worked and we subsequently used it as detailed in the book. Following this MI5 recognized that they needed a full time scientist. When I discussed this with the MI5 people [deletions] they all said that they couldn't pay enough to get a man from industry and they were not allowed to poach people from the civil service or transfer people from there. I said "What about me?"

9. They then returned to the no-poaching problem. Finally it was suggested by Cumming that I leave the RNSS and join Marconi's for a while and then move from there to MI5. I was assisted in this scheme by my father who was then engineer in chief of Marconis.

MI5 initially offered me a job at about 1000 pounds less than what I was paid at the RNSS. One of the matters discussed was pension. Since I had been a civil servant for fourteen years I had accrued certain entitlements in respect of my pension which was covered by the Federated Superannuation Scheme for Universities (FSSU) which covered all governmental scientists. This was a scheme which was paid into by the scientists and the Government contributed double the contribution of the scientist. If you left before it matured you lost your entitlement to the Government's contribution. In 1954 the union had succeeded in negotiating with the Government for members of the FSSU to have their entitlements, including the governmental contribution, transferred effectively to the Civil Service scheme which was much more generous, although it was subject to the same proviso that if you retired before the scheme matured the governmental contributions were lost. In the Civil Service scheme however there was no contribution by the employee. I had to decide in 1954 whether to go over to the Civil Service scheme, and at the same time MI5 were asking me to join. The MI5 people were adamant that these entitlements could not be transferred over to the MI5 where they said pensions were in line with those granted by the Civil Service but nonetheless entirely discretionary. They said that I would not be disadvantaged however because they would make up any difference themselves. They said that under the secret vote they were not vetted on how they paid people and they could pay me extra money as an agent or suchlike when I retired. Relying on these assurances I left the RNSS, was paid my contributions back and bought an annuity to cover Lois, my wife, if I died before I was part of the established staff, which took three years. Subsequently the Service failed to honour the undertaking and my pension therefore reflects only my twenty-one years with the Service. It is therefore about 60 percent of what it ought to be.

Wright's affidavit went into pages of detail demonstrating that none of the technical information in *Spycatcher* was even remotely current. Since *Spycatcher* was at that time officially "banned" this evidence was not received into the public transcript. The short point of Wright's evidence on this score however was that all of the radio technology referred to in *Spycatcher* was at least twenty years old. It related to the days before transistorized radios and computers had completely revolutionized communications. He demonstrated, again in confidential sections, how Mrs. Thatcher's statements about Blunt and Hollis were materially false and misleading. He answered each paragraph of Armstrong's affidavits by demonstrating there was nothing in the book which caused the sort of damage about which Sir Robert had been so apparently concerned. His answer to the Government's evidence about the dangers of identifying MI5's informants is typical of Wright's approach:

> 38. Informants generally like their identities to be kept in the dark. However after a long period of time when the informant is dead or long since retired, there will not be any adverse impact by such disclosure. During my career with MI5, I have been aware of the identities of hundreds of informants of varying degrees of sensitivity. I have been careful to remove any reference to persons in the book who could be prejudiced by their being named. In my manuscript the only informant whose name is not in the public domain is [deleted]. For a start that isn't his real name, and secondly I think he is dead. It may be that there are some I have missed. I have repeatedly asked the Government to nominate such names, so they could be removed. The overall objection I have to Sir Robert's contentions is that they never descend from the general to the particular. My book is of historical interest only.

Wright's affidavit went on to summarize his philosophy about Soviet penetration. It was, predictably, an extreme and alarming point of view:

60. For years the secret services have assumed that their work is best done with minimum reporting and accountability to the Government and ultimately the people. When I was young I readily adopted this philosophy. I was told we can't have a formal reporting system because we will be cast in concrete. I now think this is entirely wrong. The work of protecting our society against subversion is too important to leave to the spies, as it were. The British establishment has never accepted that it was, en masse, penetrated by the Russians. It may be that the establishment fears that public debate of this problem will cause the people of Britain to have less faith in its leadership than the Establishment would like it to have. Our society is not materially different today to what it was thirty years ago. People mistakenly see the penetration problem as having been limited to a few colorful, often homosexual, Cambridge intellectuals. It went much further and deeper than that. It revealed a fundamental weakness in British society. Understanding the past will enable us to prevent repetition in the future. In my life I have seen too many people in power turning a blind eye to this sort of thing. [Deletions] And now I see Mrs. Thatcher misleading parliament over Hollis and Blunt. As an experienced intelligence officer I have taken care to ensure that my book is of historical importance only. It will compromise no operations, prejudice no sources and expose no secrets. It will greatly embarrass the Government and probably the Security Service as well. The time has come for there to be openness about the secret world, at least the secret world of so long ago.

64. [Deletions] With so many spies, there is no hope of MI5 catching them all. The answer to Soviet penetration is greater public awareness of the problem. That is the object of my book.

Much of Peter's evidence about Rothschild could not be read out in open court as it related to his years in MI5, but he was able to testify to Rothschild's loyalty

and describe the curious events surrounding his involvement with Pincher. As, for the first time, he started to
tell the story of Victor Rothschild, Chapman Pincher and
himself, the courtroom became deadly quiet and strained
to hear the old man's softly spoken words.

65. I first met Victor Rothschild in 1958. In the
years that followed I came to know him very well. He
had worked in MI5 during most of the war. He was
responsible for investigating all cases of sabotage. He
was awarded the George Medal for bravery. His second
wife Tess received a similar award for bravery in
defusing bombs. [deleted] I am absolutely certain that
neither of them at any time spied for Russia.

74. I left for Tasmania in 1976 after retiring from
MI5. I was due a lump-sum payment of Five Thousand
Pounds which MI5 delayed paying me until my birth-
day in August. I needed the money in January as I
was leaving for Tasmania before August and Victor
lent me Five Thousand Pounds. I made arrangements
for the lump sum to be paid directly to his secretary
and it was so paid in August. I corresponded with
Rothschild occasionally between 1976 and 1978. Indeed he helped me obtain a review of my pension.
The review did not result in any change. At the
moment my pension is Six Hundred Pounds per month.

75. In 1979 Anthony Blunt was exposed as a spy
following publication of Andrew Boyle's book *Climate
of Treason*. Mrs. Thatcher made a statement confirming
Blunt's guilt. This statement was gravely misleading
as I have stated earlier. I had nothing whatever to do
with Blunt's book. In my view she should not have
made the statement she did. She should have either
said nothing or else made a full and accurate statement
about the whole history of the investigation of Soviet
penetration of the British Establishment, if necessary
by the publication of a full White Paper. I believed
at the time that Mrs. Thatcher had been misled by
MI5 over the extent of those investigations. So I began

to write a dossier detailing all that I knew about those investigations, including a [deleted] analysis of the problems of Soviet penetration in the past and how the continuing problem would be met in the future. It was my intention to somehow bring this dossier to the Prime Minister's personal attention.

76. In about August 1980 I received, out of the blue, a letter from Victor. He told me that following Blunt's exposure, people were accusing him of having been another spy, on account of his friendship with Blunt. He asked me to write out a list of his achievements for MI5 which he could publish if necessary. I wrote back and told him I would be happy to do this, but I couldn't go to England as I did not have enough money. Shortly after this Victor telephoned me and told me a courier would be arriving and could I meet him at Hobart airport. We met the courier and he handed me an envelope with a first-class return air ticket to London, open-dated, and nothing else. The courier asked if I had Victor's letter. I said I did and he then asked for it back. I gave it to him.

77. My doctor advised that in view of my health, I could not travel alone. So I exchanged the first-class ticket for two economy tickets and my wife Lois and I flew to England arriving there on August 22, 1980. We went up to stay with my daughter in Yorkshire for about a week. I took the train by myself from York to Euston Station. I took a taxi to Victor's flat at 23 St James Place. We had some drinks and lunch and he explained that he needed a list of his achievements for MI5 because of the rumors circulating about him following the exposure of Blunt. I agreed to provide one and I did.

78. At the time Victor brought me to England, I had completed ten chapters of my dossier. I decided to bring them with me to England to show to Victor to see if he could get them to Mrs. Thatcher. In 1980 I still saw Mrs. Thatcher as a new broom prepared to shake out some of the dusty cupboards in Whitehall and elsewhere. I told Victor about the chapters and

what they contained in his study at his flat. I did not give them to him to read until we were in Cambridge the next day.

79. I told Victor the dossier was not complete, but that I wanted him to give it to Thatcher. I explained to him that if it went to MI5 they'd simply rubbish it and ignore it. Victor said that it was pointless formally giving it to Thatcher, as she would be obliged to give it to MI5. He said to me: "You know she was sitting on this couch only a few days ago. She doesn't understand intelligence." Victor did not elaborate. I knew him well enough to note the significance of what he had said and not to question him about it.

80. We then went up to Cambridge and Victor read the ten chapters of the dossier over the following day and a half. When I had completed my list of Victor's achievements for MI5, I had his secretary type it up and I signed a copy of it. We then discussed my dossier which Victor had read while I was writing the list of his achievements. I wrote the list over a day and a half in his sitting room, while he sat in his study reading the dossier. When I had finished the list, we discussed the list, and I added some more achievements. We then discussed my dossier. He said to me that he thought it was very good and that it was hopeless putting it through official channels. He said that he thought the dossier should be published. He said I would need a ghostwriter and that if the book made any money I would be helped with my financial problems. Rothschild asked me if I knew Chapman Pincher. I did not tell him that I had met Pincher. Rothschild said that Pincher's contacts were so good he could ensure the book was published without official interference. Rothschild also said that such a book by Pincher would probably prompt a parliamentary inquiry into the intelligence and security services.

81. He rang Pincher about 4:00 p.m. and said he would get him to come to dinner. He then went away and made a phone call and Pincher arrived at Cambridge about 6:30 p.m. Rothschild introduced me sim-

ply as Phillip. Pincher gave no indication of recognizing me. Rothschild outlined his proposal to Pincher. He said that I would provide the information, Pincher would write the book and Rothschild would use his Swiss bank to channel half the royalties to me in Tasmania.

82. I concluded in my own mind that I was being used as part of a deniable operation. It never occured to me that Rothschild would lend himself to a scheme of this kind without some degree of official approval. Victor was always very secretive and it was not done to ask him questions. He loved intrigue and conspiracies and was always engaged in secret deals and arrangements, especially with politicians. He loved to exert influence behind the scenes. His wealth and position are so great that I could not believe that he would risk it for such a scheme if it was not at least tacitly approved. I note that since his involvement in this matter has become public, he has not made any denial. It has been suggested that Victor arranged the publication of the book in order to help me financially. That is certainly incorrect. He had offered me a job with his Bank as a consultant in the past and could have done so again. Or he could have given me financial assistance without any risk to himself. Pincher [deleted] had the reputation of being a safe way to let information go into the public domain. His book *Inside Story* contains numerous intelligence secrets and he has never been charged. It struck me as particularly odd that Rothschild should suddenly seek to secure the publication of MI5's secrets about the mole-hunts, since he had always before counselled caution. Before 1980 he always used to tell me that he felt confident that he would be able to secure something through his political connections. For instance, when he was in government he used to tell me that when the time was right he would take any document I wrote and place it personally before Ted Heath. I could only conclude that his proposal was very well considered by him and subject to some sort of approval.

83. I did not suggest the idea of a book. I did not suggest Pincher as an author. My original intention was simply to bring what I knew before the Prime Minister. If I had been able to get Thatcher to read the dossier and do something about it I would have been much more content than helping Pincher write a book. I was happy to get the additional money. It was not my motivation to help Pincher, however. In due course I received a total of Thirty Thousand Pounds all of which was sent to my bank at Huonville from the Union Bank in Zurich, and this can be checked.[1] The use of the Swiss bank meant that nobody could trace the identity of the person sending me the money.

84. Pincher came to Tasmania for about a week, not three days as I thought earlier. Pincher already knew most of the matters relevant to the book. He was particularly well informed about the Hollis case. I do not know who told him, but Rothschild was certainly in a position to do so, having been told by me. He certainly had enough to write a book without me, although I did provide him with a deal of detail. It is perfectly obvious from *Inside Story* Chapter 1 pp. 16 to 18 that Victor provided Pincher with some information about me. I know this to be so because the only two possible sources for that information are Victor and myself and I know I didn't tell Pincher about it prior to the publication of *Inside Story*.

85. Pincher returned to England. We corresponded using pseudonyms. I had believed I had lost all the correspondence and said so in my answers to the Interrogatories. However on the second day of the trial here a box of papers appeared at Mr. Turnbull's office. It was from my previous solicitors, Corrs Pavey Whiting and Byrne. In that box was the correspondence with Pincher which I now recall giving them

1. The Thirty Thousand Pounds (about $50,000) was barely sufficient to pay off the debts Wright had run up on his unsuccessful horse breeding business.

over a year ago when the injunction was placed on
the book.

86. Pincher did not at any time show me a synopsis
or a complete manuscript. I did not see the book until
it was published. I was very disappointed with Pincher
because the last chapter of the book concluded that
there was no need for an inquiry. This conclusion was
quite contrary to my views. I did provide Pincher with
some information about Soviet penetration after the
publication of *Their Trade is Treachery*. Pincher and I
in fact discussed a second book on intelligence matters
which would deal with Soviet penetration issues on
both sides of the Atlantic. He did not tell me he was
going to write a second book *Too Secret Too Long;* in
fact he denied that a second book would be written.
I received no money from Pincher, or anyone else, in
respect of that second book.

Peter's tale about Rothschild confirmed the information
which had leaked into the public domain over the previous
weeks. Dealing quickly with the interview on Granada
Television, he concluded his affidavit with some personal
remarks:

91. Lastly I want to stress that my patriotism is
undiminished. I worked for my country for more than
thirty years and shouldered many heavy responsibilities. I believe my achievements especially in the scientific modernization of intelligence and in the im-
provements of Anglo-American relations are proof of
my service to the country. I was awarded the CBE in
1972. I have become an Australian citizen as has my
wife. Notwithstanding my many years of hard work
for Britain, I believe that my greatest and most important work has been in exposing the way Britain's
leaders have shut their eyes to the problems of Soviet
penetration. As Pope Gregory VII observed: *Dilexi
iustitiam et odi iniquitatem. Propterea morior in exilio;*

translated means: I have loved Justice and hated In-
iquity. Therefore I die in Exile.

It had been a long job reading his affidavit and Peter
was tired. He looked up from the paper and the tears
were plain in his eyes. The judge seemed affected and
adjourned the court twenty minutes sooner than was
customary.

Peter climbed down from the witness box. "You've
done well, Peter," Greengrass told him. "That'll show
the bastards," he replied.

The next day it was Peter's turn to be cross-examined.
He was nervous as we walked to court across the park.
"Mrs. Thatcher will want him to really tear me to pieces."

"Theo is nature's gentleman. He has none of my coarse
advocate's tricks."

"But she will insist on him accusing me of lying."

"Are there any lies in your affidavit?"

"No."

"Well take heart, Peter, you have nothing to fear."

"Now I know how Philby felt," Peter muttered.

"It took them another ten years after the interrogation
to find him out," Greengrass observed, to general hilarity.

Simos was faced with a difficult task. It was plain that
the British had not provided Theo with anything like the
detailed brief he would need to take Peter to task. Had
they wanted to destroy him, they would have needed a
couple of experienced intelligence officers feeding Theo
questions the way Greengrass was feeding them to me.
Instead Theo gave the distinct impression of having barely
read *Spycatcher* itself.

So instead Theo skirmished with Wright. He asked
Wright why he had not disclosed to the Court that he
had rediscovered the Wright-Pincher correspondence as
soon as it reappeared. Wright was a little nonplussed and
I intervened to say that the fault was mine, if fault there
was. The letters did not seem relevant to the case the

Government was trying to prove and Wright gave full particulars of the matter in his affidavit. As Theo labored on with this small point, the judge's patience was sorely tried.

Tuesday, December 9, 1986

His Honor	What is the purpose of the question Mr. Simos? I merely point out that if the suggestion is that the defendant is guilty of some misdemeanor in failing to answer interrogatories, a far greater comment can be made about the plaintiff who, if I may say so, had to be dragged into this court every time as the result of its interpretation of issues in interrogatories.
Mr. Simos	Of course we do not accept that with respect.
His Honor	Perhaps you do not, but that is my view Mr. Simos.

The next issue Simos took up with Wright was his press statement of November 25, 1986 when he responded to the inspired reports in *The Times* that he had received money for his part in the publication of *Their Trade is Treachery.* We had knocked the statement together in a great hurry and in it Wright said that at the time he was introduced to Pincher he was "terrified of getting into trouble." Simos asked him whether he had been terrified at the time. Wright said he hadn't, but acknowledged there was an inconsistency. Simos then endeavored to discover the names of those who had helped Wright with the preparation of the manuscript. I successfully objected to this. It was an attempt to elicit admissible evidence of the role of Greengrass, which we were anxious to suppress, for his own sake.

Theo wound up with a question about Thatcher.

Q.	I want to put to you that Mrs. Thatcher's two statements to the House concerning firstly Blunt and secondly Hollis were accurate?
A.	They were certainly not accurate. I was the senior case officer in both those matters.

On that odd note, Simos' cross-examination ended and I rose to re-examine. I needed to clarify the muddle about the press statement.

Q.	The statement of November 25 that Mr. Simos showed you, do you remember that?
A.	Yes.
Q.	How much time and consideration was able to be given to the drafting of that statement given the attack on you in *The Times?*
A.	Ten minutes, I should have thought, something like that.
Q.	Just turning to the arrangement with Rothschild and Pincher, you have said in your affidavit it was a deniable operation. Can you explain to his Honour what you mean by the phrase "deniable operation?"
A.	It is an operation which the authorities that had mounted it will disown it if anything goes wrong.
Q.	What would the consequences have been for you, a participant in a deniable operation, if the nature of the operation had become public and the authorities that authorized it had disowned it, as you said?
A.	In the extreme I would have been sent to prison.

Q.   Going back to Rothschild and Pincher, you have stated you believed it was a deniable operation. Can you answer that?

A.   Yes.

Q.   Did you have any concern that this operation which you believed to be a deniable one could become blown and disowned by the authorities?

A.   It was certainly deniable in the sense that Lord Rothschild would have denied having anything to do with it. If there was participation by the authorities behind it, whatever they were, I believe that both Pincher and the authorities and Rothschild would have disowned me.

Q.   Did you therefore have any apprehension of public risk to yourself at the time you entered into it?

A.   Not really because I had tremendous faith in Lord Rothschild.

Q.   If Lord Rothschild had disowned you . . .?

A.   Yes, it would have been too bad.

Q.   Too bad for you?

A.   Yes, for me.

Theo indicated his clients wanted formal production of the Wright-Pincher correspondence.

I had a quiet word to him. "Theo, if you want it, you can have it, but bear in mind that once you have this correspondence your chaps may have to prosecute Pincher and Rothschild. The correspondence is most unedifying. Now without that correspondence there may not be enough evidence to charge them. Have a think about it. Peter wants to protect Rothschild." Theo gave me a shrewd look, and conferred with his colleagues.

When we resumed after the luncheon adjournment he informed the judge that he did not wish to cross-examine

Wright any further and he did not wish to pursue the
question of the correspondence.

We returned to my office and a press conference.
Norman Tebbit, the chairman of the Conservative Party,
had accused Peter of "ratting on his friends" and the
old boy was seething with anger. Hitherto no one had
questioned his patriotism; even Armstrong had agreed in
a brief chat outside court that Peter was a fine patriot
. . . misguided maybe, but a patriot nonetheless.

Peter said Tebbit's criticism was "absolute rubbish."
He said: "I am extremely loyal. I have done far more
for my country, England, than most people. I have made
it clear to the British Government that I will take anything
out of the book that would damage them. They are
embarrassed because they have made a mess of it. The
book is embarrassing to them because they have told a
whole lot of lies, it's as simple as that." His angry patriotism was at its most visible there. Right or wrong he
was a loyal Queen's man to the very last.

As the reporters started to ask Peter to name the names
of other moles in the establishment, I realized we were
moving onto thin ice and stopped the press conference.
He was disappointed at being shut up, but as usual accepted my guidance with good grace.

Wright's composure in the witness box was remarkable
for a man with his disabilities. The British had chosen
not to attack him, and I was grateful for that, but I felt
at least his sincerity had shown through. He did believe
everything he said, and he did believe that by saying it
he was serving England better than its Prime Minister.
Only history will prove whether he was right.

CHAPTER 13

I HAD OFFERED TO reach a negotiated settlement over the documents issue. On Wednesday, December 10, that settlement was reached. Simos agreed to make certain admissions concerning the contents of the documents and to produce a copy of the synopsis. This synopsis was written by Pincher in December 1980 and provided by him to Sir Arthur Franks, then head of MI6. Simos read out the agreed admissions. They painted a very different picture of the *Their Trade is Treachery* affair. He admitted that on or a little before December 15, 1980 MI6 had received a synopsis.

> *Synopsis*
> *Their Trade is Treachery* (Dedicated to "The loyal members of the Security and Intelligence Services, on whom so much depends.")
> *Prime purpose*—to expose, by case records, the true extent of the Communist conspiracy to undermine the fabric of British life and the ruthless methods used by the Russians and their allies to trap the unwary into serving as spies and saboteurs.
> *Contents*
> 1. The full, unexpurgated story of the treachery of Anthony Blunt—the crimes which make him one of the most damaging spies in history, contrary to the

belief that he was small fry. His part in the Ring of
Five—including the surprising truth about Burgess,
Maclean, Philby, Driberg and others. The espionage
activities to which Blunt confessed—or gave unwitting
leads. How he "blew" Driberg, the double agent. How
Blunt saved Philby in 1951. The real Fifth Man. The
Labour MP spy who committed suicide. The truth
about Tomas Harris and the real reason why Blunt
confessed in 1964. etc., etc.,

2. The dramatic search for "moles" inside MI5 and
the Secret Service. Philby, Blake and Blunt not the
only ones. How the others were tracked down by an
official MI5-Secret Service team. The chief suspects
and those who confessed—*now all dead.*

3. The evidence that both Services are now "clean"
of Russian penetration. The steps taken to ensure that
they stay that way.

4. In the context of the search for "moles," the
truth about the Vassall Case, the Navy Secrets Ring.

5. The penetration of the Foreign Office—Maclean,
Cairncross and other exposed by Blunt. The Russian
penetration of the British Embassy in Moscow. The
attempt to suborn ambassadors.[1] The Foreign Office
and Philby. "Emerton"—the self confessed spy of whom
the public has never heard. (now dead).

6. The penetration of Parliament. The new rules
laid down by Wilson. (MPs immune to investigation).
The truth about Driberg and Henry Kerby. The MI5
inquiry into the mystery of Gaitskell's death. etc., etc.,

7. Round-up—what the facts imply. The vital importance of MI5 and the Security Service in protecting
the nation against subversion and sabotage. How the
Russians never stop—the current penetration of the
CIA.

N.B. All the information in this book has been
gleaned from authorities who are deeply concerned
about the Soviet penetration of Whitehall and its off-

---

1. Suborn: to induce a person to commit an unlawful, or in this
case, treacherous act.

shoots and believe that the public needs to be warned about its full extent and purposes. None of it—according to professional advice—can prejudice current or future operations by British agencies or damage the present image of the Security or Intelligence Services. *The security aspects of the various situations are outdated. It is the truth that is new.* It has been concealed solely because of the traditional zeal of Civil Servants to "protect" their departments.

Simos produced a copy of this synopsis and then made a number of admissions. They were in answer to a shopping list I had prepared for him.

As far as *A Matter of Trust* by Nigel West was concerned, Simos said that MI5 became aware that Mr. West was writing the book and believed that it contained information provided to him by former officers of MI5 and/or MI6 by September 23, 1982, which was also the date MI5 received the original manuscript.

As far as *Their Trade is Treachery* was concerned, Simos said that MI5 received the synopsis on or a little before December 15, 1980. It was sent to MI5 from MI6 together with a letter which stated that the writer had been informed that Chapman Pincher intended to publish, probably in February or March 1981, a book about the Security Service, a synopsis of which was enclosed.

He said that it was generally agreed in the security and intelligence services that there would be no point in trying to encourage specific deletions or changes in the text, but no reasons are expressed for this view.

He said that the manuscript was first read in February 1981 when it appeared that much of the information in it had come from former members of the security and intelligence services. By March 12, 1981 several sources had been identified, but it was stated in writing by an officer of the Service to Sir Robert Armstrong that the Service was a long way from obtaining hard usable evidence on sources, and it was stated orally to Sir Robert Armstrong that the advance copy was obtained on conditions which made it impossible to take any action about it, which view was later recorded.

So far as Chapman Pincher's second book, *Too Secret Too Long* was concerned, Simos said that the documents showed that the Security Service first knew on July 19, 1984 of the report in *The Times* as to the forthcoming book. On September 3, 1984 the Security Service was informed that Chapman Pincher was claiming that he had received material from former MI5 officers. On October 26, 1984 the Security Service had a copy of the book. The documents do not state reasons for not seeking an injunction, but state the view that the central argument is much the same as in *Their Trade is Treachery* about whether Hollis was a spy, filled out with additional detailed comment.

So far as the Peter Wright TV Interview in the "World in Action" program in 1984 was concerned, Simos said the documents showed that the Security Service had information by May 4, 1984 that there were plans for a "World In Action" program in which Wright was assisting and might take part. The Security Service had information by July 3, 1984 that Granada TV intended to show an interview with Wright in which Wright would reopen the Hollis case and, in effect, present the case against him and so advised the Treasury Solicitor in a letter of that date. Following a report in *The Times* on July 16, 1984, the day of the broadcast, the likelihood that Wright had breached the Official Secrets Act was noted and it was presumed that he had taken the precaution of remaining outside the United Kingdom jurisdiction.

Following an article in *The Times* the possibility of asking for a preview of the program and seeking to restrain publication, if necessary by means of an injunction, was discussed on the telephone between the Treasury Solicitor's department and the Security Service. The view was expressed that, if a preview was refused, going for an injunction would undoubtedly be a hard fight and if a preview was agreed the Government could be put in the position of appearing to have approved it whether or not it asked for cuts.

After that discussion the view of the Security Service conveyed to the Treasury Solicitor's department was that the interests of the Security Service would be best served by not taking action at that stage (July 16, 1984) although the question of taking legal action would need to be reconsidered if Wright returned to the United Kingdom jurisdiction.

This communication appears to have been made late in the day and the documents do not show that any further consideration was given to the possibility of restraining the broadcast of the program.

With those admissions the evidence in the case was now complete. As a condition of being allowed to fly home the previous week, Armstrong had undertaken to the court to return for further cross-examination if I required him. I advised the court that I had no further need of Sir Robert. Simos indicated he was not proposing to re-examine Sir Robert. The judge adjourned the hearing until the following Monday when submissions from counsel would begin.

The admissions made by Simos were in stark contrast with the evidence given by Sir Robert. Armstrong had said on oath that as far as he was aware the Government had not been aware of the forthcoming publication of *Their Trade is Treachery* until February 1981. Yet in December a synopsis had been forwarded to MI6 (then headed by Pincher's lunching chum, Sir Arthur Franks). As the London press were not slow to point out, either Sir Robert had yet again misled the court, or MI5 had misled him. Whitehall predictably trumpeted the deal over the documents as a great triumph. For my own part I was perfectly happy. I had always doubted that there would be much joy in the documents since Peter constantly insisted that they would be "filleted" by MI5 before they were allowed anywhere near the lawyers. "We did it all the time, Malcolm; I am sure they haven't changed," he told me.

I was however still in some doubt whether I should have fought on over the documents as a means of giving the Government an honorable justification for pulling out of the case. I had gravely underestimated Mrs. Thatcher's determination earlier on in the litigation. Was I now overestimating it? If we had obtained discovery, even after appeals, of some documents, would she have chucked it in there and then? I had taken the view that she would not have done so, and on balance I still believe I was correct.

On Monday, December 15, 1986, the trial resumed. Peter Wright gave some brief supplementary evidence to demonstrate that the synopsis had been written by Pincher on the same typewriter which he used to write his letters to Peter, a number of which were tendered as examples. Peter must have been feeling uncharacteristically modest that morning because he told the judge in his evidence in chief that he was not "an expert in typewriting." Fortunately, his cross-examination by Theo Simos enabled Peter to correct the misapprehension about his expertise.

Monday, December 15, 1986

Q.	You said you were not an expert but you have some experience. What experience have you had?
A.	On and off about twenty years.
Q.	But what did you do?
A.	Whenever a letter appeared in a case that I thought had been typed by somebody that I knew, I had a look at it first and then we used to send all typewriting and handwriting comparison problems to an expert at the Welsh University.

Q.   How many times did you have a look at it first, as it were, in relation to various letters?

A.   Every time—I wouldn't know—I dealt with hundreds of cases in MI5.

Q.   Was the expert opinion ever contrary to your own non-expert opinion?

A.   No.

Simos began his closing address. People think of counsel's addresses as long flowing speeches. Generally they are somewhat disjointed, as extracts from evidence and law reports are read to the judge. The judge himself regularly intervenes and Justice Powell was no exception. The submissions are more of a debate between counsel and judge, with the judge always playing devil's advocate testing the argument for its weaknesses. Simos adhered to his absolute argument. Wright's book was a breach of confidence and would damage MI5 even if all of its contents had been previously published. He denied there was sufficient evidence to demonstrate a conspiracy over *Their Trade is Treachery*, but said in any event, even if Government had in the past been lax in enforcing the obligation of confidence, that did not mean it should be prevented from doing so now.

He referred repeatedly to Michael Codd's evidence as proving publication of *Spycatcher* was against the public interest of Australia. Justice Powell was unimpressed. Codd had cut very little ice with him, and he let Simos know it. However it was on the *Their Trade is Treachery* affair that Simos had the roughest ride. Justice Powell plainly did not accept Armstrong's explanation for not seeking an injunction to stop Pincher publishing that book.

His Honor   I am faced with a set of facts which to me, as a lawyer, are just inexplicable and I am not provided with an answer which I can accept. Now that is not Sir Robert's

	fault. It is the fault of those who "put him up." If that is the way the British Government wants to run its case, so be it.
Mr. Simos	We submit with respect that there is sufficient information in Sir Robert's . . .
His Honor	I know what you say. I know what Sir Robert says and, as I say, I am prepared for the purposes of this argument to accept every word he says. I still say if I had been sitting up there in the Royal Courts of Justice in the Strand in the Chancery Division and you had come skidding through the door with a short Nursaw-type affidavit you would have gone out with one of my cheerio calls that said "Stop that, you wretched fellow," and, what is more important, "Give me all the evidence, before you turn up to be shot." You could not have failed in London.
Mr. Simos	Perhaps our mistake was in not applying for an Anton Piller order from your Honor.
His Honor	At the present rate of progress it may not have done you any good here but if you had got on in London you might have done pretty well. I just cannot accept, Mr. Simos, bearing in mind what happened to Mr. West [author of *A Matter of Trust* which was quickly injuncted by the Government as soon as it got wind of its impending publication]. He got hit between the eyes with a 160 mm hammer.

Simos' submissions had taken over two days and it was not until 11:00 a.m. on Wednesday, December 17, that I rose to address. Most of Theo's address had been on very technical legal matters and I had prepared extensive submissions in reply to them. However I knew that to win the case I had to win it on its merits. I had to persuade the judge that the British had not been straight with him, that they had no absolute principle of silence and that they had over the years authorized and acquiesced in other works not dissimilar to *Spycatcher*. If I could do that, I felt I could win. I started with the credit of Sir Robert Armstrong.

Sir Robert's evidence and his demeanour showed him to be a man with no regard for the truth, rather a man determined to say whatever he felt would advance the Government's cause, regardless of its truth or falsity. His evidence is worthless. Sir Robert is the classical fall guy: an ambassador for Britain, in the sense that an ambassador is a man sent abroad to lie for his country. It is not possible to shield Sir Robert from the consequences of his mendacity, but it would be unfair not to say that the real responsibility for his disgraceful conduct lies with those in London who sent him here to lie and dissemble to this court.

I then reminded the judge of the changes in testimony on *A Matter of Trust* and *Their Trade is Treachery*. I had tendered the House of Commons Hansards and submitted that Sir Robert's change in testimony had come only as a result of pressure being exerted on the Government by Neil Kinnock in the Commons.

It is submitted that the court should take the gravest view of the evidence concerning the Attorney's role in the *Their Trade is Treachery* affair. Sir Robert is the most important civil servant in Britain; he is a lucid, highly educated, intelligent and experienced man who would never have risen to his great office had he not been a master of detail. The broad brush may be all right for politicians, but it is certainly not for civil servants. His previous lack of recollection about *Their*

Trade is Treachery is hard to credit given, one, that it was a very important affair with which he was personally involved; two, that he actually received a written communication about it; three, that he knew it was going to be the subject of inquiry and examination and cross-examination in this court; and four, it is at odds with his own excellent memory on other matters. In answering Interrogatory 150 he was advised by the Treasury Solicitor's office and by no less than the Treasury Solicitor, Mr. John Bailey, and his deputy, Mr. Hogg. These men similarly must be experienced and careful, meticulous and learned in the law and practice of the great nation they serve. They sat in court throughout Sir Robert's evidence. They heard him describe their role in drawing the answer to Interrogatory 150. They heard him tell the court that it was the Plaintiff himself, Sir Michael Havers, who took the final decision, not the Government. They did not seek to correct him. They were not called to explain their part in this egregious error. The court can only conclude the failure to call these men was because their evidence would not have supported Sir Robert's later explanation.

It is therefore impossible to believe that these three men, Sir Robert, Mr. Bailey and Mr. Hogg, did not know that the Attorney-General, Sir Michael Havers, played no role in the affair of *Their Trade is Treachery*. It is impossible to believe that these answers which implicated the Attorney personally were not checked with him before they were sworn and filed in these proceedings.

However even if the court were minded to give Messrs. Armstrong, Bailey and Hogg the benefit of the doubt and to ascribe the answer to Interrogatory 150 to a degree of carelessness, there can be no doubt that Sir Michael Havers and the Prime Minister knew of Sir Robert's testimony concerning Sir Michael as soon as it was given and certainly no later than Thursday, November 20 when Mr. Kinnock first raised it in the House of Commons. The following day the

Attorney answered a written question which also showed he was aware of Sir Robert's evidence. From that time on, at the very latest, Sir Michael Havers knew that Sir Robert's testimony was false. Yet it was not for another week, after Mrs. Thatcher's reluctant answer to Mr. Kinnock on Thursday, November 27, that Sir Robert was told to tell the truth. Again it is inconceivable that even if Sir Robert had been stating his true belief on Tuesday, November 18, he or Messrs. Bailey and Hogg had not been advised by Sir Michael that he had not been personally involved. The best construction which can be placed on these answers, giving the plaintiff the benefit of every doubt, no matter how small or how unlikely, is that Sir Michael Havers allowed Sir Robert Armstrong to give evidence in New South Wales which Sir Michael knew was false. In other words if Sir Robert, Mr. Bailey and Mr. Hogg were honest and careless fools, then Sir Michael Havers was guilty of the worst form of dishonesty: he allowed another man to lie on his behalf and did nothing to correct it. This conduct of Sir Michael's is doubly grave given his status as Attorney-General. Presumably Sir Michael knows the importance of telling the truth in court; his whole life has been devoted to the law and the administration of justice. If Sir Robert is innocent of any conscious deceit, then Sir Michael's conduct is so dishonorable it is a matter the court should take into account if it reaches the stage of considering what discretionary relief should be granted.

It must be stressed however that the defense does not submit that Sir Michael was alone in this dishonest attempt to conceal the truth from this court. The court is entitled to use its common sense and knowledge of the ways of the world and must come to the conclusion that on the balance of probabilities Sir Robert and Messrs. Bailey and Hogg were aware that Sir Michael was not personally involved at the time the answer to Interrogatory 150 was sworn and at the time Sir Robert first gave evidence on this issue, on Tuesday, November 18. To find otherwise would be to ascribe a degree of carelessness to these three men quite out of keeping with their training and professional life. The court should further conclude that in any event the three men were advised of the true position shortly after November 18. Given the manner I pressed Sir Robert it is inconceivable that the matter was not raised with London and the true position discussed with Sir Michael. Finally the court should find the only reason the truth was finally told was because Mr. Kinnock put so much pressure on the Prime Minister in the House of Commons that at last a chink of truth appeared, and it is part of the evidence that it was after that answer on November 27 that Sir Robert was told to tell the truth.

Why did Sir Robert lie? Why did the British Government, its Prime Minister, its Attorney-General and its Treasury Solicitor sit by allowing the lies to be told for so long? The answer lies in the special status of the Attorney-General. The dignity, importance and independence of that post are too well known to rehearse here. The advice said to have been given about *Their Trade is Treachery* was most peculiar. It is simply nonsense to say that in applying for an injunction the Attorney would have risked exposing the source of the manuscript. It is further nonsense to say that it was necessary to nominate the precise source of Pincher's information. Any lawyer with any knowledge of this area of the law recognizes that much. But the lie is given by the nature of the evidence used to obtain an interim injunction against West. In Nursaw's affidavit, there is no reference to West's source for the information in the manuscript or to the person who gave the manuscript to MI5. Faced with this problem of improbable legal advice, the plaintiff chose to attribute it to the Attorney-General. It was just believable that unlikely advice of this kind would be accepted if it came from the first law officer of the Crown and it related to a decision peculiarly that of the Attorney in his independent role. Sir Robert repeatedly said that it was not for him to question the Attorney's advice or decision. That strained credulity a bit, but it was just believable that in the more formal world of Whitehall, the Attorney's views would be accepted without question, no matter how odd they might appear on the face of it. There was always a chance the court would accept this version of events, so long as the Attorney-General was prepared to take the rap. Once the pressure got too great, the truth emerged.

My submissions moved onto other more prosaic matters of law. I argued that there was simply no justification for restraining Wright from publishing information that was a matter of common knowledge. I repeated my offer to Simos of an agreed blue-pencilling exercise.

> If he can demonstrate a piece in that book which has not been made previously published, if he can say to us that is going to be a problem, then, subject to it being a sensible request, we will take it out.

I outlined yet again the evidence about the *Their Trade is Treachery* affair and submitted that the book must have been published as part of a covert government operation to leak the Hollis story into the public domain. If the Government's position was correct, and there was no such conspiracy, the following inconsistencies, at the very least, arose:

> (a) Why would Lord Rothschild with all his connections, wealth and respectability suggest such an unlawful enterprise to Wright and then procure the writer and act as a channel for the royalties?
> (b) Why did Rothschild fly Wright to England? If all he needed was the list of his achievements, Wright could have done that in Tasmania and sent it back with the courier.
> (c) Why would someone close to Pincher provide the synopsis to MI6, when if the Government was opposed that would be certain to draw an injunction?

(d) Why would the synopsis so provided be so concerned with assuring its reader that the book would not damage the intelligence services? A synopsis for a publisher would presumably be more devoted to emphasising the sensational features of the book, rather than its political responsibility.

(e) There was plainly a good cause of action to get an injunction on the basis of the synopsis. Why didn't the Government act?

(f) Pincher was a friendly journalist. Why not at least try to talk him round, at least get him to cut some material out?

(g) Why did someone close to Pincher provide the page proofs to MI6? If the Government was opposed, that surely would draw a hostile response.

(h) Why didn't the Government seek an injunction after it got the page proofs?

(i) Why did the Government receive and then accept such ludicrous legal advice?

(j) Why did the Government not seek the advice of the Attorney-General or some other senior lawyer? According to Sir Robert this sort of matter is in the Attorney's area of responsibility.

(k) Why did Sir Robert give false testimony about the Attorney's role in the affair and why did the Attorney allow him to do so for so long after he must have known what Sir Robert was saying about him?

(l) Why did Pincher draw a very different conclusion in his book from that favoured by Wright? Pincher's conclusion was precisely what the Government wanted to hear: no current penetration problem, no need for an inquiry.

(m) Why were the synopsis and page proofs sent to MI6, then headed by Pincher's lunching companion, Sir Arthur Franks? The logical place to send it was MI5 to which it was sent by MI6.

(n) Why did Pincher give twenty-one months warning of *Too Secret Too Long* to Sir Arthur Franks? Why did Franks report this straightaway to Sir Robert Armstrong?

(o) Why did the Government do nothing to attempt to track down the source? It was only a matter of making routine inquiries about Pincher's movements and having the police interview the local suspected informants and then Wright would be narrowed down very quickly as the principal informant.

Simos had argued that if all the principal allegations in the book were in the public domain already, how was the public interest served by their repetition in *Spycatcher*? I answered his argument in this way:

Let us look again at Winston Churchill. No doubt all the fascist sympathisers in the British establishment, all the Jew haters, would have been very happy for Winston Churchill to stop breaching the Official Secrets Act and revealing confidential information given to him by civil servants in Whitehall. Enough is enough, Mr. Churchill, we have heard enough about the German air force, we have heard enough about the Jews.

The fact of the matter is that nothing is achieved in this world, particularly politically, other than with persistence, and persistence involves repetition and it involves argument and re-argument; and there is a great public interest in that today, just as there was in Churchill's time, and just as it was not possible in 1936 to say that Winston Churchill was right or wrong—although we now know of course that he was right—so it is not possible today to say that Peter Wright is right or wrong. We may in ten years' time, in one hundred years' time, know.

The problem inherent in Mr. Simos' argument is that it misconceives the whole nature of the freedom of speech. The public interest in free speech is not just in truthful speech, in correct speech, in fair speech, in speech one point at a time and never to be repeated. The interest is in the debate. You see, every person who has ultimately changed the course of history has started off being unpopular. When the Australian

Workers Union was founded under a tree in the bush, when unionists were not permitted to even go on to squatters' properties, there were plenty of people and, I am afraid to say plenty of judges, in those far off days who supported the establishment against those people. They spoke out, and they spoke again and they said the same thing a great deal more than once and finally they changed history and there are few people today that would say the struggle of the labour movement in this country and the struggle of other people who have been unpopular—Winston Churchill if you like—was not in the public interest, because ultimately these ideas are tested in debate and it is that debate in which there is a public interest, not in having a say once and once only.

Theo rose to make his submissions in reply. His clients had given him a little speech to read, and it was vintage Lobby copy. Responding to my remarks about Havers and Armstrong, he said:

Mr. Simos	Those submissions, your Honor, of the defendants in relation to the credit of Sir Robert Armstrong and Sir Michael Havers, were extravagant, melodramatic and outrageous; inappropriate even as a jury address but doubly inappropriate as an address to a judge of this court, sitting without a jury. The submissions were baseless and unjustified and should be rejected out of hand. The submissions were full of schoolboy debating tricks, full of emotive clichés and mixed metaphors of which even a third-rate journalist could not be proud.
Mr. Turnbull	Unlike what you are saying.

Simos continued for a few more hours and on Friday afternoon the trial ended. It was something of an anticlimax. Once Armstrong left most of the excitement went with him, and tying up the legal ends in submissions lacked the drama of cross-examining the Cabinet Secretary.

The journalists went home, Peter and Lois returned to Tasmania, Lucy and I reacquainted ourselves with our children and Mr. Justice Powell retired to his chambers to write his judgment. He invited all the lawyers and journalists into his chambers for a drink after the case ended and the press contingent presented him with a framed courtroom sketch by Bill Leak showing him on the Bench surveying his court and its inhabitants. Powell was full of good humor. His quirky sense of humor and candor had rattled the British somewhat, and a lot of harsh things had been said about him. But he ran a fair and generally happy court, and he had forgotten more about equity law than his critics had ever known.

Those who felt Justice Powell had been harsh on the British overlooked the history of the case. The real damage to the British case had occurred during my cross-examination of Armstrong. The judge could not have stopped that cross-examination; it was all relevant to the issues in the case. Indeed Armstrong was cross-examined, though with somewhat less vigor, on precisely the same issues when he gave evidence in the later New Zealand and English proceedings. Powell's critics perhaps reveal more about the way they believe courts should react to powerful civil servants. If they expected an Australian judge to treat a civil servant differently from any other witness, they were bound to be disappointed.

Christmas arrived, and we repaired to the beach. As I lay on the sand in January 1987, I reflected that had I been there twelve months before, I might never have met Peter Wright.

CHAPTER 14

PHILLIP POWELL LABORED ON his judgment through January, February and March. He first read every book, newspaper article and television script which we had tendered into evidence. Then he read *Spycatcher*. He delivered his 286 page decision on Friday, March 13, 1987. I had tried to put the case out of my mind in the intervening three months. Pressure of work had helped. Kerry Packer had decided to sell his television network to Alan Bond in January and together with my partner Bruce McWilliam I had spent most of January negotiating that billion dollar sale. February found me fighting, and ultimately losing, a battle for a television station one of whose former stars was suing it for $8 million damages for breach of contract.

I became very apprehensive about the result and was feeling a little downcast as I walked through the gaggle of photographers on that March morning. My fears were groundless. Justice Powell dismissed the British Government's case and ordered it to pay our costs. My opponent, Theo Simos, was as courteous and gentlemanly as ever. "You have won a great victory, Malcolm, congratulations."

From the books and articles he had read, Justice Powell pieced together a history of the intelligence services and the various leaks of information about them over the last twenty years or so.

Powell found that Wright had not been employed under a contract, as the Government alleged. He said that Wright *did* owe a duty of confidentiality to the British Government, but that duty only extended to matter which remained confidential and the publication of which would cause real detriment to the Government. In this respect he was following to the letter a decision of the High Court of Australia; Commonwealth v. Fairfax in which Sir Anthony Mason had stated the limits within which governments can protect their secrets.

Powell did not find that Armstrong had lied to the court; his criticism of him was somewhat more muted. He described the extraordinary events surrounding *Their Trade is Treachery* and, as he had indicated during the trial, said that he could not accept the Government's explanation as to why they did not seek an injunction to stop publication of the book.

> It is no understatement to say that the evidence on this aspect of the matter . . . has been left in a thoroughly unsatisfactory state. This being so, it is hardly surprising that, in his submissions at the conclusion of his evidence, Mr. Turnbull mounted a vigorous and sustained attack on Sir Robert Armstrong's credibility, and submitted that his evidence—not only on this, but on all matters of significance—was totally unacceptable; indeed he went so far as to describe Sir Robert Armstrong as "an ambassador for Britain, in the sense that an ambassador is a man sent abroad to lie for his country."
>
> Although, after much consideration, I find myself unable to accept Mr. Turnbull's submission that Sir Robert Armstrong deliberately set out to mislead the court . . . I have nonetheless come to the conclusion that much of his evidence on matters of importance must be treated with considerable reserve.

Powell did not accept my submissions on the conspiracy theory surrounding *Their Trade is Treachery*. He did not do so for two reasons. First he said that Sir Robert's letter to Mr. William Armstrong on March 23, 1981 indicated a desire by Sir Robert to mislead Sidgwick and Jackson as to whether the Government had a copy of the book. Why would he have bothered to do this if there had been an orchestrated conspiracy between the Government and the publishers? Second, he said that Pincher in the paperback edition of *Their Trade is Treachery* seems to have delighted in the fact that MI5 had had to conceal its, no doubt, covert obtaining of the book. He went on, however, to find that the Government had been given more than adequate warning of the book and had made a conscious decision to allow it to be published, knowing that this would place into the public domain previously secret information.

As Pincher himself was later to reveal, Justice Powell was quite mistaken. Far from the publishers being unaware of the Government having a copy of *Their Trade is Treachery,* a shadowy intermediary acting on behalf of the publishers had actually given a copy of the manuscript to MI6 for the express purpose of seeking their informal approval.

Powell agreed with our submissions about the contents of *Spycatcher:*

> . . . first—as is not really disputed by the British Government—at least in general terms, if not in its ultimate detail, much of the information contained in Mr. Wright's manuscript has already been made available to the public, not only in the United Kingdom, but elsewhere, in the books and other materials which have been published over the years; and, second, that it is difficult for me to see in what respects it can reasonably be said that the publication, now, of information—even if not previously made available to

the public—relating to technological matters which
are at least twenty years old, and which have, long
since, been made obsolete by the developments in
modern technology, or relating to operations—many
of them failed—which occurred at least twenty years
ago, will, or in all probability, will, detrimentally affect
the national security of the United Kingdom.

Dealing with the many books and articles which we
had tendered in evidence, the judge observed:

> Further, it seems to me that, the British Government
> having had ample notice, in some cases, of the ultimate
> detail, and, in other cases, of the general nature, of
> the otherwise confidential information intended to be
> published or televised, and being aware that some, at
> least, of that information in fact had, or must have,
> been obtained by, or from, a person or persons, subject
> to an obligation of confidentiality to it, and appreci-
> ating that, if that information were published or tel-
> evised, the national security or the Service would
> thereby be detrimentally affected, and accordingly be-
> lieving that it was undesirable, in the interests of the
> national security or of the Service, that the information
> be published or televised, its failure, thereafter, to act
> to restrain the intended publication or televising of
> such information as was disclosed in *Their Trade is
> Treachery, Too Secret Too Long, The Spy Who Never Was,
> MI5's Official Secrets* and *Conspiracy of Silence* cannot be
> categorized as other than an acquiescence in the pub-
> lication, or televising, and, thus as a surrender of any
> claim to the confidentiality of that information.

Finally he dealt with the argument that even though
there had been leaks of information in the past, there
was a great public interest in MI5 being shown to be
leakproof, as Sir John Donaldson had said the previous
year in the English Court of Appeal.

The facts as revealed by the evidence in these proceedings, even if they do not totally deprive that view of any strength, gravely weaken whatever might otherwise have been its strength, for it would seem that, over the last five years, at least, former officers, including at least one former Director-General, Sir Dick Goldsmith-White, have felt free to disclose confidential information received by them while in the Service, and have done so without any action being taken against them; and, further, far from it appearing to be, even if not being, "leakproof," it must have been apparent to anyone who had cause to consider the matter, that, as a result of the acquiescence, or inaction, of the British Government, the Service has, for years, leaked like a sieve.

Powell rejected our argument that the British were endeavoring to indirectly enforce the British Official Secrets Act in Australia, an arcane legal argument which ultimately found more favor in the appellate courts. He found that a legal obligation of confidence existed despite the provisions of the Official Secrets Act. He held there was a public interest in revealing evidence of the many crimes and treasons described in the book.

Peter was sick in the hospital at the time the judgment came down, but shortly recovered, no doubt buoyed up by his win over "the bastards," as he now invariably referred to the British Government. In fact he had become quite passionate about it and had to be restrained from referring to Mrs. Thatcher as "a bitch" with the sort of loathing one would usually reserve for a rabid dog.

Predictably, the British Government appealed to the New South Wales Court of Appeal. Equally predictably they waited the full four weeks before they lodged the Notice of Appeal, thereby ensuring the hearing of the appeal was postponed as much as possible. The undertakings preventing Wright and Heinemann from publishing *Spycatcher* continued pending the outcome of the appeal. In the meantime, however, a copy of *Spycatcher* found its way to *The Independent* in London which on April 27, 1987 duly published slabs of the book until an injunction stopped them. On May 14, 1987 Viking Penguin Inc. in America announced they proposed to publish an American edition of *Spycatcher*. They had apparently been provided with the manuscript back in 1985 before any legal action had been commenced.

Viking Penguin is a subsidiary of Pearson plc, publishers, among many other things, of *The Financial Times* and *The Economist*. The Treasury Solicitor tried to persuade Lord Blakenham, the chairman of Pearson, to instruct his American subsidiary not to publish. Lord Blakenham insisted that the American board was independent and that he could not interfere. The British Government considered taking legal action against Viking, but decided they would have no hope in the American courts. On July 13 the book was published in the United States and was a huge success. Hundreds of thousands of copies were sold at airports, mainly to British visitors who returned to England clutching their contraband copies of *Spycatcher*. The Government resolved not to seize copies at the airport. *The Sunday Times* of London on July 12 published extracts from the American edition and the Government took contempt proceedings against *The Sunday Times*. By now *The Guardian, The Observer, The Sunday Times* and *The Independent* were all in the dock for publishing extracts from *Spycatcher*.

My life had changed dramatically in the months between Justice Powell's decision and the hearing in the New South Wales Court of Appeal. On July 1, 1987 I had established a new investment bank, Whitlam Turnbull & Co Limited. My partners in the new bank were my old friends, Neville Wran and Nicholas Whitlam. Wran was an old university friend of my mother and had recently retired as (Labor) Premier of New South Wales after a record ten years in the job. He was widely recognized as the most astute politician in Australia. Nick Whitlam had had a very successful career in banking both in Australia and abroad and had just completed a seven-year term as Chief Executive of the State Bank of New South Wales. It was an exciting new career development, although tinged with sadness since my law partner, Bruce McWilliam, did not join us in the bank and returned, as a partner, to Sydney's biggest law firm, Allen Allen & Hemsley.

On Monday July 27, 1987, the British Government's appeal to the New South Wales Court of Appeal began. The bench was the same as that which had rejected the British Government's application for special leave to appeal from Justice Powell's order of discovery on November 19, 1986: the Chief Justice, Sir Laurence Street, the president of the Court of Appeal, Justice Michael Kirby and Justice Michael McHugh. I was relieved that McHugh was back on the bench, but nonetheless Lucy and I were both gloomy about our prospects in the state Court of Appeal because we feared the conservative Chief Justice, whose sympathy for the British Government case had been apparent the previous year, would find some support from his colleagues on the bench. We were more optimistic about our chances in the Federal High Court of Australia. But that was a long way off as we wheeled our books to court for the first appeal. We constantly reminded each other that this appeal was merely a staging post on the way to the ultimate appellate court, the High Court.

We first endeavored to get the injunction lifted. I presented evidence of the extensive publication in the United States and argued that whatever may have been the situation at the trial, the contents of *Spycatcher* were now well and truly in the public domain. Even if the Court of Appeal were to find against us, I argued, they should not continue the ban on the book. Rather they should order us to pay over our profits to the Government instead. The judges heard this evidence and resolved not to consider varying the interim orders until they had heard the whole argument. So *Spycatcher* was public property in the United States, but still a banned book in Australia and Britain.

When a decision by a trial judge is taken on appeal, all the relevant papers including the transcript of the evidence is printed into bound volumes called Appeal Books. In this appeal there were twelve such books. Theo Simos again led for the Government with Bill Caldwell as his junior. An English barrister called John Laws also appeared with Simos and Caldwell. He works for the Government full-time and was apparently brought out to stiffen up the Government's legal team. He was medium height and chubby and had the rather unusual habit of staring across the court towards Lucy, who glared back, when he was not trying to prompt Simos. It was not hard to discern the strain he was enduring by not arguing the case himself. David Hogg was there as was Susan Marsh. John Bailey stayed at home.

The Court of Appeal sat in the huge Banco Court which seats over three hundred people. It is mostly used for formal occasions like swearing in new practitioners and judges. It lacked the intimacy of Justice Powell's court. I have often regretted the fact that the scores of schoolchildren who visit the Supreme Court every day are exposed immediately to the Banco Court. Judges look tiny, craggy, grey and remote. The gloomy and grave atmosphere in the court affected my two-and-half-year old daughter, Daisy. When her grandmother brought her in to see some of the proceedings, the little girl saw Lucy sitting below in the well of the court. Daisy took fright and thought something terrible must have been happening to her mother. She was quickly taken outside but her screams were still heard as she clawed at the doors.

My son Alexander, however was much more robust about courts. He came to watch some of the action in

Justice Powell's court, but insisted on wearing a toy London policeman's hat. The appearance of a four-year-old in court with a black bobby's helmet he refused to take off even brought a smile to Ivor Robert's face.

Simos went first. It was quite clear that of the three judges one or two had read all the evidence. McHugh's photographic memory was put to good work as he challenged Simos about Armstrong's evidence. Simos had a fairly easy ride, overall. The storms were reserved for me. I was quickly rocked by Michael Kirby. We had counted on him as a supporter, but his questions indicated some hostility. He expressed the view that it would be wrong for the court to overrule, on a security question, the considered opinion of the Australian Government, expressed by Michael Codd.

The judges quickly divided on the jurisdictional question. We had argued, unsuccessfully before Powell, that the whole case was an indirect attempt by the British to enforce the British law of official secrecy. We argued that it would be contrary to Australia's independence and territorial integrity if it were to allow such a political law, as that of official secrets, to be enforced within Australia. If the British wanted to silence their old spies in Australia they should ask the Australian Government to enact legislation in the Federal Parliament which would permit this to be done.

Michael McHugh appeared to be of the same mind as Justice Powell. Sir Laurence Street and Michael Kirby, however, appeared quite sympathetic to this argument. Street started to develop the idea that even though the British Government's case was prima facie non-justiciable in Australia, the affidavit from Codd made it so.

The argument continued for five days. The arctic chill from Sir Laurence Street rattled me. Lucy and Sandy Grant were similarly concerned. At the end we were quite convinced that we had lost. We felt McHugh was sympathetic but that Street, and unexpectedly Kirby, were dead against us. McHugh has a very broad Australian accent. He is a very affable judge, expressing even the most devastating remarks with a big grin. While Theo briefly addressed in reply and I nursed my wounds, McHugh became a little skeptical as Theo insisted that there was absolutely no evidence of *Their Trade is Treachery* having been covertly authorized.

July 31, 1987

> McHugh JA   Nobody can point to evidence showing the Director-General handing over the documents to be leaked, but Mr. Turnbull says that the footprints are all over the place. Robinson Crusoe did not have to see anybody on the island. When he saw the footprint, he knew somebody was there and here you have this whole chain of circumstances all pointing, says Mr. Turnbull, quite irresistably to the conclusion that the British Government lets out into the public domain what it wants to when it is favorable to it.

The Court of Appeal adjourned to consider their decision on July 31, and in the meantime the House of Lords, Britain's ultimate court of appeal, had in a majority decision a few days before, upheld the ban on *Spycatcher* in Great Britain. Not only had the House of Lords banned any publication of extracts from *Spycatcher,* it had also banned any reference to the allegations in *Spycatcher,* even if they were uttered in open court in Australia. The dire predictions of the *Sunday Times* editorialist the year before had come true. *Spycatcher* was freely available in America and Europe but in England, and Australia too, it was a banned book. In England, Wright had become a banned person. He could not be quoted, even if his words had been publicly uttered in an Australian court. People freely brought *Spycatcher* into the country, but newspapers could not quote from it. Bookshops could not sell it. *The Economist* protested at its inability to publish a review by simply publishing a blank page where the review would have been. In more graphic terms perhaps, The *Daily Star* manifested the general dismay at this unreal decision by publishing a picture of the Law Lords upside down under the headline "YOU FOOLS!." The House of Lords decision was a majority one; Lords Templeman, Ackner and Brandon being in favor of the suppression, Lords Bridge and Oliver being in favor of allowing the newspapers to publish information gleaned from *Spycatcher*. Lord Bridge in particular was critical of his colleagues' decision, writing: "freedom of speech is always the first casualty under a totalitarian regime. The present attempt to insulate the public in this country from information which is freely available elsewhere is a significant step down that very dangerous road. The maintenance of the ban, as more and more copies of the book *Spycatcher* enter this country and circulate here, will seem more and more ludicrous."

On September 24, 1987 the New South Wales Court of Appeal handed down its judgment. I was filled with foreboding. My opponents were obviously expecting victory and seemed cocky and self-assured. Sir Laurence Street first announced his opinion. He was in favor of upholding the appeal and continuing the ban on the book until such time as the Australian Government gave new evidence in the light of the American publication. I groaned inwardly. Michael Kirby then announced that in his opinion the appeal should be dismissed, then Michael McHugh said he was of the same opinion. "Accordingly," the Chief Justice intoned, "the Order of the court is that the appeal is dismissed."

We had won! But the book was not yet published. Bill Caldwell leaped up and asked for a continuation of the injunction until the British Government had had an opportunity to appeal to the High Court in Canberra. The Court of Appeal continued the injunction, but only for three days. The British Government quickly applied to the High Court in Canberra for an order continuing the injunction until their second appeal had been heard. I was tied up with some important banking business and so I arranged for Lucy's father, Tom Hughes QC, to appear for Heinemann and Wright before Justice Sir William Deane when he heard the application by the British Government on September 27, 1987. The following morning Justice Deane decided to lift the injunction. There was no longer any possible justification in banning a book which had sold nearly 750,000 copies throughout North America and Europe. The British immediately announced they would try to overturn Justice Deane's decision by appealing to the full bench of the High Court on October 14, 1987.

Sandy Grant immediately put in hand three separate printings. Heinemann flew into Australia the film from the American edition and edited it as soon as the judgment was announced. He quickly printed 20,000 copies in Ireland, 70,000 in Melbourne, and 50,000 in Chicago. The Chicago copies were flown to Holland for distribution in Europe. We were aware that the courts could reimpose the injunction on October 14 so the printers and binders worked day and night to ensure the books were on the bookstands within 14 days from the injunction being lifted. With the hearing on October 14 due the next morning copies arrived and were rushed to every major bookshop in Canberra, Melbourne and Sydney. It became an instant bestseller and reprinting commenced immediately in Dublin and Melbourne.

The court case had given the book an unrivalled publicity coverage and orders flowed in from Malta to Nigeria from the minute the British lost their appeal to the New South Wales Court of Appeal. *Spycatcher's* success astounded us all. Demand seemed impossible to fill as third and fourth printings went ahead. Within four months of publication sales of *Spycatcher* had topped one million copies.

With the book finally published in Australia, we were able to read the decision of the New South Wales Court of Appeal handed down a few weeks before. The three judges had written separate judgments. They all agreed that Wright had not been employed under a contract of employment, but after that took very different approaches to the case. Justice McHugh rejected our argument that the British were trying to enforce a public or penal law of Britain in Australia, but nonetheless held that their case was non-justiciable in Australia. Expounding a novel principle, he said that it would be embarrassing for Australian courts to hear cases which involved consideration of the public interest of other countries. Chief Justice Street was just as imaginative. He did agree with our argument that the British were indirectly attempting to enforce a foreign public or penal law. He agreed that general principles of international law would result in the case being unenforceable in Australia as a result. However, he said that this general prohibition on unenforceability was overcome in this case by the support given to the British Government by the affidavit of Michael Codd.

Of the three judges only Michael Kirby dealt with all the issues. McHugh did not discuss the evidence in any detail, finding for us on his jurisdictional point, and Street found against without examining the evidence in any detail. Indeed the Chief Justice appeared to believe that *Spycatcher* contained a great deal of confidential information, something which no one else had ever seriously contended. Kirby on the other hand dealt with all the evidence, and all the legal arguments.

> In its nature, the case is the assertion by a foreign state of the public law and policy of that State. The first law officer of that state came to this country to

do so. He brought out here the Secretary to the Cabinet. He calls in aid, for that purpose, our courts . . . It is a policy which that country is perfectly entitled to enforce in its own courts in respect to persons within its jurisdiction. Without more it is not, in my opinion, a law which this country's courts will impose upon persons in this jurisdiction. To do so would be to lend the orders of our courts to the enforcement of the public law and policy of the United Kingdom, indirectly to enforce the language and purposes of the Official Secrets Act 1911 of that country and directly to enforce the public law of silence which the duties called in aid by the appellant in our court were merely the instruments of achieving.

Even though this disposed of the case in our favor, Kirby went on to deal with the merits of the case. Kirby did not agree with my submission that Justice Powell should have held that Armstrong deliberately lied to the court. He agreed with Justice Powell on the public domain defense, holding: "Because the overwhelming bulk of that material is already in the public domain, and was so when *Spycatcher* was commissioned by Heinemann and written by Mr. Wright, I do not believe that those matters in it should now be suppressed."

The High Court granted the British leave to appeal on October 14 and the hearing of the final Australian appeal was scheduled for March 8, 1988. The urgency was now gone from the Australian proceedings, as the book was being published in Australia and by Christmas had already sold 715,000 copies worldwide. Even though Theo Simos on October 14 had unsuccessfully asked the High Court to reimpose the ban on the book (presumably by seizing copies off the bookstands) there was now no possible prospect, whatever the final result, of any ban being reimposed. The appeal to the High Court was really about money. If the British won the appeal they would recover all of the profits made by Wright and Heinemann from publishing *Spycatcher*. Thanks to the free publicity generated by the efforts to ban *Spycatcher* these profits were now huge, running into many millions.

The British continued their valiant efforts to ban the book. They successfully stopped *The South China Morning Post* from publishing extracts of it in Hong Kong. In New Zealand, however, they failed in a similar effort against *The Dominion* (both at first instance and on appeal), despite Sir Robert returning in November 1987 for a brief spell in a Wellington witness box.

Back in Britain, the newspapers were preparing for a full hearing of the case against them which began in December, 1987. So far all of the litigation had involved interlocutory orders based on affidavit evidence only. Now Sir Robert was to be cross-examined again. The English hearing was, for me, a huge disppointment. Sir Robert was handled with kid gloves, his credit was not impugned and the newspapers' very English counsel seemed as determined to distance themselves from Wright, and me, as they were to win the case.

One of the matters being considered in this case, before Mr. Justice Scott, was whether the *Guardian* and *Observer* had acted wrongfully in June 1986 when they published details of some of the allegations of criminality in *Spycatcher*. The Government's QC, Robert Alexander, submitted that the newspapers had been provided with this information by myself. The newspapers had in fact received this leak of information not from me, not from anyone at Heinemann Publishers Australia Pty Limited, but from a fellow Englishman based in London. This person had no authority from either Wright or the publishers to leak the information and was harshly castigated for doing so. At the hearing before Justice Scott, the newspapers' lawyers sat back and allowed these allegations to be made about me, knowing they were false, and doing nothing, or practically nothing, to correct them. As a result they protected the reputation of their English informant at my expense. I offered to the newspapers' solicitors that I would swear an affidavit to be filed in the proceedings disavowing any involvement in this un- fortunate, and completely unauthorized, leak of infor- mation. The newspapers' solicitors, again anxious that the truth of this matter not come before the court, rebuffed this offer and I had to content myself with a letter to *The Times*. Ultimately Justice Scott found, as he no doubt had to do, that "the journalists must have received the information on which they based their respective articles either from someone in the offices of the publishers or from someone in the office of the solicitors acting for Mr. Wright and the publishers." The judge was wrong on both counts. Needless to say the informant did not turn himself in, as it were, but was similarly relaxed about my taking the blame for his own stupidity.

The gentle approach to the Cabinet Secretary was particularly surprising since he changed his evidence once again! Shortly before the English trial began, Chapman Pincher published his own book about the *Spycatcher* affair, called *A Web of Deception*. Like all of Pincher's work it is self-serving and self-congratulatory. However it did reveal, for the first time, that the manuscript of *Their Trade is Treachery* had been given to a distinguished person, whom Pincher called "the Arbiter." He gave the book to Sir Arthur Franks, head of MI6. The Arbiter advised Sir Arthur that if the Government felt the book should not be published he would ensure that Sidgwick & Jackson would not publish it.

Sir Robert Armstrong gave evidence before Justice Scott on Tuesday, November 23, 1987. He confirmed Pincher's revelation, adding that he had not been aware of this offer by "the Arbiter" until very recently, in fact following the publication of *A Web of Deception*. He said the offer was not taken up because the Arbiter said he was sure that Pincher would simply take the book to another publisher. This rather astonishing view was apparently shared by those at MI5 and MI6 who had read the book. Pincher contradicts this, and on this point it is difficult to disagree with him. What English publisher would readily publish a book like *Their Trade is Treachery* if it knew that the Government was prepared to take action, inevitably successfully, to stop it? Charles Gray QC, for the *Guardian,* did press Sir Robert on this matter. Armstrong stuck to his particularly incredible evidence. It was not possible to take it any further with Sir Arthur Franks since the Government claimed crown privilege to prevent him giving evidence.[1] Armstrong agreed that this matter had not been revealed to the Australian court. Charles Gray QC stressed, as he cross-examined the Cabinet Secretary, that he made no personal criticism of him over this matter.

So Sir Robert had first mislead the Australian court over the role of the Attorney-General, and then had to correct that. Now it transpires he has misled the Australian court by failing to reveal this very important offer from "the Arbiter." The explanation for these inadquacies in his evidence is apparently that someone in government, someone ultimately responsible to Sir Robert, has deliberately withheld information from the Cabinet Secretary. If, as he insists, Sir Robert told the truth as he knew it throughout the *Spycatcher* litigation then one can only assume that there is either a very cynical or very negligent group of people in the Civil Service who seem determined

---

1. Crown privilege, or public interest immunity, or "executive immunity" as it is called in the United States, is when a government seeks to prevent documents in its possession being produced to a court because to do so would prejudice national security, confidentiality of cabinet meetings or good government generally. In Australia and the United States, the courts have become much skeptical of claims of this privilege and have restricted the scope of it. Not so in Britain where the Government only has to whisper "national security" and the judges meekly agree that no documents need be produced.

to tell Sir Robert as little as possible. If he is an honest man, then he appears rather like a well-educated mushroom. Frankly I am not sure what's worse.

Justice Scott presented his judgment in the English newspaper case about *Spycatcher* on December 21, 1987. He was unimpressed by Armstrong's explanations about *Their Trade is Treachery*. He wrote:

> The evidence before me has made it clear that the Government had it in its power to prevent publication of *Their Trade is Treachery*. The intermediary could have been taken up on his offer to prevent publication by Sidgwick & Jackson. An action against Chapman Pincher for an injunction restraining publication of the book on the same legal base as has been strenuously argued before me could have been instituted. I do not have doubt by that, at the least, an interlocutory injunction restraining publication until trial could have been obtained. The reasons put forward explaining the Government's inaction are shallow and unconvincing.

He was scathing about the twists and turns in Sir Robert's evidence:

> The facts surrounding the Government's decision not to attempt to restrain publication are, as they emerged in the evidence given before me, very curious. Not the least curious is that the full facts were not known to Sir Robert Armstrong when he gave evidence in the New South Wales action, notwithstanding that there must have been those in Government to whom the facts were known. Sir Robert was not fully briefed. Even now there is reason to question whether Sir Robert has been told the full story.

He held that the *Guardian* and *Observer* had been justified in publishing the allegations in June 1986 because they concerned important matters of public interest; he particularly instanced the allegation that members of MI5 had plotted to destabilize the Government of Harold Wilson. He held that the *Sunday Times* had been wrong to commence serialization of *Spycatcher* in July 1987 and ordered it to pay any additional profits from that serialization to the Government. He held that henceforth, given the wide circulation of *Spycatcher* throughout the rest of the world, newspapers were free to report its contents in the United Kingdom.

He also observed that in his opinion Wright had acted wrongly in publishing *Spycatcher* and that he would, were he to be sued in England, have to make an account of his profits to the Government. The basis of his finding appears to have been a complete misapprehension. Justice Scott agreed with the Australian judges that Wright's duty of confidentiality would not extend to information which it was in the public interest to publish, nor to information which was trivial or useless or had already been disclosed under the authority of the Government. He said that it was a matter for speculation what the result would have been if *Spycatcher* had confined itself to matters which had previously been published, because Wright, he said, had not asked for authority to publish his memoirs. He said that if the Government had refused Wright authority to publish, that refusal would have been amenable to judicial review.

The Government did not, apparently, trouble the English judge with the fact that Wright had begged it to blue-pencil his book. The whole case in Australia had in fact been a judicial review of the correctness of that refusal of authorization. Wright had asked for authority, he had asked the Government to apply its mind to his book, and it had refused to do so. In fact Justice Scott's finding was completely at odds with the absolutist claim of the Government. He found, as the Australian judges had, that the duty of confidence was qualified. He mistakenly held that Wright had not ever asked for authority. Had he known this to be the fact, I believe that Justice Scott would have reached precisely the same conclusion as did Justice Powell in Sydney.

Any joy the newspapers had from Justice Scott was short lived. The old injunctions were restored pending an appeal to the English Court of Appeal. The Court of Appeal was composed of the Master of the Rolls, Sir John Donaldson, and Lord Justices Dillon and Bingham. Even Sir John had cooled down a little by this time, observing, in a good-natured dig at himself I suspect, that the *Spycatcher* litigation had a unique quality "in its ability to raise blood pressures, metaphorically if not literally." The Court of Appeal was in favor of lifting the injunctions, but continued them pending an appeal to the House of Lords. Most important, however, they also rejected the Government's argument that Wright had owed an absolute duty of silence. They agreed it was qualified in the same way Justice Scott had held. In what must have left the Government's lawyers grinding their collective teeth, Lord Bingham even went so far as to quote, with approval, Sir Anthony Mason's statement of the limits of governmental confidentiality in *Commonwealth v. Fairfax.*

The final act of the *Spycatcher* drama began on March 8, 1988 when we assembled in Canberra before the full bench of the High Court of Australia. There had been a little consternation before the hearing over what I would wear. Australia is a federation of six States and in only two of those States, New South Wales and Queensland, are lawyers admitted as either solicitors or barristers. In the other States lawyers are admitted as "barristers and solicitors," and lawyers appearing as advocates in those States wear robes regardless of whether they in fact practice as a partner in a big law firm, or as a barrister does. I am admitted as a solicitor in New South Wales; a barrister and solicitor in Victoria and the Australian Capital Territory. Should I be on the High Court roll as a solicitor, a barrister, or a barrister and solicitor? If so, what should I wear?

I informed the High Court's registrar, Frank Jones, that I would wear whatever the High Court preferred. I was told I should appear robed, in a wig and gown. While I was puzzling over who I would borrow them from, the Registrar changed his mind, I could appear in a suit. So I did, and Lucy, recently admitted to practice, was readily given permission by the court to join me at the Bar table, thus getting the formal recognition for her work that she had deserved.

The High Court hearing coincided with Whitlam Turnbull's biggest assignment since its establishment. In September 1987 Warwick Fairfax had launched a bold takeover bid for his family newspaper company, John Fairfax Limited, publishers of Australia's most prestigious newspapers including *The Age of Melbourne, The Sydney Morning Herald and the Australian Financial Review.* But the stockmarket crash of October 1987 had brought with it some big problems in repaying the two billion dollar debt he had incurred to buy back the family business. In January 1988 Whitlam Turnbull was called in to help and we quickly arranged a five hundred million dollar loan to keep the company afloat and then proceeded to negotiate major asset sales. We were right in our element negotiating with Rupert Murdoch, Robert Holmes a Court and Robert Maxwell. My years of working with Kerry Packer had taught me a lot about dealing with business titans and I put that experience to good effect for Warwick Fairfax.

The High Court appeal went much more smoothly than the hearing before the Court of Appeal. The only hiccup was at the outset when Sir Anthony Mason suggested that the High Court should adjourn until it had heard what the House of Lords would say about the English litigation. I urged the court that Wright had waited long enough for an end to the litigation, and after a brief adjournment the judges agreed.

The judges gave every indication of not wanting to become embroiled in the facts of the case. That was a great pity. The latest revelations about the role of the "Arbiter" in the *Their Trade is Treachery* affair now put it beyond doubt that our claims about a conspiracy were accurate. The book had plainly been unofficially vetted by MI6 and MI5, and the efforts to deny this were, as Justice Scott observed, "shallow and unconvincing." However, it is not the role of the ultimate appellate court to determine knotty issues of fact; their role is to articulate important matters of legal principle. The problem my opponents faced was that the evidence from the trial was so bad, from their point of view, that unless the High Court was prepared to agree with the British Government's absolute approach to governmental secrecy, there was little chance they could win.

The High Court judges were faced with a difficult dilemma. They could not accept the British Government's doctrine of absolute and undiscriminating secrecy since it would involve overruling one of their own decisions, and since that doctrine had not even been adopted in England. If Wright's obligation of confidence was limited to real secrets which were not in the public domain and which would cause real damage to Britain if they were published, then the High Court could not find for the Government without performing the same detailed analysis of all of the evidence including all the previously published spy books in precisely the same way that Justices Powell and Kirby had done in Australia, and Justice Scott had done in England. That was even less palatable. It involved redoing all of the work of the courts below, and could only result in a finding against the Government. Who now could safely hold that *Their Trade is Treachery* was published against the wishes of the Government? Practically, there were only two ways the High Court could conclude the appeal without re-examining all of the evidence. One was to revoke the grant of special leave and simply say that the case raised insufficient matters of principle to justify its consideration by the High Court. The other was to conclude that this case was one which an Australian court should not enforce for all of the arguments we had raised about justiciability. It was clear from the first few minutes of the appeal that this last course was most favored by the judges.

Why, they kept on asking Theo Simos, should Australian courts enforce the British law of official secrecy? More important, why should they entertain arguments about the public interest of the United Kingdom. The whole exercise was pregnant with possible sources of embarrassment. Simos argued that the court should accept the evidence of the Australian Government of the matter. Very well, the judges replied (occasionally in unison) what happens when the Australian Government's evidence is so unreasonable as to be unacceptable by a court? Then the embarrassment is compounded. Simos responded by saying that the courts should refuse to entertain cases like this unless the Australian Government confirmed the plaintiff Government was an ally. Worse and worse the judges replied. Why should the Australian Government be placed in the position where it had to say whether a particular foreign Government was an ally or not?

I said as little as I could about this public international law argument; it was obvious the judges were keen on it and there was little I could add to it. So I concentrated on the evidence, addressing for a day and a half on the factual background to the case, seeking to convince them that the British case had no merits on the facts. Advocates often forget that judges are human beings. Even though courts occasionally find in favor of unmeritorious parties because of a legal technicality, they don't like doing so and my address was designed to ensure the judges would not have second thoughts about dismissing the appeal when they got back to their chambers. I wanted them to be convinced that the British Government did not have a leg to stand on, no matter how you looked at the case. Once they felt the British didn't deserve to win, they wouldn't have any qualms about dismissing the appeal on a technical point of law.

We made a subtle change to our submissions about Armstrong's credit in the High Court. Before Justice Powell and the New South Wales Court of Appeal we had argued that Armstrong had lied in his evidence. However in the High Court I told the judges that I no longer sought to establish Armstrong had actually lied. There was no doubt that even if Sir Robert had thought he was telling the truth, people in Whitehall knew it was false and allowed him to continue with it in the hope it would not be found out. "If Sir Robert was not a perjurer, then he was unquestionably a proxy for perjury," I told the seven High Court judges.

We left the High Court after three days of argument very confident of success. The judges retired to write their judgments. We had feared they would reserve their judgments for six months, but on Tuesday, May 31 Frank Jones telephoned and told us the judgments would be handed down on Thursday, June 2, 1988. The High Court unanimously dismissed the British Government's appeal and ordered it to pay the legal costs of Wright and Heinemann. The High Court had dismissed the case on the grounds that it was an attempt to enforce the penal or public laws of Britain.

Lucy's public international law argument had won the day! The profits from *Spycatcher* were now safe. The British Government had been completely vanquished. Lucy, Sandy Grant and I shared a bottle of champagne. We telephoned Peter, who was delighted. When we returned to Sydney later that afternoon we found half a dozen bottles of champagne waiting for us from the Wrights. I gave many interviews about the case, debated a Tory backbencher on British television, he in a London studio and I in Sydney. I watched amazed as the British Government's spokesmen in London argued that they had really won the case, since the High Court had only dismissed the appeal on a legal point and had not denied that Wright owed a duty of confidentiality to the British Government. They omitted to note that Wright had never denied he owed such a duty of confidentiality; he had simply insisted that *Spycatcher* did not, because of its contents, breach that duty.

In fact the judgments of the High Court had achieved the complete reverse of what the British Government had sought. By suing Wright they had hoped to establish a precedent which would show that former British intelligence officers could not evade their duties under the Official Secrets Act by travelling abroad. We had always concentrated our efforts on our argument that this particular book, *Spycatcher,* was not one which should be suppressed. Had the High Court found for Wright on the same basis as Justice Powell had found for him, the next would-be Peter Wright would have had to go through the same lengthy and expensive exercise to prove that his or her book was also not worthy of suppression. However the High Court's judgment has slammed the shutters down on any further cases of this kind being brought by a foreign Government in Australia. Referring to the public international law principle which we had argued before them, the judges wrote: "The principle of law renders unenforceable actions of a particular kind. Those actions are actions to enforce the governmental interests of a foreign state. There is nothing . . . that could justify the making of an exception or qualification for actions by a friendly state. The friendliness or hostility of the foreign state seeking to enforce its claims in the [Australian] court . . . has no relevant connection with the principle . . . So far as friendly states are concerned, the remedy, if one is thought to be desirable, is to be found in the introduction of legislation." The result is that as the law in Australia now stands a British intelligence officer could travel to Australia and publish with impunity the most up-to-date secrets imaginable. By their bloody-minded refusal to reach a sensible compromise the British Government has created a legal precedent which can only be overcome by legislation of the Australian parliament. Justice Brennan, who wrote a separate concurring judgment, was even more explicit: "It is for the Parliament, not for the Courts, to say whether Australian security and foreign relations can be served by enforcing obligations of confidence owed to a foreign government with respect to that government's intelligence secrets and confidential political information."

This parliamentary solution was proposed by Gough Whitlam when he gave evidence at the trial. I would hope that the United States, Australia, Canada, New Zealand and Britain will enact complementary legislation which enables each country's intelligence and defense secrets to be protected in the courts of the others. This legislation could not embody the absolutist doctrines for which Sir Robert Armstrong contended in the Peter Wright case. In order to be acceptable in America and Australia it will have to contain sensible criteria, similar to the current practice of the Central Intelligence Agency, so that former intelligence officers are free to publish books of historical interest only, and are restricted only when they seek to reveal information which is both secret and of current operational significance. The Australian intelligence agencies are already using a similar vetting system to that of the CIA. The courts of the country in which suppression is sought will need to retain the ultimate right to allow the publication of intelligence information belonging to another country, if the court believes that its publication is in the public interest.

Britain's absolute doctrine of official secrecy and its cynically inconsistent application has much more in common with the practices of the Soviet Union than with those of its intelligence partners among the Western democracies. Pursuing this doctrine through the Australian courts has only made inevitable a change in the British official secrets doctrine to a sensible and discriminating system similar to that employed in the United States.

But that inevitable change must await the retirement of Mrs. Thatcher as British Prime Minister. She has continued the battle in England with a vengeance worthy of her great idol, Queen Boadicea. She has proposed changes to the Official Secrets Act which will make it even more restrictive than it is now. No former intelligence officer will ever be able to speak about his work and no newspaper or television station will be able to quote him. Former intelligence personnel will become "non-persons" and any newspaper that dares to quote them will run the risk of criminal prosecution.

In October, 1988 however, the House of Lords grudgingly agreed that *Spycatcher* could be published in England. They did so with great reluctance and only because of the worldwide publication outside Britain. The English law lords demonstrated how political the British judiciary had become. One of them said Wright was as great a traitor as any of those he had criticized in his book. Certainly one could be excused for thinking that he was an even worse traitor than Philby. Philby's autobiography had never been suppressed in England and within weeks of the House of Lords decision another biography of Philby containing extensive quotes from the old traitor was published without hindrance in Britain.

The law lords even went so far as to invite other publishers to print "pirate" editions of *Spycatcher* so that Wright would be deprived of royalties. They asserted that no British court would assist Wright in protecting his copyright in his own work. They said that if Heinemann or Wright earned any profits from publishing *Spy-*

catcher in England, those profits could be confiscated by the Government.

William Heinemann Limited in the United Kingdom wisely did not publish the book in England, but its Australian subsidiary has imported hundreds of thousands of copies of the book and it is a best seller in England as it has been everywhere else.

I was in England, promoting the English edition of this book, when the House of Lords gave their decision. It was an extraordinary feeling to be such a famous figure in another country. Lucy and I were invited to lunch by the English Law Society[2] and I addressed two hundred of its members later that day. I spoke about official secrets at the Oxford Union, returning as "a great man" to the chamber where, as a student, I had listened to so many other "great men" not so many years before.

My move into investment banking had an ironic side to it. Had I remained in legal practice, the notoriety from the case would have been an enormous boost to my legal firm, but being a "world famous advocate" does not necessarily translate into lots of investment banking business. Whitlam Turnbull is owned 75% by myself, Nick Whitlam and Neville Wran with the balance held by a big United Kingdom financial services group, British & Commonwealth Holdings plc. We have concentrated on providing corporate advice, mainly to large corporations, and often in the context of mergers and takeovers. Our work has been very interested and varied, ranging from restructuring the newspaper empire of Warwick Fairfax to merging two large stevedoring companies to masterminding a boardroom coup to secure control of a large Australian gold mining company. Our clients have included many English corporations, which don't seem to object to engaging the tormentor of Sir Robert Arm-

2. The professional body which regulates the solicitors in the UK, equivalent of the American Bar Association.

strong and quite a few American ones which I suspect rather approve of my robust rejection of Britain's attempt to patronize the Australian courts (something she stopped doing to American ones in 1776!).

Inevitably the enormous publicity surrounding *Spycatcher* has led journalists to renew their predictions of a bright political career for me. I am a member of no political party, but despite my very good friends in the Labor Party and despite the fact that my two partners, Neville Wran and Nicholas Whitlam are both Labor Party members, I feel that my own libertarian philosophy fits better with the free enterprise political parties. But in Australia today we have a federal Labor Government which is employing a more free enterprise approach to Government and the economy than did any of its "conservative" predecessors.

The *Spycatcher* affair has galvanized my determination to see Australia rid itself of its remaining constitutional links with Britain. The titular head of state of Australia is still the Queen of England. Indeed ever since Gough Whitlam's radical government of 1972–1975 the Queen is officially Queen of Australia. But all those countries of the former British Empire which still retain the Queen as their Head of State, such as Australia, Canada and New Zealand, recognize that the Queen is Queen of England first. I firmly believe that Australia must have its own head of state who is an Australian. I similarly believe that we should change our flag which currently carries the Union Jack in the top left hand corner.

These views are regarded as somewhat radical in Australia today, but as I give speeches about Australian republicanism and nationalism I sense a growing sense of pride as Australians realize that in the difficult and dangerous world of the late twentieth century they can rely only on themselves and cannot look to nostalgic links with Britain, or America for that matter, for salvation. When we finally cut the last constitutional links with

Britain, I have no doubt that the *Spycatcher* case will be remembered as a great watershed in the history of Australian nationalism.

Peter Wright grows old and his memory fades. He gave a different version of his story of the Wilson Plot in a television interview. In *Spycatcher* he had claimed that he had stopped others from plotting against the Prime Minister. In the television interview he said that he was the ringleader, and at the end the only one prepared to threaten Wilson for exposure as a Russian agent. Where does the truth lie? I suspect Peter is now too old and sick to be able to tell us for sure. His triumph has come a little late for him to relish it as he should be able to.

Amid all the abuse and hatred the English have laden upon him, he is still a patriot, still determined to awaken Britain to the menace of international communism and the KGB. Perhaps in the age of glasnost this is outmoded, but it is sincerely felt, of that I am sure.

Peter's greatest satisfaction lies in knowing that at least his Queen has not deserted him. In 1976 when he retired he was awarded a Royal honor, Commander of the Order of the British Empire, or CBE. Mrs. Thatcher has repeatedly asked the Queen to strip Peter Wright of that honor just as Anthony Blunt was stripped of his knighthood. And Her Majesty has repeatedly declined to do so.

INDEX